"Historian John Roth has crafted a compelling inside look at the seventy-five-year saga of one of the enduring Anabaptist-Mennonite church institutions. Readers of all stripes will meet the fascinating personalities who led the organization along a twisting and turning path that led to what came to be Everence."
—**STEVE BOWERS**, former vice president of marketing for Everence

"From the perspective of a Mennonite agency that is blessed to be served in many ways by Everence, John Roth's eloquent telling of the larger story of faithfulness to the values of mutual aid in this organization's founding and history gives me even deeper appreciation for the resources and stewardship that Everence provides today."
—**KAREN E. LEHMAN**, president/CEO of Mennonite Health Services

"I had the privilege of reviewing early drafts of this book and then discussing the key themes with John Roth. Because I had worked at MMA/Everence for thirty-two years, I thought that I knew most of the stories and had participated in discussions concerning all aspects of mutual aid. However, I was stretched in my thinking by the way Roth connected the various mutual aid themes with a biblical grounding. This book will give the reader an increased understanding of Anabaptists' mutual aid and stewardship practices and, most importantly, why mutual aid is a key and vibrant element of our faith through changing times."
—**STEVE GARBODEN**, former interim president and senior vice president for Everence

"Throughout the history of the church, Christians have sought to care for one another and have worked to create ways to give aid to those in need. John Roth masterfully tells of the birth of a new innovative organization, created to help the church care for those in need in the changing landscape of the twentieth century. Today, Everence continues to seek creative and innovative ways to assist Anabaptist churches in meeting the spiritual and financial needs of their members. The Brethren Church is blessed to be a partner with Everence in this endeavor."
—**STEVEN COLE**, executive director of The Brethren Church

Where the People Go

Where the People Go

COMMUNITY, GENEROSITY, AND THE STORY OF EVERENCE

John D. Roth

HERALD
PRESS

Harrisonburg, Virginia

Herald Press
PO Box 866, Harrisonburg, Virginia 22803
www.HeraldPress.com

Library of Congress Cataloging-in-Publication Data
Names: Roth, John D., 1960- author.
Title: Where the people go : community, generosity, and the story of Everence /
   John D. Roth.
Description: Harrisonburg, Virginia : Herald Press, 2020. | Includes
   bibliographical references and index.
Identifiers: LCCN 2020011602 (print) | LCCN 2020011603 (ebook) |
   ISBN 9781513806785 (paperback) | ISBN 9781513806792 (ebook)
Subjects: LCSH: Everence (Organization)—History. |
   Mennonites—Charities—History.
Classification: LCC BX8128.W4 R68 2020 (print) | LCC BX8128.W4 (ebook) |
   DDC 267/.1897—dc23
LC record available at https://lccn.loc.gov/2020011602
LC ebook record available at https://lccn.loc.gov/2020011603

WHERE THE PEOPLE GO
© 2020 by Herald Press. Released by Herald Press, Harrisonburg, Virginia
   22803. 800-245-7894. All rights reserved.
Library of Congress Control Number: 2020011602
International Standard Book Number: 978-1-5138-0678-5 (paperback);
   978-1-5138-0679-2 (ebook)
Printed in United States of America
Cover and interior design by Merrill Miller
Cover photos: composite using an image by bowie15/iStockphoto/Getty Images
and portraits of staff and members compiled by and used with permission of
Everence.

Scriptures taken from the Holy Bible, New International Version®, NIV®.
Copyright © 1973, 1978, 1984, 2011 by Biblica, Inc.™ Used by permission of
Zondervan. All rights reserved worldwide. www.zondervan.com The "NIV"
and "New International Version" are trademarks registered in the United States
Patent and Trademark Office by Biblica, Inc.™

Every effort has been made to secure permission from the photographers and
subjects whose images are depicted in this book. However, at press time the
source of some materials remains unknown. They are included with the intention that acknowledgment will be made in future editions as such information
becomes available.

24 23 22 21 20   10 9 8 7 6 5 4 3 2 1

Contents

"The test of any organized program of mutual aid is not the form of its organization or of its operations, but rather its purpose, its objectives, and the spirit with which it is carried on. Does it encourage its participants to seek first the kingdom of God? Does it promote Christian stewardship? . . . Does it encourage each participant to bear his own burden as much as he can and gladly do what he can to help to bear his brother's and his neighbor's burden?"
—Guy F. Hershberger

"We respond to God's love by service in all areas of life. So we must assist and prod ourselves, our congregations, our institutions, and our government to care for all people as together we work to promote health and relieve suffering in the name of Christ."
—Healthcare Access statement,
MC USA delegate assembly (2005)

Introduction

The scene has become one of the iconic images of American culture, as comforting and familiar as a calendar photo of Yellowstone National Park or Mount Rushmore: a swarm of sturdy, bearded laborers—many of them poised precariously on rafters—are scattered across the skeleton of a half-built barn. Against the backdrop of cornfields, well-tended gardens, and a simple white clapboard home, the structure rises, miraculously, in a single day, as an entire community converges to lend their aid after a fire. For many Americans, the Amish barn raising has come to represent a host of ideals that embody the best qualities of our shared humanity—community, trust, hard work, and the comforting assurance that we are surrounded by friends who will generously offer their help in our hour of need.

To the outsider, the Amish barn raising appears simple, orderly, and spontaneous. A large group of men and women appear at sunrise, work hard, enjoy huge meals, and return home by sunset, basking in the satisfaction of helping a neighbor and the pleasure of witnessing the transformation of a charred foundation into a beautiful barn. Behind the event, however, is a remarkably sophisticated organization: key leaders collaborate on dates, budgets, and various complex supply chains to ensure that the necessary materials will be available at just the right time. A foreman organizes and oversees an elaborate division of labor that aligns tasks with appropriate skills. Seasoned carpenters ensure that corners are square and joints secure. Meanwhile, Amish women also engage in a carefully choreographed plan to fuel the labor with hearty meals, served up in shifts so that the work continues without interruption.

But the most crucial element of an Amish barn raising—without which the whole enterprise would collapse—is a profound sense of community, woven together by deeply held religious convictions, shared traditions, and a thick web of personal relationships. More than anything else, it is this awareness of interdependence that makes the principle of helping each other in times of need—what is often called "mutual aid"—both possible and joyful. And it is this tangible expression of community that makes the scene of an Amish barn raising so fascinating to modern viewers.

Thanks to technology and social media, modern Americans have endless opportunities to connect with each other across vast distances. Yet, people today are feeling lonelier and more isolated than ever before. According to a 2017 congressional report, Americans are much less likely today to trust other people—or the government, the press, schools, labor unions, big business, and the medical system—than they were fifty years ago.[1] All around us, political relationships are strained to the breaking point, economic disparities between rich and poor are growing, race relations are as fraught as ever, and traditional expressions of neighborliness and community are increasingly called into question. Although life expectancy in the United States has increased significantly during the past seventy-five years (from age sixty-two to age seventy-nine), anxieties related to health insurance, medical costs, elderly care, and end-of-life questions have made it clear that merely prolonging life is not the same as a prolonged life of security and dignity. Modern Americans own more things than ever before; yet suicide rates continue to rise, along with prescriptions for anxiety medication, addictions to reality-numbing drugs, and mass shootings that almost always have their source in the suffering that arises from intense isolation and alienation.

In the face of these powerful forces, the Anabaptists—a 500-year-old faith tradition that includes members of the Hutterites, the Old Order Amish, and many varieties of Mennonites—have sought to preserve communal forms of economic sharing and mutual dependence.

The principle of mutual aid is deeply embedded in the broader Christian tradition. Indeed, some expression of communal assistance and solidarity is an important part of every religious tradition. But the concept has found particular emphasis among Anabaptist groups, where practices that foster community are regarded as essential expressions of the gospel. Many of these forms of mutual aid are informal—spontaneous assistance in the form of quilting bees or a readiness to share labor, tools, meals, money, or counsel. But other practices of community dependence have been more formal: the Hutterite tradition of shared possessions, for example; or Amish self-funded medical assistance plans; or "fire and storm" insurance programs among conservative Mennonite groups; or themes of stewardship, generosity, and charitable giving among more acculturated Mennonites. Regardless of the form, a commitment to sharing one another's burdens has been an unmistakable element of the Anabaptist tradition since its inception in the tumult of the Protestant Reformation nearly five hundred years ago.

In the middle of the twentieth century, a new organization emerged among Mennonites in North America that brought a greater level of organizational sophistication to the principle of Christian mutual aid. Formed in 1945, Mennonite Mutual Aid (MMA) initially focused on providing low interest loans to Mennonite and Amish young men who were returning from Civilian Public Service camps, where they had done "work of national importance" as an alternative to military service during World War II. Very quickly, however, MMA proved to be a dynamic and enduring organization, well-equipped to channel the principle of sharing in other ways within a growing denomination. Already in 1946, the fledgling organization extended the scope of its loan program to include Mennonite refugees from Europe rebuilding their lives in South America. Within a decade, MMA had spawned a host of subsidiary organizations: a burial aid plan, a healthcare plan, a widows' and survivors' aid plan, a program to loan money to church schools, a "thrift accumulation" or savings program, automobile insurance, a foundation for charitable giving, and a reinsurance company to serve other, smaller Mennonite mutual associations. Within another decade, MMA, now incorporated as a "fraternal benefits" association, had moved fully into automobile, health, and life insurance, while also providing retirement plans for church workers and businesses, and a philanthropic branch that funneled millions of dollars back to needy individuals and institutions.

In subsequent decades, as many Mennonites moved off the farm and into suburban contexts shaped by higher education and professional employment, MMA shifted its focus from mutual aid to stewardship, symbolized by a growing emphasis on a more holistic approach to health, money, time, and talents. By the end of the twentieth century, the organization confronted new challenges in the form of dramatically escalating medical costs, the ongoing national debate over healthcare reform, changes in the regulatory environment, and shifting cultural expectations regarding financial security, retirement, and end-of-life medical interventions. Along the way, MMA expanded its membership far beyond Mennonites to include all groups associated with the Anabaptist tradition, and eventually to all individuals who could affirm its key theological commitments.

Today, MMA—now known as Everence—has responded to the needs of its members by expanding its focus to encompass financial planning, socially responsible investments, a trust department, and banking services. With offices across the United States, in 2020 Everence employed some 380 people and managed assets of more than $4 billion.

In 1943, Mennonite church leaders debated over the best way to respond to the financial needs of their members in the face of rapid cultural and economic changes. Orie Miller, a trusted business leader and widely-respected church administrator who would become MMA's first president, argued strenuously in favor of creating a new church-related institution that could address those needs. "In this changing situation," he wrote, "the church means to go along with its members and to help them wherever in conscience they need to go."[2] Miller's argument that church institutions should reflect the needs of their members—following "where the people go"—has been a central theme in the story of Mennonite Mutual Aid/Everence ever since. Throughout its entire history, Everence has defined itself as an extension of the church, deeply anchored in the Christian faith as expressed in the Anabaptist-Mennonite tradition. Most of the people it serves are members of the thirty-plus groups who identify with Anabaptist-Mennonite or peace church traditions. A network of over 1,100 congregational advocates help to distribute millions of dollars in Everence Sharing Fund grants to needy people in local settings. Since 2013, Everence has distributed more than $395 million in charitable giving through its Sharing Fund, church loan program, community development investments, MyNeighbor credit card, and the charitable gifts managed by the Everence Foundation. And Everence continues today as a program agency of Mennonite Church USA, with close ties to related groups such as Mennonite World Conference, Mennonite Economic Development Associates, Mennonite Health Services, and Mennonite Central Committee.

At the same time, throughout its history Everence has continuously adapted in response to the changing needs and expectations of its members, following "where the people go." Some critics may see this deeply held commitment as merely pandering to the market, particularly as program emphases have shifted from direct forms of mutual aid to themes of stewardship and generosity in the context of financial planning. Yet expressions of Christian faithfulness are never static—the gospel is always being incarnated in the shifting realities of particular times, places, and cultures. Church institutions that refuse to adapt to the needs of their members and to the changed context of their culture will rightly become irrelevant. When Orie Miller committed MMA to "go where its members go" he qualified that commitment with the words "wherever *in good conscience* they need to go." Throughout its history, the leaders of Everence have wrestled daily with that balance—following where the people lead, while also devoting a great deal of attention to questions of faith and conscience, and to the themes of stewardship, generosity, and community.

This book tells the story of a complex church-related financial organization as it has negotiated seventy-five years of profound social, cultural, and economic change. Some of that story focuses on the details of its various programs and the visionary leaders who created them. Some of the story explores the dynamic relationship between Everence and the Anabaptist-Mennonite churches out of which it emerged. Part of the story traces the dynamic cultural context of healthcare, insurance, and investment management, including the legal and regulatory environment, the societal strains associated with the healthcare debate, the shifting economic sensibilities of members, and the organizational complexities of a professional financial services organization.

But mostly this is a history of an idea—a deeply rooted Christian conviction that the amazingly abundant love of God, expressed most clearly in the life and teachings of Jesus and the witness of the early church, is still accessible to Christians today. The generous outpouring of love that Christians have received from God only becomes visible in the world today to the extent that it is shared with others. For those in the Anabaptist-Mennonite tradition, that spirit of generous love has consistently found expression in the gathered community, the living body of Christ, in the form of openhanded giving and receiving, what many have called mutual aid. That same generous spirit has also extended outward wherever there is need—in our neighborhoods, our communities, our country, and indeed the world.

It should be stated that the ideals of love, generosity, and community cannot be contained in a single program, institution, or denomination. They always transcend the unique forms in which they are expressed. But at the same time, those same ideals are meaningless until they are embodied in concrete, specific, and particular ways. Church-related institutions and programs are essential to the Christian witness.

This is the story of one such church-related institution—the stresses, strains, and stubborn idealism of a living organization as it embraced the challenge of expressing deeply held spiritual commitments, however imperfectly, in institutional forms in the midst of rapid cultural change.

Chapter 1 maps out the biblical basis of economic generosity—particularly in the teachings of Jesus and the example of the early church—and its various expressions among different Anabaptist groups since the origins of the movement in the sixteenth century. What, if anything, changes as the ideals of mutual aid and stewardship take institutional forms that extend beyond the local congregation? Chapter 2 describes the origins of Mennonite Mutual Aid in the context of the Great Depression, the economic transformations brought about by World War II, and internal debates within the Mennonite Church about investments, insurance, and institutions. Chapters 3 and 4 trace the details of MMA as a rapidly growing organization—the emergence of a host of subsidiary companies, the ongoing debates over insurance, and the struggle to gain legal recognition as a fraternal benefit association. Chapter 5 describes the national healthcare crisis of the late 1970s and 1980s, and a shift in understanding as church members expressed increasing reluctance to fund traditional forms of mutual aid. Chapter 6 details the remarkable financial recovery of MMA in the 1990s, the emergence of stewardship as a central marker of its organizational identity, and a growing emphasis on financial services, including socially responsible mutual funds. Those themes are carried forward in Chapter 7, which describes broadening definitions of membership, a more sophisticated approach to marketing, and the name change to Everence when MMA joined with the Mennonite Financial Federal Credit Union. Chapter 8 reviews the priorities of the organization today and some of the challenges it faces as it looks to the future.

Definitions of Mutual Aid

In the course of the twentieth century, Mennonites and other Anabaptists in North America settled on the term *mutual aid* to describe the various ways that church members assisted each other in times of need. As these forms of assistance shifted during the second half of the century from face-to-face sharing within local congregations to more institutional forms of support, church leaders became increasingly self-conscious about definitions. Was mutual aid to be understood as something distinct from other forms of benevolence like generosity, or stewardship, or service? At a conference sponsored by MMA in 1996, sociologist Don Kraybill argued that the term *mutual aid* should be understood very precisely as "a reciprocal responsibility, based on biblical teaching, to provide material aid to other church members who face special economic and physical hardships."[3] For Kraybill, it was crucial that the term be reserved for relationships in the context of formal *membership*, that the assistance offered focused on *material* needs, and that there was an expectation of *reciprocity*—that is, the person receiving assistance was also expected to share when others had need. Kraybill's concern was to give the concept of mutual aid sufficient precision to serve as a standard for assessing whether various institutions in the contemporary church were doing "true" mutual aid.

Kraybill's narrow definition of mutual aid may have served the needs of a social scientist, eager to define relationships in terms of a fixed standard; and it might also have helped the ethicist, formally trained to make such distinctions. But within the long historical sweep of the Christian tradition and Anabaptist-Mennonite practice, people and institutions have not confined their mutual aid efforts to this narrow definition. Using this definition, Kraybill and others argued that assistance offered to people who were not members of a particular church—such as that provided by Mennonite Disaster Service—did not qualify as mutual aid. Neither did forms of support within the group that focused on emotional, social, or spiritual needs. Thus, medical care fit the definition as a physical need, but mental health services did not. Yet the biblical themes of *koinonia*, stewardship, and generosity are much richer than a narrow definition of mutual aid might suggest. And, as we shall see, groups within the Anabaptist-Mennonite tradition have always expressed their understandings of mutual aid in a wide variety of ways.

To be sure, words like *stewardship* or *generosity* may not provide the same precision as Kraybill's definition of mutual aid; but this book will focus more on the many and varied expressions of Christian generosity and community across time and culture rather than establishing a fixed ideal of mutual aid and then assessing which expressions qualify according to that definition.

Over time, various groups and individuals within the Anabaptist-Mennonite tradition have expressed their ideals in a wide variety of ways, sometimes disagreeing sharply with each other about how the principles of love and generosity should be put into practice. Yet those very debates suggest that something important is at stake in the conversation. And it is these enduring tensions—more than settled orthodoxy—that ensure the renewal of received traditions by calling each generation to the task of discerning how to put their convictions into practice.

A Word about Sources

Writing the history of a seventy-five-year-old organization presents several unique challenges in terms of sources. The official records related to Everence— e.g., board minutes, financial reports, periodical articles, newsletters, and marketing materials—exist in great abundance. Most of these can be found in the Mennonite Church USA Archives, or in a somewhat less organized fashion at the Everence corporate office. Public records such as these are very useful for tracing the basic narrative of the story; but they often hide as much as they reveal. Board minutes, for example, noting that "a vigorous discussion ensued" offer a strong hint that the matter under consideration was controversial, but say little about the nature of the controversy or who represented which position. The same is true with press releases or the numerous periodicals generated by the Everence marketing staff. The information found in these sources is highly valuable in factual information, but it rarely reveals the nuanced complexity or internal debates behind those facts. During the early years, the organization's president, Orie Miller, oversaw the day-to-day operations of the company from Akron, Pennsylvania, which meant that he was in almost daily correspondence by mail with the staff at their office in Goshen, Indiana. Buried in the hundreds of letters he exchanged with the home office—preserved in folders of carbon copies printed on thin onionskin paper—are often personal insights into the inner workings of the office, or the emerging context of larger strategic decisions as they were being considered. The correspondence of Guy F. Hershberger, an early proponent of MMA, an intellectual thought leader for the Mennonite Church, and a member of the MMA board for many years, also provided useful information regarding the early years.

When we move into the 1970s, however, these sorts of records become much more scattered or vanish altogether. For example, much of the correspondence of Harold Swartzendruber—longtime general manager and eventually president of MMA—has apparently disappeared. Nor do we have the office correspondence or personal records from Dwight Stoltzfus and James Kratz, the two leaders who succeeded him. Howard Brenneman, whose presidency coincided with the emergence of the personal computer, left few paper trails, preferring to conduct most of his business face-to-face. The introduction of email also meant that the trove of information preserved in traditional forms of correspondence would not be readily available to the modern researcher.

The published memoirs of several individuals—including Harold Swartzentruber, Christian L. Graber, and Edgar Stoesz—provided welcome additional perspectives, as did the scholarship of other historians, most notably Theron F. Schlabach's exhaustive biography of Guy F. Hershberger and John Sharp's more popular book on Orie Miller's life. Other Mennonite pioneers in the field of mutual aid—Howard Raid, J. Winfield Fretz, John Rudy, Daniel Kauffman, Lynn Miller, and others—have also left a legacy of published reflections on Christian stewardship. A collection of scholarly essays—*Building Communities of Compassion*—commissioned in 1996 for the 50th anniversary of MMA, provided additional helpful information.

As an organizational history, this account of Everence focuses largely on decisions made by leaders and on the larger social, economic, and religious context within which those decisions were made. Largely absent from this history is a clear sense of the experience of ordinary employees at Everence.

What was it like to be a member of the "Mutual Aires," an office octet that sang in Sunday evening services in the 1950s? What were the working conditions of the secretaries who labored over the IBM punch card machines in the 1960s, or the clerks who sorted through the enormous mail bags that arrived every day at the 110 Marilyn Avenue offices? What was going through the minds of employees in the 1970s and 1980s during the two-minute interlude, signaled by a bell chime, designated as a time for morning prayer? How did the hundreds of congregational representatives communicate information regarding healthcare plans or updates on the Sharing Fund application process to their fellow congregants? What did sales representatives, working out of distant offices scattered across the country, think about their commission structures or the mandates coming from the company headquarters? How did the employees in the IT department regard their counterparts in marketing or church relations? What was it like to be a member of the Missionary Church, working in an office dominated by Mennonites?

All these questions, and dozens more, are also part of the history of Everence. Yet, regrettably, this account does not adequately capture those experiences. To have included all this would have required access to a very different set of sources and would have added a considerable number of pages to an already lengthy book.

Acknowledgments

I am deeply grateful for the willingness of Everence employees and board members—past and present—to make themselves available for interviews, which helped to bring personal perspectives and welcome nuance to the story. Nearly fifty individuals consented to a conversation with me, and sometimes several conversations. Memory, of course, is not always as trustworthy as written documents; but these conversations helped make the records come alive and often added a valuable human dimension to the sometimes tedious information preserved in board minutes, official correspondence, and financial balance sheets. My thanks must begin with them: Jim Alvarez, Herman Bontrager, Jane

Bowers, Steve Bowers, Howard Brenneman, Beryl Brubaker, Brian Campbell, Chad Campbell, Eunice Culp, Rod Diller, Leonard Dow, David Gautsche, Steve Garboden, Judy Martin Godshalk, Bruce Harder, Bill Hartman, Kent Hartzler, Steve Herendeen, Ken Hochstetler, Chad Horning, Marlo Kauffman, Steve Kauffman, Delmar King, Ted Koontz, Peg Leatherman, Rosalyn and Roger Ledyard, John Liechty, Madalyn Metzger, J. B. Miller, Larry Miller, Lynn Miller, Martin Navarro, J. Lorne Peachey, Mark Regier, Sid Richard, Vyron Schmidt, Jack Scott, Karl Sommers, Kent Stucky, Colin Saxton, Carol Suter, Sara Alvarez Waugh, Michael Zehr, Phil Zimmerman, and Bill Zuercher.

Several individuals, including Steve Bowers, Eunice Culp, Steve Garboden, Judy Martin Godshalk, Ken Hochstetler, Chad Horning, Madalyn Metzger, Laura Miller, Hannah Geyer Roth, Mary Roth, Ruth Miller Roth, Karl Sommers, and Philip Zimmerman read through portions or all of the manuscript as it was being written. I am deeply grateful for the generosity of their time and the gift of their critical insights. I have been spared numerous misunderstandings and outright errors thanks to their gentle corrections. And I thank Jace Longenecker, who doggedly sorted through and categorized the many photos for this book.

Finally, I wish to express my special gratitude to Judy Martin Godshalk, Marketing Manager at Everence, who has shepherded the logistical and conceptual details of this project from the very beginning, as well as to Ken Hochstetler, current CEO and president of Everence. Ken's love of history has been evident throughout this project, not simply as a way of knowing more about the organization he is leading, but out of a desire to understand more deeply the role and witness of a church-related institution in a rapidly changing cultural context.

Increasingly, new Everence staff members are as diverse as the clientele that Everence now serves. I hope that this book may provide them and other readers with a deeper understanding of this remarkable organization and a renewed appreciation for its commitment to "the best of business and the best of church."

ONE

The Word Made Flesh

The Theology and Practice of Mutual Aid in the
Anabaptist-Mennonite Tradition

*E*arly in March of 1528 a group of some two hundred refugees, recently exiled from the Moravian city of Nikolsburg for their religious convictions, laid out all their earthly belongings and committed themselves to share their possessions freely with each other in the spirit of the early Christian church. Led by "one-eyed" Jacob Wiedemann, the group was part of a much larger movement of religious radicals known as Anabaptists (or "rebaptizers") who had fled to Moravia in the late 1520s seeking refuge from persecution.

Most Anabaptists had started out as followers of Martin Luther. They were inspired by the reformer's defiance of Catholic tradition, persuaded by his appeal to "Scripture alone" (*sola Scriptura*), and eager to follow the teachings of Christ as they encountered them in the Gospels. But the Anabaptists broke with Luther and other mainstream reformers over several key issues.

The most fundamental difference focused on baptism. The Anabaptists understood the Christian life to begin with repentance, followed by a voluntary decision, like that of Jesus' own disciples, to follow Christ in daily life. Thus, in contrast to both Catholic traditionalists and the Lutheran, Calvinist, and Anglican churches that emerged out of the sixteenth-century Reformation, the Anabaptists advocated the practice of adult baptism instead of infant baptism.[1]

Other Anabaptist convictions were no less radical. Based on the life and teachings of Jesus, the Anabaptists practiced an ethic of love that extended even to the enemy. In keeping with Christ's admonition in the Sermon on the Mount, they also refused to swear oaths or use courts to defend their legal rights. The Anabaptists pursued a disciplined life, reminiscent of a Benedictine monastery. They told their members that followers of Jesus could expect to suffer as Christ did, even to the point of death. Not least, they believed that the Christian life entailed a new view of possessions—followers of Jesus should share their money and property with each other freely, as if all were members of the same family.[2]

In the years following its origins in the Swiss city of Zurich in January 1525, the Anabaptist movement expanded rapidly. But just as quickly, it encountered fierce opposition. Within two years the majority of its most dynamic missionaries and leaders had been killed, and scores of its members fined, tortured, imprisoned, or forced to flee their homes.

For a time, the feudal lords of Moravia—today part of the Czech Republic—opened their territories to hundreds of religious refugees, offering them safe haven despite their unorthodox beliefs. But even in Moravia, the principles of religious toleration had its limits. When an Anabaptist group in Nikolsburg refused to pay taxes earmarked for war with the Turks, they aroused the anger of the local prince. When they refused to swear oaths of loyalty to defend the territory with arms, or to acknowledge that magistrates who did so could be a Christian, the ruler's patience was stretched to the breaking point. In March of 1528, the prince ordered Wiedemann and his group to leave.

Thus it was that the bedraggled group of refugees "took counsel together in the Lord because of their immediate need and distress." Then, "each one laid his possessions [on a cloak] with a willing heart . . . so that the needy might be supported in accordance with the teaching of the prophets and apostles."[3] Within a few years the group, now settled in Austerlitz, formalized its commitment to mutual aid by establishing a highly-organized community of goods that rejected all private property. Under the leadership of Jacob Hutter, they became known as the Hutterites.[4] In the decades that followed, various Anabaptist groups would express their commitment to mutual aid in very different ways. However, the basic conviction that followers of Jesus would share their possessions freely and generously became a central theme in the Anabaptist tradition, one that continues to inspire many different Christian groups still today.

Established in 1945, in the context of the Mennonite tradition, Everence traces its theological origins to this early Anabaptist movement.

In the course of its five-hundred-year history, two themes in the Anabaptist-Mennonite tradition are particularly relevant for understanding the practices that have shaped Everence throughout its seventy-five-year history. The first is a clear conviction that the Christian faith necessarily entails an earnest and ongoing conversation about economic practices—the biblical teachings on community, stewardship, and generosity. The second theme, just as pronounced, is that Christians in the Anabaptist tradition have expressed their convictions regarding economic practices in a wide variety of ways. As culture, context, and concerns have evolved across the centuries, patterns of Christian mutual aid and stewardship have likewise evolved. Everence traces its roots to these traditions of continuity and change.

An Anabaptist Theology of Mutual Aid

Although significant differences soon emerged among the Anabaptists, all groups regarded economic sharing as a core conviction, as central to their Christian identity as adult baptism. Repeatedly—in confessions of faith, interrogation records, letters, and even hymns—the early Anabaptists argued that the Christian faith could not be separated from economic questions of buying and selling, borrowing and loaning, possessing and sharing, charity and mutual aid. They believed that followers of Jesus should take seriously Christ's command not to "lay up treasures on earth" (Matthew 6:19), or the example of the early church of having "goods in common," (Acts 2; Acts 4), or Paul's encouragement to "bear one another's burdens" (Galations 6:2). One of the earliest descriptions of Anabaptist church life, for example, included this clear admonition:

> Of all the brothers and sisters of this congregation none shall have anything of his own, but rather, as the Christians in the time of the apostles held all in common, and especially stored up a common fund, from which aid can be given to the poor, according as each will have need.[5]

Their theological arguments for sharing earthly possessions were remarkably similar. They began with the conviction that God created humans in God's own image to honor God by living in relationships of trust and transparency. God had entrusted the world to humans, calling on them to be stewards of creation. This was the purpose for which humans had been created—and God pronounced it good.

Yet the Anabaptists were not naive about the reality of sin. In the opening chapters of the Bible, sin arises from the concept of "mine" and "thine," and the associated posture of the clenched fist, rather than the open hand. "For as the sun with its shining is common to all," wrote Ulrich Stadler, an early Hutterite leader, "so also the use of all creaturely things. Whoever appropriates them for himself and encloses them is a thief and steals what is not his. For everything has been created free in common."[6] As a result of a sinful self-centered understanding of possessions, we have all become refugees and aliens from Eden, living estranged from God and each other, and at war with nature.

But that's not the end of the biblical story. The Bible, the Anabaptists believed, is an account of God's effort to restore humanity to our created purpose. Even if we have a deep inclination toward selfishness, possessiveness, and greed, humans also have an equally deep desire to live as God intended—in relationships of intimacy and generosity. The biblical story, as they saw it, was an invitation by God to unclench our fists, to be freed from the anxieties of possessiveness, and to trust in God's extravagant bounty and goodness.

Thus, throughout the Hebrew Scriptures, God called Abraham and his descendants to become a community that put its trust in God. No matter what the circumstance, God always provided for the material needs of God's people, sometimes in miraculous ways, such as when Moses commanded the water to gush forth from a rock (Exodus 17:6), or when manna fell from the skies to feed the hungry children of Israel (Exodus 16:1-36), or in the promise of a land "flowing with milk and honey" (Exodus 3:8, 17). In return, God's people demonstrated their trust in God's provision by offering sacrifices of their finest crops or animals—literally burning their possessions at the altar. Ultimately, the faithfulness of God's people was measured by the care they extended to the most vulnerable in their community: the poor, the widows, the orphans, or the strangers and aliens who were passing through (Deuteronomy 10:18). The Hebrews described the flourishing that arises from rightly ordered living as *shalom.*

The shalom that God intended found its fullest expression in the person of Jesus Christ. For the Anabaptists, the incarnation—the Word made flesh in the person of Jesus—was the hinge of the entire biblical story. In Christ, the new Adam (1 Corinthians 15:45), God offers a wayward humanity the possibility of being restored to life the way God intended at creation itself.

Repeatedly, the message of Jesus was to let go of possessions—give and you will receive; don't worry about the future; don't hoard up treasures on earth; give to all who ask. These were not merely encouragements to adjust one's attitude toward possessions; they were invitations to participate in concrete acts of extravagant generosity. Jesus, for example, explicitly warned his disciples against "storing up treasures on earth" (Matthew 6:19-21); he suggested to the rich young ruler that true freedom in Christ is possible only if he was ready to sell his possessions and give to the poor (Mark 10:17-22); and he affirmed the gesture of the woman who poured out expensive oil on his feet as an expression of worship (Mark 14:3-9). At the heart of the gospel is an invitation to share possessions freely—even exuberantly—with others and to live in the childlike trust that God will provide for your daily needs.

These same qualities were part of the early church as it took shape after Christ's ascension and the gift of the Holy Spirit at Pentecost. For the first Christians, the decision to follow Jesus—to become a "new creature in Christ" (2 Corinthians 5:17)—meant letting go of the sin of possessiveness. Sharing of material goods in the context of community—what would later be called mutual aid—was an essential mark of the Spirit's presence. One of the first official acts of a new community in Jerusalem was to identify deacons to tend to the needs of widows and the poor in their midst. Repeatedly, Paul exhorted new believers to share generously with each other, and he issued sober warnings against church members who celebrated the Lord's Supper while ignoring differences in wealth (1 Corinthians 11:17-32).

Behind this posture of generosity and trust in the early church was a desire for *koinonia*—a rich word appearing often throughout the New Testament that means fellowship, sharing, partnership, or communion. Because believers "share in" (*koinonia*) the divine character of Christ (e.g., 2 Peter 1:3-6), they are called to express *koinonia* with each other. Thus, the early Christians described in Acts 2 "devoted themselves" to the *koinonia*:

> All the believers were together and had everything in common. They sold property and possessions to give to anyone who had need. Every day they continued to meet together in the temple courts. They broke bread in their homes and ate together with glad and sincere hearts, praising God and enjoying the favor of all the people. (Acts 2:44-47)

As a result of this tangible expression of *koinonia* "the Lord added to their number daily those who were being saved."

The apostle Paul made a similar connection in his letter to the Corinthians. As recipients of God's generous gift of mercy and grace, the churches in Macedonia would naturally share "generously" and "cheerfully" with the needy saints in Jerusalem (2 Corinthians 8-9). One of the earliest compilations of Christian doctrines, a text known as the *Didache*, included the following instruction: "Never turn away the needy; share all your possessions with your brother and sister, and do not claim that anything is your own." "The evidence is conclusive," writes one scholar of the period, that early Christians "held the sharing of wealth to be an essential part of the Christian community."[7]

Although the Catholic Church eventually made its peace with private property and the later feudal structures of inequality and power, the radical economic teachings of Jesus refused to disappear, particularly among monastic orders, who have preserved the principles of shared possessions, mutual aid, and voluntary poverty until today.

Despite the deep anxieties of sixteenth-century princes that the Anabaptist teachings on economics were a threat to social stability, in reality the Anabaptists were simply carrying forward a set of principles deeply embedded in the biblical story and the broader Christian tradition. "Freely you have received," Jesus instructed his disciples, therefore you should "freely give" (Matthew 10:8).

Diversity of Anabaptist Witness

Agreeing on the principles of *koinonia*, however, does not resolve the question of how those convictions will find expression in daily life. For example, when Jesus said "Give to all who ask" or "Give no thought for tomorrow," what did he actually mean? Even earnest Christians like the early Anabaptists, who were determined to take the words of Jesus seriously, quickly recognized that some interpretation would be necessary. Here is where the story becomes more complicated.

HUTTERITES: COMMUNITY OF GOODS

For the Hutterites, the biblical mandate was clear: all sin can be traced to the desire to possess things. They rejected private property in the conviction that the gathered body of believers (*Gemeinde*) only became the body of Christ if it literally held all things in common (*Gemein*). The most radical of the Anabaptist groups, the Hutterites rejected all private property, refused to pay war taxes, and adopted a communitarian life that erected a clear boundary between their communities and the surrounding society.[8]

Contemporary descriptions of Hutterite colonies as "beehives" or "dovecotes" were intended to be derogatory; but such metaphors were appropriate descriptions of well-ordered communities that elevated common good over personal good. In Hutterite colonies, membership in the church was inseparable from the economic, educational, and cultural life of the community, in which there was no private property. "Everyone, wherever he was," according to the *Hutterite Chronicle*, "worked for the common good to

A detractor imagined Hutterite communal living in the sixteenth century as chaotic and noisy like a dovecote (house). USED BY PERMISSION OF MENNONITE HISTORICAL LIBRARY, GOSHEN COLLEGE

A Hutterite pamphlet showing the positive view of their early Anabaptist faith community, which continues today to hold all possessions in common. USED BY PERMISSION OF MENNONITE HISTORICAL LIBRARY, GOSHEN COLLEGE

supply the needs of all and to give help and support wherever it was needed. It was indeed a perfect body whose living members served one another."[9] In the 1870s the Hutterites immigrated from Russia, where they had migrated several generations earlier, to North America. Today, around forty-five thousand Hutterites, living in some 420 colonies in the western states and provinces, continue to practice the Anabaptist principle of community of goods.

SWISS BRETHREN: MUTUAL AID WAS ESSENTIAL . . . BUT VOLUNTARY

Many Mennonites and Amish in North America today, especially those living east of the Mississippi River, trace their spiritual roots to another sixteenth-century Anabaptist group known as the Swiss Brethren. The Swiss Brethren shared many basic convictions with the Hutterites. They practiced adult baptism, rejected the oath and the use of the sword, and sought to put the teachings of Christ into daily practice. And like the Hutterites, they assumed that faith could only be lived in the context of a community of believers that practiced some form of economic sharing.[10]

Nevertheless, the Swiss Brethren argued that mutual aid could not be coerced. While community of goods was a very fine thing, it should be a *voluntary* expression of Christian love and not an absolute principle of Christian faithfulness. "I don't reject property," insisted Hans Hausimann, an emissary from the Basel congregation commissioned to baptize in Bern. "In the beginning of Christianity everything was in common. But it is no command."[11]

In a similar way, Hans Pauli Kuchenbecker, a Swiss Brethren in Hesse, included several articles on mutual aid in his 1578 confession of faith. "Newborn Christians and children of God," wrote Kuchenbecker, "can buy, own and use their own property *as long as they help the poor and extend aid*." Another article in his confession offered even clearer teaching on the congregation's responsibility "to support our poor members and comrades in the faith, old and sick, widows and orphans, and to show love to other needy people."[12]

As a marginalized and persecuted people, the Swiss Brethren lacked the resources and civic space needed to create a highly structured form of mutual aid. They did, however, develop guidelines for regulating the economic activities of church members. In 1568 when representatives from congregations throughout Switzerland and South Germany met at Strasbourg to seek a common position on matters of faith and practice, eight of the twenty-three articles of agreement addressed economic issues.[13]

Each congregation ordained a deacon (*Armendiener*) to tend to the needs of widows, orphans, and the poor. According to one job description, deacons "are to distribute to the poor the gifts received for this purpose, so that the giver shall remain unknown as Christ teaches."[14] Other expressions of mutual aid among the Swiss Brethren included economic support for ministers and their families, and travel funds to assist refugees. An entry in the church record book from the congregation in Montbeliard in Alsace suggests a system in which several members cared for an elderly person on a rotating basis.[15]

By refusing to make community of goods an absolute principle, the Swiss Brethren joined a measure of both Christian voluntarism and pragmatic flexibility to mutual aid, which sometimes prompted fierce debates with the Hutterites, who regarded economic equality as an essential principle of the gospel.

DUTCH MENNONITES: WEALTH AND THE PRINCIPLE OF GENEROSITY

Anabaptists in the lower Rhine and the Netherlands pursued yet another model of mutual aid. Like the Hutterites and Swiss Brethren, Anabaptists in northern Europe affirmed an understanding of Christian faith that had direct consequences for daily life. "It will not help a fig," insisted Menno Simons, a leader of the early Dutch Anabaptist movement, "to boast of the Lord's blood, death, merits, grace or gospel if the believer is not truly converted from his sinful life." Becoming "like minded with Jesus" implied a commitment to actually live like Jesus. "True evangelical faith," Menno wrote, "cannot lie dormant. It clothes the naked, it feeds the hungry, it comforts the sorrowful, it shelters the destitute, it serves those that harm it, it binds up that which is wounded, it has become all things to all people."[16]

Menno, from whom Mennonites would later derive their name, shared with his Hutterite and Swiss Brethren cousins a conviction that faith would inevitably lead to a new perspective on wealth and possessions. "How is it possible," Menno asked rhetorically, "for the love of God to dwell in a person who has this world's goods, sees his brother in need, and then closes his heart to compassion for that person?"[17] Menno did not think it was impossible for a Christian to be a merchant or retailer, but he frequently warned against the temptations that went along with such occupations.[18]

The context of Anabaptism in the Netherlands, however, was very different from that of either the Hutterites or the Swiss Brethren. In 1581 the newly-formed Dutch Republic gave Mennonites limited freedoms. During the centuries that followed, Dutch Mennonites were fully engaged in nearly every aspect of society. In the world of business, for example, their work ethic, frugality, honesty, and networks of family and congregational connections made them leaders in a host of profitable industries—especially in shipping, salt production, textiles, and the manufacture of decorative tiles—earning them the nickname "the worker bees of the Dutch state." Mennonites gained widespread recognition for their engineering skills, harnessing wind power to drain the polders and reclaim fertile farmland from the North Sea. In the printing industry, Mennonites took the lead as publishers, mapmakers, artists, and writers.

Wealthy Dutch Mennonites were quick to apply their entrepreneurial and organizational skills to meet the needs of church members who were less fortunate. In the middle of the seventeenth century, for example, the Waterlander congregation in Amsterdam had ten deacons or "ministers of the poor," who met on a weekly basis to hear appeals for financial or material assistance from members of the congregation and to tend to the needs of widows, orphans, and the elderly.[19] The deacons offered financial advice, settled financial disputes, resolved bankruptcy cases, supported housing costs for orphans, and administered homes for widows and elderly members. They even provided medical care for members, sometimes paying a physician a retainer for his services with the understanding that he would treat members without charge. These same deacons received bequests to the congregational poor fund. And they were expected to invest excess funds and endowments, often loaning money at interest to members who sought capital for their own business ventures.[20]

Dutch Mennonites extended this same generous spirit and highly organized form of mutual aid to needs outside their congregation, particularly to their Swiss Brethren "cousins in the faith" who were imprisoned, forced from their homes, and dispossessed of their farms throughout the seventeenth century. For the Dutch Mennonites, who were living in a context of religious toleration and economic growth, personal wealth supported a host of church-related projects that addressed the needs of the poor, supported theological education, and funded numerous philanthropic initiatives.

By the middle of the sixteenth century, all Anabaptist groups understood themselves to be stewards, not owners, of God's creation; all thought of their community as a form of *koinonia*; and all assumed that sharing possessions was an inevitable response to God's own generosity. But even though they agreed on these core principles, they applied them in very different ways that changed over time as circumstances and contexts shifted.

The contrasting understandings of wealth and possession that were evident among the Hutterites, Swiss Brethren, and Dutch Mennonites raised a host of interesting and complicated questions that have continued to shape Anabaptist-Mennonite groups ever since. The creative tensions embedded in this extended conversation provide a useful context for understanding the story of the formation of Mennonite Mutual Aid in 1945 and the seventy-five-year journey that has led to the work of Everence today.

Mutual Aid and the Emergence of Church-Related Institutions in North America

When Anabaptist-Mennonite groups emigrated to North America in the eighteenth and early nineteenth century their primary identity as a religious community—along with their understandings of mutual aid—focused on the local congregation. In contrast to the Catholic Church, Mennonites had no pope whose authority transcended geography and culture. In contrast to the Lutheran Church, which had settled on the Augsburg Confession of 1530 as its authoritative lens for interpreting Scripture, Anabaptist-Mennonites had adopted a range of confessional statements, none of which had an all-encompassing authority. Unlike the Anglican (or Episcopal) Church, Mennonites did not have a well-defined hierarchy of bishops, nor did they embrace a high view of the sacraments, which could anchor the mystical unity of the church.

Instead, the Mennonites who first settled in the regions around Philadelphia in 1683 brought with them a view of the church that was strongly oriented to the local congregation and a thick web of family relationships, ethnic folkways, oral traditions, and shared practices. To be sure, religious beliefs mattered to colonial Mennonites; but the primary expression of their religious identity focused on face-to-face relationships in the local faith community, not in formal organizations or in abstract doctrine.

This congregationalist orientation was shaped in part by historical experience. Since their origins in the radical wing of the Reformation, many Anabaptist-Mennonites had lived under the constant threat of persecution at worst, or as a tolerated minority at best. In times of active persecution, survival dictated that congregations met in secret, often in small groups to avoid detection. As tolerated minorities, they no longer faced direct threats to their lives; but the price for survival was a deep sense of being a people at the margins. These Mennonites and Amish tended to live in isolated hamlets, worshiping in homes, as congregations comprised largely of extended families. Their pastors—uneducated and unsalaried—were selected from within the community. As a result, they placed a high value on tradition and localism, and accepted their identity as a people apart.

Somewhere in the back of their minds, Anabaptist-Mennonites living in colonial America knew they were part of a larger church—a universal church that was bigger than their congregations. But they experienced the body of

Christ most tangibly in the concrete, face-to-face relationships of the local faith community—in regular worship, in sharing their possessions, in dressing modestly, speaking sparingly, resolving conflicts peacefully, and in countless other daily practices of Christian discipleship.

As other Christian traditions organized themselves into denominations—with national assemblies, church offices, and institutions like seminaries and mission boards—Anabaptist-Mennonites expressed their identity in more organic ways. They shared a distinctive dialect of German long after many other immigrants had given up their mother tongues. They had a common sense of history, preserved in texts such as the *Martyrs Mirror*. And some of the distinctive features of their faith—such as adult baptism, refusal to swear oaths, or their commitment to nonresistance—clearly set them apart from their Catholic, Lutheran, and Reformed neighbors. In the late eighteenth century, the American Revolutionary War forced Mennonites into a heightened awareness of their shared identity as they struggled to find consensus on a host of new and difficult questions: Could they pay war taxes? Should they swear allegiance to the British monarch? How should they respond to the formation of local militias? In sorting out answers to these questions, their first impulse was to do so as a congregation or as a people rather than as a denomination.

This decentralized, informal approach to church organization and authority served Mennonite communities reasonably well, especially when they were forced to the margins of European society. In the more tolerant context of North America, however, as memories of state church oppression receded, the traditional patterns of church life seemed increasingly anachronistic.

CHALLENGE TO TRADITION

One early sign of growing frustration with these informal and local understandings of identity were the reforming efforts of John H. Oberholtzer. From an early age, Oberholtzer was an accomplished locksmith, owner of a printing press, and eventually the editor of several religious newspapers in Berks County, Pennsylvania. In 1842, as the newly-ordained minister of Swamp Mennonite Church, Oberholtzer began to challenge the inherited patterns of Mennonite tradition.[21] He especially chafed at the informal structure of the Franconia Mennonite ministers' meeting or conference, which he regarded as poorly organized—since they had no formal policies to structure their decision-making and did not keep minutes of their meetings.

In October 1847, Oberholtzer led a group of young ministers to break with the Franconia Conference. In keeping with the progressive spirit of the

Lutheran and Reformed churches around them, he envisioned a healthy church primarily in organizational terms, with clearly defined roles, procedures, and lines of authority. Already in 1844 he had written a constitution for Swamp Mennonite Church, codifying the habits and assumptions of congregational life into the formal language of policy. The new Eastern Pennsylvania Mennonite Conference that he started also had a written constitution with detailed bylaws, and Oberholtzer was adamant that a secretary take minutes at their meetings.[22]

Oberholtzer envisioned other organizations as well. He organized a children's Bible study course, introduced a new catechism, and developed warm relationships with neighboring Lutheran and Reformed pastors. In 1850 he oversaw the creation of a formal plan for "the poor and suffering members of the Christian community"—one of the first mutual aid associations formed by Mennonites in North America. Ten years later, at a gathering in Donnellson, Iowa, he took a leading role in founding the General Conference of the Mennonite Church—a loose alliance of progressive congregations that soon organized a host of new institutions, including a mission board, a seminary, and a publishing house.

Even as traditional Mennonites—now sometimes referred to as (Old) Mennonites to distinguish them from the General Conference Mennonites—

Traditionally, only the congregation provided mutual aid to its members in need because Anabaptists didn't cooperate at a regional or national level. MENNONITE CHURCH USA ARCHIVES

John Oberholtzer oversaw the first plan among U.S. Mennonites to help "the poor and suffering members of the Christian community." MENNONITE LIBRARY AND ARCHIVES, BETHEL COLLEGE.

were resisting the innovations Oberholtzer sought to introduce, other forces were at work that also strained the fabric of their communities. Steadily rising land prices in Pennsylvania and Virginia had prompted hundreds of Mennonites to follow the broader westward movement, attracted by the promise of cheap land, open prairies, or simply the lure of adventure. As the U.S. government forced the removal of native peoples from the territories west of the Appalachian Mountains, Mennonites followed, settling on the frontier in Ohio, Indiana, and Illinois. Scattered across vast distances, some settlements managed to establish small churches; but many struggled to maintain ministers and found themselves spiritually isolated.

Casting an even deeper shadow over the church, as well as the nation as a whole, were the divisive politics of slavery and the bloody civil war in the early 1860s. Mennonites found themselves geographically on opposite sides of the Civil War, uncertain about their traditional commitment to nonresistance, divided by the debates over slavery and states' rights, and ravaged by the physical trauma of violent, pillaging armies. By 1865, when the war came to an end, the Mennonite church as a whole seemed fragmented. Traditional Mennonite leaders found themselves increasingly out of step with the surrounding culture: they advocated peace and humility in an age of chest-thumping expansion; they still spoke German when the future was clearly English; they harbored lingering uncertainties about commerce at a time when young entrepreneurs were seeking their fortunes. While other groups were establishing a vast network of denominational colleges, they worried that higher education would only lead to pride and acculturation. "If the young people go to church at all," a dispirited leader wrote, "they go not to the Mennonite churches but to others, where not everything looks so dead."

Yet the Mennonite church did not wither away. Beginning in the 1860s, and through the next century, Mennonites in North America underwent a series of fundamental transformations in their understanding of the church and Mennonite identity. At the heart of that transformation was a growing readiness to adopt the new forms of organization—and the institutional culture that accompanied them—that John Oberholtzer had been promoting several decades earlier.

New Forms of Church Life and Identity: The Rise of Institutions

One central figure looms over the organizational transformation that took place in the last quarter of the nineteenth century: John F. Funk. Like Oberholtzer, Funk was an inquisitive, creative, and restless entrepreneur from eastern Pennsylvania who spent his life seeking to renew the Anabaptist-Mennonite tradition he had inherited by adapting it to the changing culture of his time. In 1857, the twenty-two-year-old Funk moved from his insular Mennonite community in Bucks County, Pennsylvania, to the bustling city of Chicago, where he established a successful lumber company. A year later, he had a conversion experience at a Presbyterian revival meeting and soon became an enthusiastic supporter of urban ministries associated with Dwight L. Moody. In 1860 Funk returned to his congregation in Pennsylvania to be baptized. After his return to the Midwest, Funk devoted the rest of his life to bringing the organizational zeal he had encountered among progressive Christians in Chicago into alignment with the theological convictions of his Mennonite upbringing.[23]

In 1864 Funk established a periodical intended primarily for members of the (Old) Mennonite Church. Published in both English and German, the *Herald of Truth* introduced its scattered readers to their history and identity. He promoted a new English translation of the *Martyrs Mirror*. His articles featured early Anabaptists, including Menno Simons, and especially the stories of Anabaptist martyrs. And Funk included regular updates from correspondents on local congregational news, along with spirited debates on church-related topics.

In October of 1873, Funk issued a rousing call to readers of the *Herald of Truth* and its German counterpart, *Herald der Wahrheit*. For more than a year, the papers had printed reports that a large number of Mennonites in South Russia were exploring the possibility of emigrating to North America. In an editorial, Funk called on every congregation to support the immigrants financially, either with an outright gift or an interest-free loan. Funk directed his appeal "not just to one branch of the church, but all the different branches. Let us in this matter, at least, join hands and work together for the common good of the church, for the extension of the Kingdom of Christ. . . . Let us show our faith by our works. . . . Almost everyone could spare a dollar for such a cause, and some who are rich and have much of this world's goods, can give a great deal more." "Our church," he urged, "should certainly be able to raise $20,000 or $30,000 for their poor brethren who must leave their country for conscience' sake."[24]

North American Mennonites responded generously. As funds began to arrive, Funk organized an inter-Mennonite committee called "Mennonite Board of Guardians" to handle the money and coordinate details. The task was not easy. Early on, the group debated whether the contributions were to be considered gifts or loans—and, if the latter, what the appropriate terms should be. Committee members also differed on details regarding logistics, who to trust in negotiating land deals, the best locations for resettlement, and exactly how the money should be distributed. The project grew more complicated when leaders in the established Mennonite communities in eastern Pennsylvania expressed distrust for an initiative being led by upstarts in the Midwest. Hesitant to send money to Indiana for disbursement, they formed their own committee to oversee the funds raised in their region. But coordinated effort to address the needs of the immigrants moved forward.

Between 1873 and 1880 some eighteen thousand Mennonites from Polish Volhynia and South Russia—about one-third of all the Mennonites in the region—relocated in North America, mostly settling in Kansas, Nebraska, South Dakota, and Manitoba. The organized support of Mennonites in the United States proved crucial to the venture. By 1881, the Mennonite Board of Guardians had distributed nearly $40,500, while the Pennsylvania group contributed another $44,000.[25]

In many regards, there was nothing unique about Funk's initiative to persuade Anabaptist-Mennonites to support their cousins in the faith. Countless immigrants in the nineteenth century relied on the generosity of their co-religionists to make the transition to their new lives.[26] Once settled in their new homeland, these communities continued to support each other by assisting widows and orphans, exchanging financial advice, extending loans, providing

John F. Funk rallied the Mennonite church in the United States to help groups of Anabaptists immigrate from South Russia (Ukraine today). MENNONITE CHURCH USA ARCHIVES

job placements, and sharing in the cost of funerals. But for Mennonites, the Board of Guardians symbolized a new type of church-related organization that was to have profound consequences in the coming century.

At the heart of this new organizational activity was an emerging sense of what sociologist Benedict Anderson has called an "imagined community."[27] Although Anderson coined the term for his analysis of modern nationalism, the concept is useful in other contexts as well. For Mennonites living in the Midwest, the emergence of church-related institutions helped to foster a sense of connection that went beyond the face-to-face context of a closely knit agrarian community. These connections were increasingly abstract or "imagined," constructed by the shared experience of reading of a church periodical, contributing to a church-related organization, or benefiting from the services of a church-related institution.

When Mennonites living in small settlements in Ohio, Illinois, or Iowa learned of the plight of the Mennonite immigrants from South Russia in the pages of the *Herald of Truth*, they recognized these previously unknown individuals as brothers and sisters in their family of faith. Readers had already encountered historical essays in the paper suggesting that Mennonites in distant Russia were connected—in spirit and theology, though not directly by blood—to the Swiss and South German Mennonites who had emigrated to America several generations earlier. They came to realize that Russian Mennonites also knew the stories of the *Martyrs Mirror*; that they, too, claimed some affinity with the writings of Menno Simons and could trace their origins to the same Anabaptists of the sixteenth century. The implicit message was clear: what the Russian Mennonites were now experiencing is what "we" also once experienced.

Since no single congregation in the United States was prepared to take responsibility for handling the details of their immigration, those readers were ready to create a new kind of organization—the Mennonite Board of Guardians—to collect and distribute resources to help them. The Board of Guardians did the work of the congregation on a larger scale—representing their collective interests, multiplying their small contributions, and concentrating expertise in logistical details and complex negotiations that individual congregations could not do on their own.

Although the Board of Guardians was short-lived, it marked the beginning of a new type of organization: a "church-related institution." Few participants at the time could define exactly what was happening; yet the energy generated around this new collective form of mutual aid was unmistakable. It pointed in the direction of a host of other Mennonite church-related institutions that would soon transform the character and meaning of "church."

The Golden Age of Institutions (1890–1950)

Starting in the last decade of the nineteenth century, the character of the wider Anabaptist-Mennonite community in North America was profoundly transformed by the emergence of dozens of church-related institutions, more or less similar to the Board of Guardians.

Among the earliest initiatives were a host of mission organizations—as many as sixteen foreign programs between 1880 and 1930. These included the General Conference Mennonite Church outreach to the Arapahoe, Hopi, and Cheyenne peoples; (Old) Mennonite "home missions" in Chicago; a host of overseas missions by the newly-established Mennonite Board of Missions and Charities and several regional conferences of churches. All of these projects required organization: appeals for funds, oversight boards, administrative logistics, theological expertise, and training in language and culture. These skills, in turn, required a ready supply of educated young people who were prepared to assume these tasks.[28]

Thus, parallel to the emergence of mission institutions, Mennonite groups also organized educational enterprises. As with missions, the General Conference Mennonite Church took the lead. In 1868, they established the Wadsworth Institute, a seminary in Ohio, which bore the official name

"Christian Educational Institution of the Mennonite Denomination." In the following decades, Mennonites in Kansas, Indiana, Ohio, and Virginia established at least ten high schools or colleges, which would go on to produce thousands of administrators, educators, doctors, nurses, missionaries, theologians, and relief workers.

Others took up Funk's interest in publishing, often to promote these institutions and keep their supporters informed of their work. Thus, in addition to the *Herald of Truth*, the *Herold der Wahrheit*, and the *Mennonitische Rundschau*, a periodical that Funk started for newly-arrived Russian Mennonite immigrants, historian James Juhnke has identified at least fifteen other Mennonite periodicals or local newspapers in Kansas alone.[29] Meanwhile, various communities also established nearly a dozen hospitals between 1890 and 1930, as well as a host of local orphanages, homes for the elderly, and even mental asylums.

During the early decades of the twentieth century, Mennonite identity in North America was undergoing a profound transformation, marked especially by a rapid embrace of new forms of organization that enabled individuals and congregations to collaborate in a shared mission. Amid this enthusiasm for institution-building, three organizations merit particular attention since each was to have a formative impact on the emergence of Mennonite Mutual Aid in 1945.

GENERAL CONFERENCE OF THE (OLD) MENNONITE CHURCH

For centuries, the preferred organizational model of Mennonite congregations in the Swiss and South German tradition had been the "ministers' meeting" or "conference,"[30] in which local ministers and bishops met for conversation. These conferences varied significantly in formality and authority. The conference that formed around Lancaster, Pennsylvania, for example, developed a strong bishop board, which sought to maintain a shared set of beliefs and practices within all its congregations. Other conferences, especially in the Midwest, tended to be less structured. By the 1890s some sixteen regional conferences had emerged among the (Old) Mennonites. Now, inspired by the organizational energy unleashed by Funk and others, some leaders were looking for more formal connections with each other. In November of 1897, seventy bishops and ministers gathered at the Pike Meetinghouse in Elida, Ohio, to consider the formation of a broader church body. Their goal was to bring about "a closer unity of sentiment on Gospel principles."[31] With strong support from regional conferences in the Midwest, the group reconvened the following year in Wakarusa, Indiana, and formally organized itself as the "General Conference" of the Mennonite Church—a most unfortunate name since it virtually guaranteed confusion with the General Conference Mennonite Church that had formed in 1860.[32]

Leaders insisted that they did not intend to usurp the authority of regional conferences or local congregations. But from the beginning, the General Conference exerted its control over emerging church institutions, particularly in the areas of mission, publication, and education. The General Conference's first moderator, Daniel Kauffman, was quick to recognize the power of print in shaping the "imagined community" of the (Old) Mennonite Church. For nearly forty years (1905 to 1943), he served as editor of the church's periodical, the *Gospel Herald*, speaking authoritatively on church doctrine and practice through his editorials and control of the paper's contents.[33] Kauffman also exercised enormous influence on most of the boards of the new church-related institutions, and he emerged as an arbiter of orthodoxy on all manner of theological concerns. The ministers and bishops who gathered for the biennial meetings of the General Conference oversaw the work of the Mennonite Publishing House; they exercised enormous influence over Mennonite colleges through the Board of Education; they appointed members to the Mission Board; they addressed controversial issues by appointing study committees; and they interpreted and enforced the recommendations on doctrine and practice that emerged from those committees. As a testimony to its growing authority, the General Conference represented the (Old) Mennonite Church to the U.S. government on legislative concerns, especially on conscientious objection. Significantly, the two oldest and largest conferences in the east—Franconia and Lancaster—did not formally join the General Conference, choosing instead to maintain their own authority. Nevertheless, bishops from both groups frequently attended and even voted in the General Conference sessions.

Between 1898 and 1971, when a new model of organization emerged, the General Conference of the Mennonite Church gradually came to embody the official voice of the (Old) Mennonite Church. Any new organization—such as Mennonite Mutual Aid when it came into existence in 1945—would need to answer to its authority.

MUTUAL AID SOCIETIES

Through the first half of the nineteenth century, most forms of sharing within the Mennonite community were local, ad hoc, and spontaneous. Members responded as needs emerged. But by midcentury some communities were calling for a more formal approach. Already in 1850, for example, John Oberholtzer had urged his congregation to create a mutual aid plan for the "poor and suffering members of the community."[34] Eight years later, Mennonites in Wellesley, Ontario, formed the Amish Mennonite Storm and Fire Aid Union to protect members against catastrophic property loss, soon to be followed by the Sonnenberg Mutual Insurance Association of Dalton, Ohio, in 1859, and the creation in 1866 of the Mennonite Mutual Aid Society among General Conference Mennonites in Bluffton, Ohio.

Each of these fledgling efforts carried with it some controversy. Although most members in these new societies were from the same congregation and the impulses behind the initiatives were deeply religious, the new organizations were not identified exclusively with the congregation. In today's language we might call them parachurch organizations that operated parallel to the church, but were ultimately controlled by boards whose authority was, formally at least, independent of the ministers.

Interest in mutual aid societies grew exponentially during the last half of the nineteenth century following the first wave of Mennonite immigrants from South Russia in the 1870s. During their sojourn in South Russia, Mennonites had organized in colonies—essentially self-governing commonwealths. Although the church remained the dominant social institution, Mennonites in Russia developed their own schools, hospitals, and orphanages. They built roads and bridges, established grain elevators and market exchanges, published books and newspapers, and formed music and literary societies.

They also developed numerous institutions for mutual aid. These collective forms of economic assistance had a deep history, going all the way back to seventeenth-century Prussia. Indeed, the earliest known Mennonite mutual aid society dates to 1623, when a series of fires among the Mennonite communities in West Prussia prompted a group in the Tiegenhof congregation to organize the Tiegenhöfer Private Fire Plan (*Tiegenhöfer Privat Brandordnung*).[35] Another fire aid plan, started around 1725 among Mennonites living nearby, became the model for numerous future mutual aid societies. In these associations, administered by volunteers, members assigned their own value to their property; premiums were levied only after a loss; and assessments were calculated according to the value each member had identified for their property. Generally, the community provided labor for rebuilding the damaged structure, with the aid society paying the cost of materials.

As descendants of these Prussian Mennonites, colony leaders in South Russia modeled their own mutual aid societies on the same basic plan. Virtually every colony, for example, had a communal storehouse of grain that was available to the poor or families facing unexpected hardships.[36] Every colony also had fire and storm insurance plans, a widows and orphans fund, a burial aid society, and numerous other agricultural cooperatives for sharing labor, capital, risks, and profits.[37]

When large numbers of Russian Mennonites migrated to North America, they brought with them a long tradition of mutual aid societies and the administrative policies and formal procedures needed for success. They arrived at precisely the moment when groups long established in North America were just beginning to develop their own organizations for mutual aid.

By the early twentieth century, Mennonite mutual aid societies were proliferating in North America. According to one count, various groups of Mennonites and Amish Mennonites had formed nearly forty associations by 1920. Almost all of them were organizations with small capitalizations and modest premiums.[38] But they were institutional forms of sharing—with boards, constitutions, and bylaws—that went beyond the spontaneous, face-to-face forms of mutual aid within the congregation, and were ultimately regulated by written policies to which even the bishops were subject.[39]

None of these expressions of mutual aid were unique to the Mennonite tradition—other religious and ethnic groups had similar plans. However, the strong emphasis on community in Anabaptist-Mennonite theology, combined with an equally strong commitment to the life and teachings of Christ, strengthened and sustained these communal practices of sharing.

MENNONITE CENTRAL COMMITTEE

Many of the mutual aid societies that emerged in communities before 1920 were local institutions, focused exclusively on the needs of church members within their immediate vicinity. But North American Mennonites were also increasingly aware of human suffering elsewhere in the world. In the late 1890s, for example, the (Old) Mennonite Church formed a Home and Foreign Relief Commission to raise funds in response to a famine in India; in 1899, the General Conference Mennonite church formed a similar Emergency Relief Commission. Immediately after the end of World War I, yet another Relief Commission for War Sufferers collaborated with Quakers to support postwar reconstruction in France.

In the spring of 1920, news circulated in church papers of a famine among Russian Mennonites in the Ukraine who were already devastated by the Bolshevik Revolution and ensuing civil war. In response, leaders from the (Old) Mennonite Church, the General Conference Mennonite Church, and the Mennonite Brethren church agreed to join their relief efforts into a single organization with the prosaic name of Mennonite Central Committee (MCC).[40] The formation of MCC had a wide-ranging impact. Not only did it provide a significant amount of relief aid; it also gave expression to an "imagined community" that enabled an even broader coalition of Anabaptist-Mennonite groups to collaborate in a common mission.

MCC's mission was rooted unmistakably in the local church; yet the scope of its vision and administration was always larger than any single group. Moreover, from the beginning MCC administrators were forced to deal with the complexities of power, including negotiations with governments, balancing the expectations of diverse constituencies, and making hard choices about the distribution of limited resources in situations of seemingly infinite need. Celebrating its 100th anniversary in 2020, MCC has become one of the church's most visible institutions—a complex, far-reaching network that brought together numerous Anabaptist groups into a common cause of service "in the name of Christ."

Critique of Institutions: The Medium Is the Message

The remarkable variety of church-related organizations that emerged during the course of the twentieth century—missions, relief, service, education, publication, mutual aid, etc.—gradually came to define the public face of the church. The new institutions gave a visible, positive, and relevant witness to the theological convictions of the Anabaptist-Mennonite tradition. They enabled individual congregations to connect to worlds beyond their regional and national borders. They fostered a coherent collective identity within the landscape of American denominationalism. And they creatively channeled the energy and talents of young people into the service of the church.

Not surprisingly, the leaders who devoted their lives to these new institutions and the flurry of transformational activity around them regarded them as an unmitigated success. John F. Funk characterized the era as the "Great Awakening" of the Mennonite Church, a term that quickly became a standard description in history texts.[41] Guy F. Hershberger, a Mennonite sociologist and leading church figure in the midtwentieth century, declared that "the new vision of the gospel, the church, and the Christian life which came as the fruit of Funk's labors was nothing less than a . . . 'recovery of the Anabaptist vision.'"[42] Other historians of the church have characterized the energetic organizational fervor as a "renewal," or a "revival," viewing these new forms of Mennonite engagement with the world as solid evidence of an unmistakable evolution of Christian faithfulness.

Toward the end of the twentieth century, however, scholars began to sound a new, more critical, note in their assessment of this transformation. In part, this skepticism reflected a cultural mood that was critical of all institutions. Although published already in 1932, Reinhold Niebuhr's *Moral Man and Immoral Society* gained a new relevance in the years after World War II as the world struggled to come to terms with the Holocaust and the blind allegiance that many well-educated German Christians had given to institutional structures that systematically perpetuated mass murder on a targeted group of people. At the heart of Niebuhr's argument was his claim that groups of people—acting in their institutional or organizational roles—are much more likely to behave immorally than they would as individuals. Niebuhr's book, the historical experience of Nazi Germany, and the irrational fears unleashed by the McCarthy anti-Communist hearings in the 1950s, began to raise serious questions about the moral limits of institutions in general, particularly the way that the individual conscience could be overwhelmed by institutional groupthink.

The 1960s witnessed a further cultural backlash against the dehumanizing qualities of institutions. With the rapid rise of large corporations in the post–World War II economy, a growing number of social critics began to describe institutional culture as faceless bureaucracies—impersonal extensions of the industrial factory floor. In an effort to maximize productivity and efficiency, organizations reduced employees to "inputs," whose value was assessed in purely quantitative terms.

In 1964, the social theorist Marshall McLuhan summarized many of these concerns in a book titled *Understanding Media*, in which he popularized the phrase "The medium is the message."[43] McLuhan's main focus was on new forms of modern communication, particularly television. In it, he argued that the *medium* of communication—that is, the form by which a message is transmitted—is actually more important than its intended meaning or content. The fact that television, for example, can transform evening conversations among family members into a passive and largely solitary experience of watching a flickering image is much more significant than the content of the program the family is watching. For McLuhan, the public debate over the potential religious or educational value of television was largely irrelevant. What mattered was the transformative effect of the medium itself—in this case, television—on the viewers.

For critics of institutions, McLuhan's argument that "the medium is the message" offered a powerful tool of analysis. It suggested that the very structure of modern institutions—organized around strategic goals, rationalized workflow, quantitative measures of success, and compartmentalized areas of expertise—had an inherent logic that operated independently of the moral purpose that the institution was intended to serve.

Precisely because the logic of organizational culture seems so self-evident, operating at a largely unconscious level, it is almost impossible to challenge, even though it might be at cross purposes with the stated goals of the institution. The moral implications of this insight were less troubling for secular institutions, which often focused explicitly on the "bottom line" of profits. But for church-related institutions—who perceived themselves to be an extension of the faith commitments of the church—McLuhan's argument sounded more ominous.

Not surprisingly, this broader cultural critique of institutions in the 1960s and 1970s found its way into Mennonite scholarship as well. Historian Theron Schlabach was one of the first to sound the alarm. In a landmark essay in 1977, Schlabach cautioned against the triumphalist tone that had become part of the narrative of Mennonite institution-building.[44] In Schlabach's account, the shift to organizational forms of church life—the era of Mennonite institution building—was part of a larger process of acculturation into mainstream American society that brought with it the loss of a distinctive identity and witness.[45]

Other scholars critiqued the rise of Mennonite institutions by highlighting the negative effects that modernization—particularly the transition from a rural to an industrial society—has had on human relationships. In traditional rural or village communities (*Gemeinden*) relationships tend to be small-scale and face-to-face. In the Anabaptist-Mennonite tradition, the congregation—also called a *Gemeinde* in German—functioned like an extended family or village. Of course, it included all the squabbles, conflicts, and pettiness associated with family relationships; but those relationships were also infused with a sense of vulnerability, intimacy, sharing, and trust. For Mennonites, this concept of the congregation as *Gemeinde* was not just a quaint artifact of early modern European society; it also reflected deep theological commitments that shaped their understanding of mutual aid, generosity, and care for the vulnerable.[46]

With the rise of modernity, however, these local, intimate relationships were transformed. Modern societies operate by the principles of a corporation (*Gesellschaft*) rather than a community (*Gemeinde*). Corporations place a premium on rationality, efficiency, and the consistent application of policies and procedures over individual needs or idiosyncrasies.

In church-related organizations, the shift from *Gemeinde* to *Gesellschaft* often follows a discernable, even predictable, pattern. Many church institutions are founded by highly motivated Christians who are strongly committed to a particular moral cause. In pursuit of that cause, the group defines a mission statement, organizes a board, and plunges into the work to which they have been called. Over time, however, especially as the organization grows larger, integrates more people, and faces competition, this initial vision begins to fade.

As new challenges emerge, the handbook of procedures and policies expands. Overhead costs grow and the need to maintain the internal structure of the organization begins to consume more energy, diverting attention from the original mission. The organization slowly develops its own traditions, routines, and culture that are increasingly resistant to change. Boards devote more attention to the complexities of their fiduciary responsibilities, risk management, and long-term preservation of assets. The organization is likely still doing good work—or at least, it is still involved in some aspect of its original mission. But something vital to the original vision has changed. A *Gemeinde* has become a *Gesellschaft*; organizational logic has prevailed.

Some organizational theorists have described this phenomenon as *isomorphism.*[47] As organizations become more complex and more attentive to the markets in which they are operating, they tend to imitate peer institutions who are doing similar work. Initiatives that emerge in church settings slowly shift their point of reference from the church to other organizations in their field. Thus, for example, the original mission statements of many church organizations like colleges, hospitals, or retirement centers are often explicitly religious, sometimes citing Bible verses to support their work. The bylaws require board members to be adherents of a particular faith tradition. The organizational ties to the church are visible and meaningful. Over time, however, these organizations recognize that they are competing in contexts where the language and logic of the church can easily seem irrelevant or even problematic.

It's not just that a church-related hospital, for example, is competing with a neighboring hospital for patients (or "market share"), though this challenge is real. But they are also operating in a complicated legal and regulatory environment; they depend on professional expertise within a rapidly changing medical context; and they must meet accreditation requirements expected of all hospitals. Thus, it should not come as a surprise that over time, administrators of the church-related hospital realize that they have more in common with administrators of other hospitals than they do with the church leaders who founded the institution.

Without explicitly intending to, church-related organizations gradually adapt to the corporate culture—the technical vocabulary, salary scales, specialized skills, unwritten attitudes and assumptions—of other organizations similar to them. Slowly, the significance of their church connections becomes a distant memory. This shift in identity is rarely the intention or fault of any particular leader; it simply is the natural progression of institutions to be isomorphic—"The medium is the message."

These critiques of institutions are sobering, particularly in light of distinctive Anabaptist-Mennonite beliefs and practices that seem to be in tension with many aspects of modern organizational culture.

But the arguments are not fully convincing.

First, it is ironic that the most vigorous critics of modern Anabaptist-Mennonite institutions almost always draw on historical perspectives and theological insights that were made possible only by institutions themselves—their church-related colleges, seminaries, academic journals, and publishing houses. Terms like *isomorphism*, or the application of McLuhen's analysis, or the language of *structural violence* are themselves a reflection of ways of thinking that emerge only within academic circles.

Moreover, few if any of the most vocal critics are inclined to step out of these institutional worlds and return to a premodern way of life. A small industry of Mennonite scholarship, for example, has emerged around the Old Order Amish, extolling the virtues of Amish communal identity, their resistance to modern individualism, and the ideals they embody of yieldedness and humility. Yet that research relies heavily on resources—grants, libraries, academic training, sabbatical time—that are made possible only by modern institutions. And few scholars of the Old Order Amish are ready to exchange their computers for draft horses. A reflexive suspicion of institutions—whether by the rural traditionalist, the radical activist, or the academic theologian—can easily mask a nostalgic sentimentalism.

The criticism can also reflect a certain naivete about the fact that institutions of some form or another are woven into virtually every aspect of life. Every human craves the intimacy of face-to-face encounters where we are fully known. But the moment a social organization—be it a congregation, a neighborhood, a parent-teacher organization, or a service project—seeks to coordinate the efforts of a larger number of people across geographical distance, some form of organization will emerge and it may develop into an institution. Institutions are virtually inescapable.

Gift of Institutions

There are also more positive arguments for modern institutions. As with many other denominations, Anabaptist-Mennonite institutions have enabled scattered congregations to fulfill their mission by collaborating around shared goals. No single congregation is likely to publish the *Complete Works of Menno Simons*, a hymnal, or a Sunday School curriculum; a denominational publishing house, on the other hand, has the resources and expertise to pursue such tasks. If responding to the devastation of natural disasters in a distant community is part of a congregation's Christian witness, then the structure provided by Mennonite Disaster Service makes it possible to share resources more efficiently than if every congregation tried to organize its own response. If, in the changing context of the church, formal training of pastors becomes a priority, then a group will either create its own seminary or it must accept the fact that within a generation those distinctive teachings will likely disappear— replaced by the theological traditions of pastors trained in other seminaries. Institutions enable and require the concentration of power—that is, resources, expertise, and creativity—that can be used for constructive ends.

Throughout the twentieth century church-related institutions have served Anabaptist-Mennonite congregations as both bridges and boundaries for engaging with the dominant culture. This process, of course, was never simple. Institutions are always the sites of power struggles and conflict. Yet, from the broad perspective of history, these denomination-wide institutions enabled the church to navigate a tumultuous century of change remarkably intact. Publishing houses, hymnal committees, high schools and colleges, seminaries, mission boards, and mutual aid societies all nurtured a sense of identity and purpose whose impact was felt far beyond the Anabaptist-Mennonite community.

Finally, just as we would expect churches in other parts of the world to reflect the cultural context of their setting, so too Anabaptist-Mennonites in North America will inevitably express their faith within the cultural contexts of their day. Of course Christians always face the challenge of critical discernment. But a wholesale rejection of the culture—as if there is a pure Anabaptist-Mennonite way of existing in the world, untainted by cultural context—is naïve. The Spirit is always expressed in the particularity of cultural forms.

The debates among the Hutterites, Swiss Brethren, and Dutch Mennonites regarding different forms of economic sharing point to a deep tension in the Anabaptist-Mennonite tradition that would also deeply shape the history of Everence. Was the church, and its expression of mutual aid, to be understood primarily in terms of face-to-face relationships nurtured over time in small agrarian communities, often within networks of interrelated families? Or was the church also an organization with formal structures and clearly delineated procedures that could reliably meet the needs of many members in different locations?

Few themes capture these tensions better than the story of mutual aid and the church's effort to express the deeply held values of economic sharing and Christian stewardship in a structured, organized way. Mennonite Mutual Aid—the forerunner to Everence—was born in response to a very specific need within the church. The organization's rapid growth in the second half of the twentieth century reflected the profound demographic, economic, and cultural transformations that were taking place in American society, and the ongoing effort of its leaders to respond faithfully and creatively to those changes.

This is the story of Everence. But behind it is a larger story of earnest, imperfect Christians, seeking to bear witness to their faith in a changing world.

TWO

"…Where the People Go"

Origins and Early Years of MMA
(1935–1949)

*O*n August 21, 1935, leaders of the Pacific Coast Mennonite Conference sent an urgent petition to the Executive Committee of the Mennonite Church, asking them "to consider the advisability of organizing a Church-wide plan to care for needy widows."[1] Exactly one week earlier, the U.S. Congress passed the landmark Social Security Act of 1935. Although the United States was the only major industrial country at the time without a national system of social security, public debate over the legislation had been intense. Compared with similar systems in Western European countries, the Social Security Act that President Roosevelt signed into law was actually quite conservative. But for the first time in the nation's history, the federal government took responsibility for the economic security of the aged, the temporarily unemployed, dependent children, and people with disabilities.

Mennonite leaders had followed the debate surrounding the legislation quite closely and most were nervous about developments. Already in April, immediately after the House of Representatives voted in favor of the bill, the Ohio Mennonite and Eastern Amish Mennonite Joint Conference formally requested the Mennonite Church to develop "a means whereby our people would be able to lay away for the future money to be properly invested by some of our able brethren and paid back by way of annuities, funeral expenses, etc."[2] Now that federal Social Security had become reality, the Pacific Coast leaders were reiterating the call for the church to develop an alternative plan—one that they hoped would "eliminate the need of accepting State relief."[3]

There was little question that the problems the Social Security Act aimed to address were real. Throughout the nineteenth century, widows and the elderly were among the most economically vulnerable groups in the United States, with few safety nets beyond family and local charities. The effects of the Great Depression had been devastating, exposing widespread poverty among the elderly, widows, orphans, and people with disabilities in one of the wealthiest countries in the world. The Social Security Act of 1935, part of Roosevelt's Second New Deal initiative, was designed to help the nation recover from the Depression and to manage the rapid social and economic changes brought on by industrialization and urbanization.

Anabaptist-Mennonite groups were also struggling with these same social upheavals. But care for the poor and vulnerable in their midst, they believed, should be the responsibility of the Christian community, motivated by the New Testament principles of compassion and generosity, and expressed in the context of the local congregation. Although church leaders understood only dimly the social, economic, and political transformations that were unfolding around them, they had a strong intuition that if the church did not provide an alternative response to the economic challenges its members were facing, the programs of the federal government would inevitably lead to new forms of dependency on the state that would make the church less relevant.

It would take the Mennonite Church a full decade to develop a response to the Social Security Act of 1935. But the events set in motion by the national debate on care for the vulnerable sparked a parallel conversation within the church—a conversation that ultimately led to the creation of Mennonite Mutual Aid, Inc. (MMA) in the summer of 1945 and the beginnings of a remarkable financial organization known today as Everence.

The Roots of Mennonite Mutual Aid

The story of MMA's slow beginnings in the years leading up to 1945—and its sometimes conflicted history in the seventy-five years since then—was deeply shaped by a long, uneasy relationship that Anabaptist-Mennonites in North America had with wealth. As a persecuted and marginalized people in Europe, they had claimed the biblical motif of "strangers and pilgrims" as a key part of their identity. A favorite verse of the early Anabaptists—cited frequently in interrogations, confessions of faith, hymns, and devotional literature—came from the opening lines from Psalm 24: "The earth is the Lord's." In claiming this verse, they were making a political statement—their allegiance was ultimately to God, not to worldly princes or nation-states. But citing "the earth is the Lord's" was also an economic declaration. Everything that might be understood as a human possession, they taught, actually belonged to God. Humans were only stewards of the earthly resources entrusted to them. Therefore, they should hold those possessions lightly, sharing them freely with whoever was in need.

Most Mennonite immigrants in the eighteenth century arrived to the shores of the New World with only minimal resources, many of them forced to work initially as indentured servants. Yet within a generation almost all of them had established an economic foothold, often with the financial assistance of family and church members. Mennonites in eastern Pennsylvania had settled in Skippack along the banks of the Schuylkill river, and then quickly migrated north and westward to the rich soil of Lancaster and Berks counties where they gained a reputation as hard-working, sober-minded, and thrifty farmers.

As later generations of Mennonites and Amish moved westward, they demonstrated a keen eye for fertile soil and established thriving agrarian communities in the Kischoquilla Valley of Pennsylvania, the woodlands of Holmes and Wayne counties of Ohio, the Black Swamp of Fulton County, Ohio, and the rich farmland along the tributaries of the Elkhart River in northern Indiana, before moving further west to settle large tracts of land in Illinois and Iowa. For most of the nineteenth century, Mennonites in the United States were predominantly an agrarian people. By leveraging the virtues of frugality and hard work, a tradition of large families, generations of accumulated wealth, and land dispossessed from Native peoples, Mennonites were, relatively speaking, a wealthy people, even if much of that wealth was invested in farm equipment and land rather than in more conspicuous forms of consumption.

A key element in that economic success was a long tradition of mutual aid. Newly-arrived immigrants drew heavily on the social capital of established Anabaptist-Mennonite communities—profiting from the counsel, personal loans, shared labor, and outright charity that other members of the community provided them. Because members of the community trusted each other, they preferred to lend and borrow money privately within their own communities rather than rely on banks for credit. Young farmers and small business owners could generally turn to family or church members for low interest loans. Defaulting on those loans was virtually unthinkable; or if the losses were beyond anyone's control, they tended to be absorbed communally rather than resulting in the financial ruin of an individual family. Other forms of mutual aid within the community went beyond formal economic exchanges to include spontaneous sharing of time, labor, and material resources of the sort common to many groups on the frontier: quilting bees, husking parties, barn raisings, shared labor at harvest, and a deacon's fund to provide for the needs of widows and orphans.[4]

To be sure, these Mennonites and Amish were deeply integrated into the larger economy as well. They took their crops to market and followed larger economic trends with great interest. Mennonites were not opposed in principle to banks; nor were they averse to profits or troubled by the fact that some families were clearly wealthier than others. But they were deeply shaped by religious convictions that valued simplicity and frugality. Most communities exerted strong social pressure against ostentatious displays of wealth. And Mennonites tended to be skeptical of merchants who made their living by "buying low and selling high," preferring to plow profits back into land and to manage capital largely within extended families or among members of the church.

THE VARIETY OF ANABAPTISTS IN NORTH AMERICA IN THE EARLY TWENTIETH CENTURY

At the turn of the nineteenth century, the Anabaptist-Mennonite family in North America included five main groups. The largest body, the (Old) Mennonite Church, consisted mostly of descendants of Swiss or South German immigrants who had arrived in the eighteenth and early nineteenth centuries.

The next largest group, the General Conference Mennonite Church, began in eastern Pennsylvania as part of the John Oberholtzer division in 1860 that had advocated for a more progressive form of church organization. Their numbers grew significantly in the 1870s with the addition of many immigrants from South Russia.

A third group, the tradition-minded Old Order Amish, were not as visibly distinct in 1900 as they are today. Most small farmers at the turn of the century used horses, one-room schoolhouses were common in the countryside, and rural electrification was still a novelty. Over time, however, the Amish resistance to cultural change would heighten the distance between them and other Anabaptist-Mennonite groups.

In the 1870s several thousand Hutterites (Anabaptist, but not originally Mennonite) had settled in the western states, migrating from South Russia. Although many quickly gave up the practice of community of goods,[5] three Hutterite groups retained the practice and went on to flourish in the coming decades, albeit often at a far remove from the larger Anabaptist-Mennonite family, keeping alive the vision of a Christian community where all property was shared.

Lastly, the Mennonite Brethren had formed in 1860 as part of a revival movement in South Russia and migrated to North America in two large waves—the first in the 1870s and then in the 1920s after the Bolshevik Revolution. The Mennonite Brethren settled largely in the western states and Canadian provinces.

In addition to these groups, a host of other smaller Anabaptist-Mennonite denominations also emerged—among them, the Amish Mennonites, the Beachy Amish, the Conservative Mennonites, Church of God in Christ (Holdeman) Mennonites, and a dozen more—as each sought to retain particular cultural or religious practices as a form of resistance to acculturating pressures of the American "melting pot."[6] And beyond these streams other groups such as the Brethren in Christ, the Church of the Brethren, and later the Missionary Church also identified some part of their heritage with the Anabaptist tradition.

Despite the distinctive traditions and practices reflected in these diverse groups, all shared some sense of being part of a shared theological tradition. And all of them were committed, in one form or another, to the principles of community, stewardship, and generosity.

A Society Transformed

World War I marked a decisive moment for the Anabaptist groups who had settled in the United States. Initially, popular sentiment was strongly opposed to American intervention in a European war. But when President Wilson declared war on the Central Powers on April 2, 1917, the national mood changed dramatically. For Anabaptist groups—most of whom were committed to pacifism, closely associated with German language and culture, and generally wary of any involvement with the government—World War I became a painful test of their identity. Almost overnight they were forced to respond to the mass conscription of their young men, pressured to buy war bonds, and confronted with public accusations of treason for speaking German.[7]

The congregational focus of most Anabaptist groups made it difficult for them to formulate a unified or collective position in response to these pressures. Many individuals and groups in the Anabaptist-Mennonite tradition allowed themselves to be absorbed into the national spirit of patriotic unity. Others, however, insisted on their loyalty as Americans, even as they stubbornly refused to buy war bonds and encouraged their young men not to cooperate in military training. For these groups, wartime experiences with lynch mobs, burned churches, and, in several instances, martyrdom reinforced a sense of separation from the American cultural mainstream and a suspicion of the state that would linger for generations.[8] The war clearly disrupted the staid agrarian routines of Anabaptist groups, forcing them to think more carefully about basic questions of theology and communal identity: To what extent would they conform to the pressures of the national culture? How should they relate to government? What would be the markers of their distinctive witness?

In the decades after World War I, the nation as a whole underwent a profound transformation. The war had spurred the rapid expansion of industry, which called for new forms of labor, work discipline, and assembly line efficiencies. Millions of Americans were leaving rural farming communities to seek a better life in the city. Increased productivity and rising wages resulted in a growing market for consumer goods, fueled by increasingly sophisticated forms of advertising. These changes contributed to the slow unraveling of traditional networks of family and community relationships that had characterized rural America in general, and Anabaptist-Mennonite communities in particular.

The Great Depression introduced still more unsettling changes. In the months that followed the panic on Wall Street on October 24, 1929—now known as "Black Tuesday"—agricultural prices collapsed, thousands of factories closed, and millions of ordinary people lost their life savings. At the height of the Depression in 1933, at least 25 percent of America's workforce was unemployed and some five thousand banks had gone out of business. The Depression, combined with the devastating impact of the Dust Bowl, prompted a generation of young people to leave the farm in pursuit of other forms of employment in towns or cities. It also underscored the growing role of government in the lives of ordinary people. President Roosevelt's New Deal helped to address the crisis of unemployment by creating thousands of jobs funded by the government. The introduction of the Social Security Act revolutionized how Americans thought about old age and retirement.

Many Anabaptist-Mennonites initially reacted to these government programs with skepticism, worried that they would usurp the role of the church and the local community in caring for the needs of their members. Though it was difficult to discount the benefits of such things as rural electrification, water and sewage treatment plants, antimonopoly legislation, or the restoration of confidence in banks brought about by the Federal Deposit Insurance Corporation, many Anabaptist-Mennonite groups remained suspicious of the New Deal.

Anabaptist-Mennonites were equally ambivalent about financial institutions. The collapse of the global economy reinforced a traditional suspicion of banks, stock markets, big business, and the world of high finance. At the same time, however, farmers in the late 1930s were badly in need of capital. The growing mechanization of farming reduced labor costs and led to higher crop yields, but it also meant that farmers needed to borrow money as they exchanged their draft horses for tractors and purchased other expensive implements that were necessary if their farms were to be profitable.

World War II only accelerated the trend. During the 1930s, Mennonites, in collaboration with Quakers and the Church of the Brethren—the three largest of the "historic peace churches"—had appealed to legislators and the executive branch of the government for the creation of an alternative to military service that would be under civilian (i.e., church) oversight. The program that eventually

Anabaptist leaders jointly represented their peace position during World War II to the federal government, including (left to right) Robert M.R. Zigler (Church of the Brethren), Orie O. Miller (Mennonite Church), and Paul Furnas (Religious Society of Friends). MCC PHOTO COLLECTION, MENNONITE CHURCH USA ARCHIVES

emerged was known as Civilian Public Service (CPS). Between 1941 and 1947, some twelve thousand Anabaptist-Mennonite draftees accepted assignments in "work of national importance" in 152 camps throughout the United States and Puerto Rico.[9] The CPS men served without wages, and the cost of maintaining the camps was borne by the sponsoring churches. Many served longer than regular draftees and were not released until well after the end of the war. But by all accounts, the program was a success in that it enabled a generation of Anabaptist-Mennonites to give public witness to their convictions regarding pacifism in a form that the government could affirm.

Still, the cumulative impact of the social, economic, and cultural changes between the outbreak of the First World War and the end of World War II was profoundly unsettling for many Anabaptist-Mennonites. Even though their groups shared fully in the rising standards of living that characterized the economy throughout the twentieth century, they continued to consciously cultivate boundaries that separated the church community from the encroaching world.

DENOMINATIONAL IDENTITY: THE GROWING AUTHORITY OF INSTITUTIONS

Just as new government programs were exerting greater authority over the daily lives of many Americans, a parallel shift in authority was slowly unfolding within the (Old) Mennonite Church as well. The General Conference of the Mennonite Church had been envisioned in 1898 as an advisory body, subordinate to the regional conferences that comprised the gathering. Since ministers from the area conferences convened as a larger group only every two years, the Executive Committee functioned as its administrative arm between sessions.[10] In its biennial meetings, the General Conference conducted much of its business through several boards—the Mennonite Board of Education (1905), the Mennonite Board of Missions and Charities (1906), and the Mennonite Publication Board (1908). By the 1920s, the Executive Committee, and the various subcommittees it appointed to carry out its work, had consolidated control over the institutions overseen by these boards and clearly claimed an authority that far exceeded that of the individual conferences. This shift in power was due largely to the energetic interventions of Daniel Kauffman, a bishop based in Scottdale, Pennsylvania. In addition to serving as moderator of the General Conference on numerous occasions, Kauffman was a powerful speaker, teacher, writer, and administrator. But his real influence came through a keen understanding of the new forms of authority in the growing number of church-related institutions and the various committees appointed to do the work of the General Conference. At one point Kauffman was a member of no fewer than twenty-two committees and boards, wielding extraordinary influence on the decisions of the church's institutions.[11]

At the heart of the growing authority of church-related institutions in the first half of the twentieth century was a profound paradox. Kauffman and his generation of leaders were deeply troubled by the changes they perceived in Mennonite thought and practice: the influence of Liberal theology, the challenge World War I posed to the doctrine of nonresistance, the inroads of consumerism and fashion that eroded values of simplicity, and a general sense that their communal identity was being eroded on all sides. In an effort to protect traditional Anabaptist-Mennonite communities from the dramatic changes taking place in American society, Kauffman and others turned to the newly created institutions. In their vision, church-related colleges, a denominational publishing house, and churchwide committees devoted to themes like "Young Peoples' Problems" or "Peace Problems" were bulwarks to defend a distinctive identity against the encroachments of modernity.

Yet this was a strategy fraught with tension. In these new ventures, to whom were the new institutions accountable? Were the institutions reflecting the desires and priorities of the local congregations and regional conferences, or were they shaping those desires and priorities?

What Kauffman and others in his generation of leaders could not see was that the very institutions he intended to protect from modernizing influences bore within themselves the seeds of the threats he sought to contain.[12] Institutions intended to reinforce boundaries also became bridges, exposing young Mennonites to new worlds far beyond the cultural and religious assumptions of the communities that created them.

The creation of Civilian Public Service is a helpful example. In the face of overwhelming public support for the Great War, CPS camps provided a generation of conscripted young Anabaptist-Mennonite men with a way to demonstrate their commitment to the principle of biblical nonresistance while providing service of national importance. Yet the CPS experience also had the unintended consequence of accelerating Mennonite acculturation into the world. In scores of CPS camps scattered across the country, hundreds of young men from different geographical communities, church affiliations, and theological orientations were brought together in proximity. There they forged new friendships, were exposed to new ideas, and encountered new social realities, including a new awareness of widespread mistreatment of the mentally ill. Some returned to their home communities ready to resume the farm work they had left behind. But for many others, the experience gave them a new understanding of the country's social problems, a deeper appreciation for the faith of people in other Christian traditions, a hunger for further education, and a glimpse of the world beyond their rural communities.

Something similar happened in the growing number of Mennonite colleges. Kauffman envisioned church-related colleges as training schools of biblical and doctrinal orthodoxy. And they did indeed pass along the fundamentals of the faith. But colleges also opened up young people's minds to questions and ways of thinking that went far beyond the horizons of their home congregations. From the perspective of the Mennonite professors, trained in the liberal arts, this kind of open confident engagement was exactly what the church of the future needed if it was going to survive. Yet the denominational leaders who oversaw the colleges intended them for a very different purpose.

Addressing Economic Questions in Changing Context

FORMATION OF A STEWARDSHIP STUDY COMMITTEE

This, then, was the context that prompted leaders of the Pacific Coast Conference and the Ohio Mennonite and Eastern Amish Mennonite Conference to call on the General Conference in 1935 to develop a churchwide plan to care for widows and "the worthy poor" that could serve as an alternative to the national Social Security program.[13] The Executive Committee took the petitions seriously, recommending the appointment of a five-person Stewardship Study Committee, with a mandate to "make a study of Christian stewardship as it affects our financial obligations and practices." The committee was to propose a plan to the next General Conference in 1937 for an organization that "would provide for necessary medical care, hospital bills, funeral expenses, etc, of the worthy poor of the Church."[14]

It was no accident that the Executive Committee called on Christian L. (better known as C. L.) Graber to serve as secretary of the committee. A promising young accountant from Iowa, Graber had taken on the role as business manager of Goshen College in 1924, energetically raising funds that enabled the school to survive. In 1931, at the height of the Great Depression, he took a temporary leave from the college to assume control of the bank in his hometown of Wayland, Iowa, that was facing foreclosure.[15] Through a series of bold moves and persuasive appeals to key shareholders, Graber successfully negotiated a solution to save the bank, earning him a reputation in the church as a financial wizard.

Two years later, however, when the General Conference convened in Turner, Oregon, for its biennial meeting, the report from the Christian Stewardship Study Committee was deeply ambivalent. The committee noted that the church's Mission Board already had a Relief Committee and Emergency Relief Fund to meet the needs of the poor "where local congregational aid" was insufficient. It recognized that there was a genuine need among church members for "a savings system, aid for accident, storm or fire; relief in time of misfortune; and aid in time of sickness and burial." And it noted with concern that since "life insurance is making inroads in our church . . . some systematic help should be given by our church to provide benefits such as people expect to receive from life insurance companies." Such aid, the report continued, "could be provided on a Church-wide basis with a very simple organization, similar to the existing property aid organizations."[16]

But the report was also filled with cautions. Behind the comment that "life insurance is making inroads into our church" was a deep-seated concern that may sound odd today: Mennonites in the 1930s and 1940s were adamantly opposed to insurance of all types, but especially to life insurance. The full intensity of the debate over insurance would not occur until the 1950s; but for many Mennonites at the time, insurance suggested a crassly impersonal economic calculation of human vulnerability. Whereas mutual aid reflected a covenantal trust in God and one's community, insurance was based on legal contracts, statistical calculations, and premiums. Life insurance magnified all of these evils by actually putting a price on a human life.

These were the cautions in the Stewardship Study Committee's report of 1937. Any potential burial aid plan, the committee agreed, would need safeguards to keep it from "becoming a life insurance company, from fostering covetousness, and from encouraging vain display at time of funerals." And any future savings plan should avoid association with life insurance or "get rich quick schemes." The report did affirm the storm and fire plans that several regional conferences had already formed, and called for further study regarding a churchwide auto accident plan.[17] However, it offered no specific proposals for the conferences who had requested help from the General Conference two years earlier, and did little to address the deeper concerns that programs like Social Security could make church-based forms of economic sharing obsolete. It concluded by recommending further study.

Moving from general observations and encouragements to the implementation of an actual churchwide mutual aid program proved to be difficult. The initiative was helped considerably by the historical and theological work of J. Winfield Fretz, who completed a master's thesis at the University of Chicago Divinity School in 1938 titled "Christian Mutual Aid Societies Among the Mennonites."[18] In the essay, Fretz summarized the long-standing theological rationale for economic sharing and described in detail how Mennonites, particularly in South Russia, had put these ideals into practice in a wide variety of cooperatives and fraternal benefit societies. As Fretz saw it, mutual aid was not a plan to care for the poor so much as a fundamental element of the faith—a quality of relationships that should be part of every healthy Christian community. Fretz was an enthusiastic popularizer, and he found ready audiences for his mutual aid message, particularly in congregations with Russian roots where these ideas sounded familiar. His efforts in the late 1930s gained a hearing among (Old) Mennonite Church leaders, especially from Guy F. Hershberger, a fellow sociologist who keenly recognized the challenges modernity posed to traditional Mennonite community life and was eager to explore creative alternatives.[19]

REPORTS, PROPOSALS, AND NONACTION

Emboldened by the work of Fretz and Hershberger, in August of 1939 the Study Committee on Christian Stewardship proposed the creation of two new churchwide entities—a Fire and Storm Loss Association and Death and Burial Aid Association—both to be organized under the Mennonite Board of Missions and Charities.[20] The report recommended that these organizations be chartered to do business across the country, but located "in one of our middle states" with the goal of assisting smaller regional conferences who did not yet have such plans. Mennonite Church General Conference delegates, meeting in Allensville, Pennsylvania, affirmed the Fire and Storm Loss plan, but called for still more study on the Death and Burial Aid, since some ministers feared that it would open the door to the introduction of commercial life insurance.

Neither plan moved forward.[21] On September 1, 1939, Germany invaded Poland, triggering a series of events that would eventually lead the United States into war. For the moment, Mennonite leaders focused their attention on the pressing questions of military conscription and preparations for the new Civilian Public Service camps. Complicating matters, in the spring of 1940 the Mission Board reported that it had declined to oversee the Fire and Storm Loss plan, turning the matter back into the hands of the Stewardship Study Committee.

Five years after leaders from Ohio and Oregon had requested action on a churchwide response to the Social Security Act, the Executive Committee still had nothing to show for its efforts. When the General Conference of the (Old) Mennonite Church met again in 1941, the Stewardship Study Committee worried that "unless the Church provides some organized medium of fellowship through which mutual burdens of fire, storm, accident, hospitalization and death can be borne, more and more of our members will seek such fellowship with other groups."[22] At the very least, it warned, the church needed to be attentive to new economic realities. In the context of wartime prosperity among farmers, the Study Committee identified "an acute need for the teaching of Christian stewardship." "Much money is lost through unwise investment," it observed in its report, "not only to the individual but to the Church which could profit by its use if conserved through the wise management of an experienced board."[23] The group now declared its support for the creation of a churchwide annuity plan in which people could give a sum of money to a church agency with the promise of a fixed return until their death.[24]

In the meantime, the experience of World War II had brought into sharp focus a host of new questions about Mennonite engagement with modern society. The General Problems Committee, a powerful subcommittee of the General Conference,[25] shifted its full attention to topics related to nonresistance and nonconformity. As one of the committee's most insightful members, Guy F. Hershberger recognized the complexity of these questions, insisting that they had implications far beyond a refusal to participate in the military. In 1939, Hershberger had turned his focus on "applied nonresistance" to the question of unions and labor relations, and persuaded the Executive Committee to create a new Committee on Industrial Relations. Now, in 1941, Hershberger had become convinced that the church's commitment to nonresistance was inseparable from issues related to larger economic realities. Hershberger was clearly impatient with the tentative approach of the Stewardship Study Committee in addressing these fundamental questions. "The church does not yet realize as it should," Hershberger wrote on behalf of the Committee on Industrial Relations, "the possibility for fostering the Mennonite—and we believe the Christian—way of life through such means as effective organization for Mutual Aid, hospitalization, medical care, the cooperative purchase of land to assist young farmers in need of help, and the cooperative operation of community industries for New Testament business and social ethics."[26]

In one sentence, Hershberger had described Mennonite Mutual Aid as it would look a decade later.

Yet still nothing moved forward. Overshadowed by the churchwide focus on the administration of Civilian Public Service camps, the work of the

Stewardship Study Committee receded even further into the background. Indeed, in 1943 C. L. Graber reported to the General Conference that the committee had not even met during the preceding two years, mostly because of ill health of its chairperson, J. C. Frey. Complaining that "it has never been clear what the full responsibility of this committee is," Graber went on to state that the church already had a Relief Fund overseen by the Mission Board, the Publishing House was already printing articles and tracts on the theme of stewardship, and several regional conferences already had their own fire and storm or auto aid organizations.

But the 1943 report also called attention to a significant new challenge facing the church—namely, the economic "rehabilitation"[27] of the men in CPS who would be returning home at the close of the war. "If no guidance and support are available," the report warned, "the men will be likely to drift to cities and to isolated areas to become involved with labor unions, government support plans, etc., with resulting loss to our Church."[28] As before, however, the report provided no concrete proposals for how the church might address the challenges facing postwar CPS volunteers. It concluded on a pessimistic note:

Guy Hershberger, with his wife, Clara, recognized the challenges modernity posed to the traditional faith community and envisioned an organization like MMA a decade before it formed. PAUL F. HERSHBERGER

The committee has learned that no national organization of a mutual aid nature is possible. Such organizations can only exist under state charter and can only spread out from such a beginning. For that reason we have not been able to effect an organization for mutual aid in case of sickness, accident, or death.[29]

Seemingly, efforts to create a churchwide structure for addressing the economic needs of its members had come to a full stop.

Other church leaders were growing frustrated with the Stewardship Study Committee, none more so than Hershberger, who had been pressing the church for action on a mutual aid program for nearly a decade. On Oct 16, 1943, Hershberger's Industrial Relations Committee was scheduled for a meeting at the home of Orie O. Miller, an influential church leader, in Akron, Pennsylvania. In addition to Miller and Hershberger, who served as secretary, the committee also included P. L. Frey and John R. Mumaw. C. L. Graber from the Stewardship Study Committee was also present, as was Harold S. Bender, who represented the Peace Problems Committee. Hershberger was determined to move the work assigned to the Stewardship Study Committee forward with a concrete plan. "We didn't mention the [Stewardship Study] Committee," Hershberger later recalled, "but I had decided I was going to come to that meeting with a concrete proposal that we need a new church board. . . . I said the General Conference should organize it like they had organized the Mennonite Board of Education, the Mennonite Board of Mission, and the Mennonite Publication Board."[30]

MENNONITE MUTUAL AID PROPOSED

Miller was in the habit of taking a short nap after lunch. But after the break, he returned to the meeting ready for action. According to Hershberger, Miller "pulled his little notebook out of his vest pocket and he had three points. . . . He always had three points; that's the way he worked."

Miller began by first noting that "our old and century-long Mennonite ways of living are breaking up, and new patterns are being set." His second observation was that the "war [was] hastening this process and adding new elements through CPS." His third point would become something of a slogan, capturing well Miller's understanding of how of church-related institutions should function. "In this changing situation," he asserted, "the Church means to go along with its members and to help them wherever in conscience they need to go and can go."[31] Miller concluded by stating matter-of-factly that "we need to convince [the Executive Committee] to create a board . . . And we'll call it Mennonite Mutual Aid."

Orie Miller, with his wife, Elta. In proposing the creation of MMA, one of Miller's observations became an iconic statement on how the organization would come to see itself: "In this changing situation, the church means to go along with its members and to help them wherever in conscience they need to go and can go."
JOHN W. MILLER

With Miller's full support, Hershberger persuaded the other members of the Industrial Relations Committee to endorse his proposal: "That the committee favors the creation of a new organization to be known as Mennonite Mutual Aid." The proposal further affirmed that the organization should be of churchwide service, it should be a program board of the Mennonite Church, it should be "incorporated as a nonprofit, no-stock corporation," and it should be funded "through borrowing from brethren who desire to invest their money in the welfare of the Mennonite church."[32] The committee envisioned a board consisting of twelve members, six to be appointed by the (Old) Mennonite Church General Conference and six by the board itself, and proposed that one of the first tasks of the new organization would be to help CPS men adjust to civilian life, once the war had ended.

For the first time in eight years, a plan seemed to be emerging that had the attention and support of key leaders. But the group still faced sobering challenges. In addition to the difficulty of selling the program to the regional conference leaders, there was the very practical problem that the General Conference had just met, and was not scheduled to reconvene for another two years. But Miller had a strategy for this challenge as well. On December 4, 1943, he took the proposal to the Executive Committee, who gave their blessing to the plan on the condition that at least six of the (Old) Mennonite

Church regional conferences approve the idea and that it receive the formal blessing of the General Conference at its next biennial meeting. Along with Graber, Hershberger, and Miller, two additional leaders—Allen Erb and Aaron Mast—were given the authority to move the plan forward.

In the months that followed, Hershberger launched a promotional campaign in the *Gospel Herald*, publishing a steady stream of articles making a theological case for a churchwide approach to mutual aid.[33] Hershberger also oversaw the creation of a small brochure titled "Mennonite Mutual Aid: A plan for the organization of a new board to carry on an effective program of mutual aid within the Mennonite Church."[34]

Graber committed himself to personally attend every regional conference that was meeting in the spring and early summer of 1944.[35] By the end of July, however, he was forced to acknowledge that the barnstorming tour had not gone very well. After presenting the plan to seven conferences, only the Ohio and Eastern Conference and the Indiana-Michigan Conference had given their unqualified approval.[36] "I definitely feel I haven't done very well," Graber reported to Orie Miller. The Lancaster bishops expressed "no interest in the plan for the present." The Franconia bishop board "seemed rather passive" and postponed a decision. The Virginia Conference had expressed concern that the plan be made exclusive to the (Old) Mennonite Church, and withheld action, recommending that a decision be made the following year.[37] The Pacific Coast Conference, one of the groups that had originally appealed to the General Conference for a churchwide plan, "looked with favor" on the proposal but called for further study. The Dakota-Montana Conference and Southwestern Pennsylvania Conference both tabled the proposal for further discussion.

Fortunately for the advocates of the plan, a crisis in the (Old) Mennonite Church General Conference over conference polity and issues related to dress regulations prompted the conference moderator, Alan Erb, to call for a special session of the General Conference in 1944, a year earlier than the group was normally scheduled to meet. Even though they were still far from receiving approval from the six conferences they needed, Hershberger and the others managed to shoehorn their proposal into the agenda in time for the August meeting. At the gathering, Hershberger revealed that he was not above backroom strategies. As he described the meeting thirty years later, he and Miller presented the plan to the delegates "in the evening with very little discussion." The vote was scheduled for the next morning. "So I got an idea," Hershberger recalled. "I knew that Simon Gingerich, the old bishop, was in favor of at least some mutual aid. I got a hold of him and got him to acknowledge that he supported [the plan]." Then he asked Gingerich, "'When the right moment comes, would you be ready to get up, and say that you're for this, and why you're for it, and make a motion to adopt it?' he said, 'Well, yes, I'll do that.' And he did."[38]

CHANGED TACTICS TO FINALIZE THE PLAN

Members of the General Conference adopted the motion by a vote of seventy in favor and twenty-one opposed. But the wording of the resolution authorized the incorporation of Mennonite Mutual Aid only "after assurance of cooperation from the required number of [regional] conferences and subject to the General Conference Executive Committee approval."[39] Thus far, the proposal had been formally approved by only two of these conferences. As Miller reported to Graber, the committee still faced the challenge of getting at least four more conferences "lined up favorably."[40]

"I feel you should consider someone else taking the rest of the [regional] Conference sessions from now on," Graber responded. "From now on it has to be 100%."[41] Hershberger would later express his frustration with Graber, who, he claimed, focused on the details of the plan without addressing the "basic reason for such a program—that it is basic to our whole Mennonite way of life."[42] The stalling tactics in Virginia and Oregon, he observed, were not surprising, "since they are afraid of everything new as being something worldly." But Hershberger was optimistic that the Southwest Pennsylvania Conference would come on board "unless Shetler and Kniss bring out some bogies."[43] Some of the resistance, Hershberger acknowledged, reflected a long-standing suspicion of any centralized initiative that might shift authority from congregations and conferences to the General Conference. But there was also principled opposition. In September 1944, John Snyder, an accountant from Oregon who had been working with MCC, responded to Hershberger's public relations campaign in the *Gospel Herald* with a sharply critical article titled "Is Mutual Aid Scriptural?" In it, he vigorously denounced all forms of insurance and argued that even the traditional fire and storm societies were "a means of maintaining the financial status quo of their members."[44]

In strategizing for those regional conferences that were scheduled to meet in the fall, Hershberger was blunt, revealing his readiness to resort to bare-knuckled tactics, at least by Mennonite standards. The key, he suggested was to "find one or two key men and sell them on this thing in advance to the conference, getting them to see that it is up to them to put it through their conference." Hershberger then named the key individuals in each of the remaining conferences.[45]

The tactics, it appeared, paid off. On September 8, Graber reported that the Iowa-Nebraska Conference had approved the plan "without opposition." Soon thereafter Hershberger, who presented the proposal to the Illinois Conference, also reported a positive outcome, followed by the Missouri-Kansas Conference a week later. But by the time the last regional conference had convened for its annual meeting, the committee had still only secured five affirmations.

Once more the future of the proposal seemed to be imperiled by the complexities of church polity and the inherent conservatism of local and regional leaders. And once again, key leaders found a way to move forward despite the impasse. At a meeting of the Executive Committee in March of 1945, Alan Erb, its moderator, agreed that the work of the proposed organization was of urgent importance and suggested that the plan could go forward even without the formal support of a sixth regional conference. Erb only stipulated that it be approved at a special meeting of the Executive Committee that would include representatives from each of the conferences. The Executive Committee then moved to confirm the appointment of a six-member Mutual Aid Committee, consisting of Orie O. Miller (chair), C. L. Graber (treasurer), Guy F. Hershberger, Simon Gingerich, John Alger, and H. A. Diener.

So it was that on May 31, 1945, the Executive Committee, meeting with representatives from the church's nine regional conferences, along with representatives from the Franconia and Lancaster conferences who were not part of the (Old) Mennonite Church General Conference—twenty-seven people in all—convened in the Adelphian Hall at Goshen College to discuss the fate of Mennonite Mutual Aid.

Only a few weeks earlier, on May 7, Germany had surrendered to the Allied forces. Although fighting on the Pacific front would continue for several more months, all those in the room recognized that with the end of war seemingly imminent, the CPS program would also soon conclude. So even though talk of the need to "rehabilitate" CPS volunteers back into civilian life with loans and vocational counseling had only recently entered the conversation, the MMA committee now offered it as the primary reason for the urgency to move forward. By the end of the day, the assembled group approved a carefully worded resolution, drafted in language worthy of an attorney:

> Whereas the proposed program known as Mennonite Mutual Aid as presented to the 1944 special session of General Conference was approved, and whereas it has had formal endorsement in principle by five district conferences and with no negative vote by any other district conference, and inasmuch as there seems

to be a favorable sentiment expressed by representatives appointed by each conference district at a meeting of the MMA called at Goshen College on May 31, 1945, and whereas there is an urgent need for CPS rehabilitation, and although the stipulated number of conferences for endorsement has not been met; and whereas the purposes and procedures of MMA have undergone changes which have eliminated some of the necessity for district conference approval, therefore, we the Executive Committee of General Conference do authorize the immediate organization of Mennonite Mutual Aid, the Mennonite Mutual Aid committee to be the incorporators and initial board of directors.[46]

That meeting in May—followed by the successful incorporation of Mennonite Mutual Aid, Inc. as a not-for-profit company in Indianapolis on July 19, 1945—marked the formal beginning of an organization that would profoundly shape the trajectory of the Mennonite Church in the last half of the twentieth century.[47]

In the short term, the church approved the creation of Mennonite Mutual Aid as a response to the economic needs of the young men and families in Civilian Public Service. But as historian Theron Schlabach has insightfully argued, "it was also the product of a small handful of new leaders who had mastered modern organizational techniques and believed deeply that the Mennonite community needed a new approach to the social welfare of its people. More than anything else, they saw MMA as a new and better way to help preserve the fragile and changing Mennonite community they feared would soon disappear."[48] Significantly, Schlabach also observed that the efforts of those leaders symbolically represented a generational transition from the older, more conservative leaders, to a younger generation of progressives.

From Concept to Program: The "Invention" of Mennonite Mutual Aid

On a warm fall day in October 1945, six men gathered for a meeting at 1413 South 8th Street in Goshen, Indiana. The office in which they were meeting was once the living room of a home that Goshen College, located only a few blocks to the south, had recently purchased and was in the process of converting into student apartments.[49] As their first official act of business, the group began with a ritual that would continue for at least another decade. Though dressed in suits and ties, and accustomed to a culture of formality, the men knelt awkwardly between the chairs in the small room for a period of earnest prayer.[50]

As its second act of business the group took its first vote, moving to formally disband itself as the "Mutual Aid Committee" of the (Old) Mennonite

Church, and to reconvene as the board of directors of a newly-created organization called Mennonite Mutual Aid. The men then proceeded to elect officers. To no one's surprise, the group elected Orie O. Miller to serve as the organization's first president. Miller, who had chaired the Mutual Aid Committee, was a veteran churchman and consummate administrator. In addition to overseeing the operations of the Miller Hess Shoe Company in Akron, Pennsylvania, he served as the executive secretary and treasurer of Mennonite Central Committee, the secretary of Eastern Mennonite Missions, the secretary of the (Old) Mennonite Church's Peace Problems Committee, and in various capacities on a host of other churchwide boards. To all of these tasks, Miller brought a deep personal faith, a profound understanding of the nuances of Mennonite culture, an adroit bureaucratic sensibility, and a confident working style, quite comfortable with managerial authority and assertive decision-making. Miller would serve as MMA's president for the next seventeen years, overseeing a period of remarkable expansion.[51]

A second crucial member of the original MMA board was C. L. Graber. A raconteur, entrepreneur, and consummate salesman, Graber never hesitated to test the boundaries of established traditions. As Orie Miller reportedly once said, "I like to see Graber manufacture ideas; the task for the rest of us is to decide which are usable."[52] At the October meeting, the board appointed him as treasurer and part-time manager of MMA, a position he was to hold until 1954, even though he spent much of that time outside the office focused on a wide range of other projects.

Guy F. Hershberger had also been a key player in the steps leading to the October meeting.[53] Only a year earlier, Hershberger had published his magnum opus, *War, Peace, and Nonresistance*—a sophisticated translation of Mennonite peace theology in a manner that remained true to the tradition of nonresistance while also engaging with the pressing social and ethical questions of the day, including labor issues, civil rights, poverty, and litigation. Though not a gifted public speaker, Hershberger was the deepest thinker of the group and the most broadly read. As chair of the Industrial Relations Committee, which had taken the initiative to move the discussions of mutual aid from theory to practice, Hershberger looked at the new mutual aid organization as the primary vehicle for implementing many of the reforms that he envisioned for the church. More than anyone else, it was Hershberger who pressed for an expansive reading of the MMA mandate during the first decade of its rapid expansion.

The other members of the original board—H. A. Diener, Simon Gingerich, John H. Alger, and John L. Yoder, all of them well-known pastors—were solid churchmen, selected at least as much for the gravitas they lent to the organization as for their business acumen.

As the board reviewed its mandate, the magnitude of the work ahead must have felt daunting. Only a few weeks earlier, Japan's surrender brought an official end to World War II. The most urgent task—indeed, one of the main rationales for the organization's existence—was to develop a plan for helping Civilian Public Service workers, who would be facing considerable financial challenges, reintegrate into their home communities following two, three, or even four years out of the general workforce.

But the articles of incorporation that formally empowered Mennonite Mutual Aid envisioned a much broader range of activities than merely providing loans to young men temporarily in need of capital. In the coming years, the MMA board would return to this mandate repeatedly as it dramatically expanded the scope of operations.

According to the statement approved at the May 31 meeting, MMA was expected to:

1. assist CPS men who need help in establishing a home and a means of livelihood;
2. assist others, especially young married couples in establishing a home and means of livelihood;
3. provide for aid in case of property loss, sickness, or death;
4. provide financial and vocational counsel;
5. provide "a means by which brethren with money can invest it where it can be used to aid other brethren who are in need."[54]

As time would quickly prove, the freedom afforded by the mandate to provide assistance in the event of "property loss, sickness, or death," to provide "financial counsel," and to create "a means by which brethren with money can invest," opened up a wide range of potential services for a church increasingly enmeshed in the marketplace.

In the course of the next fifteen years, the MMA board would oversee the creation of no fewer than seven different corporations in an effort to provide church-based solutions to the financial needs of its members. Each of these bodies had its own board, its own articles of incorporation, its own constituency, and its own particular challenges as it tried to balance theological commitments, marketplace realities, and a host of legal and regulatory restrictions, while remaining firmly under the supervision of the Mennonite Mutual Aid board and the authority of the General Conference of the (Old) Mennonite Church.

CREATING AN ORGANIZATION: RAISING FUNDS AND THE START OF A
LOAN PROGRAM

Today, Everence—the successor to Mennonite Mutual Aid—has become a
thriving and diverse financial organization with nearly 380 employees and
managing assets of more than $4 billion. In October of 1945 the MMA pro-
gram consisted of two small rooms and working capital of $8,750, raised by
a significant private contribution from Orie Miller and donations of church
members who had responded to Hershberger's appeals in three *Gospel Herald*
articles published in September.

Miller, president of the organization, would work from his home office in
Akron, Pennsylvania. Graber served as the part-time general manager, dividing
his time between Goshen College and the MMA office down the street.
Somewhat surprisingly, none other than John M. Snyder, the vocal critic of
Hershberger's initiatives, signed on as the organization's assistant manager and
accountant. As Snyder saw it, providing low interest loans to returning CPS
volunteers did not qualify as insurance. A little more than a year later, however,
as MMA began to consider other programs, he resigned in protest. Snyder's
replacement—Graber's son-in-law, Harold Swartzendruber—would go on to
serve the organization for the next three decades, eventually as its president.

Once the basic details of organizational structure had been addressed—
office space secured, letterheads embossed, and a skeleton staff in place—the
first priority was to devise a plan for offering loans and financial counsel to
ex-CPS volunteers who were trying to establish a financial foothold after
their release from service. The model for this initiative was the Servicemen's
Readjustment Act of 1944, better known as the G.I. Bill, which provided a
range of benefits for returning World War II veterans. Though Mennonites
could not compete with the generosity of the G.I. Bill, which included
significant grants for college tuition, they did recognize the financial challenges
young volunteers faced as they returned to ordinary life. [55]

When news of the fund appeared in the *Gospel Herald*, requests for loans
began to arrive almost immediately. This meant that between the first board
meeting on October 24 and the announcement of the first loan on December
14, the fledgling organization needed to develop a policy for evaluating loan
requests and, even more crucially, for raising the funds they would need to
operate the program.

Application forms were simple: they identified the purpose of the loan and
the requested amount, and asked applicants to supply letters of recommendation
from two pastors, as well as collateral or cosigners to secure the loans. Most

of the first loan requests were for agricultural needs—tractors or other farm implements, livestock, land, or barns. The accompanying letters of support invariably focused on the applicants' moral standing in the community— their character, family ties, or perceived spiritual maturity—rather than their business acumen or the likelihood of economic success.

The more pressing question late in 1945 was determining where the money needed for operating costs and capital would come from. In a *Gospel Herald* article published in early 1946, Graber identified five sources of potential revenue.[56] First, MMA would accept gifts from regional conferences or individuals, who, he noted, could claim them as deductions "from income for the calculation of Federal Income Tax." Second, MMA would offer "participation certificates" in units of $500 which had no guaranteed rate of interest and could only be paid to the investor's estate—essentially making them a form of burial insurance, although that language did not appear in the promotional literature. As a third source of revenue, church members could purchase "preferred certificates" in increments of $100 that would pay an annual interest rate of 4 per cent. These were basically annuities that could be sold to another investor, but the principal would remain with MMA. Graber also anticipated generating funds through debenture notes, or loans, which needed to be repaid to the investor within five years. These loans could be issued in any amount, at interest rates that were not

Ruth Keim was among the few early staff members who kept MMA running out of a small office in a converted house.

MENNONITE MUTUAL AID, Inc.

C. L. GRABER, MANAGER
HAROLD L. SWARTZENDRUBER
ASSISTANT MANAGER
PHONE L-1 AID

1413 SOUTH EIGHTH STREET
GOSHEN, INDIANA
October 7, 1949

Max Miller
Purdue Electric Farm
Route 1
Lafayette, Indiana

Dear Max:

Our Board of Directors met and have considered your application for a loan to purchase a used car. They have asked that before further consideration is given on the loan that the following information should be given to us:

1. Are you marrying a Mennonite girl?
2. Will your marriage change your "pay plus room and board"?
3. Will you be able to pay $50.00 after your marriage?
4. Will your father co-sign the note?

We will appreciate your prompt reply to these questions and you may expect to hear from us more promptly than we have so far.

Sincerely yours,

MENNONITE MUTUAL AID, INC.

Harold Swartzendruber

hls

Personal as well as financial questions were common in the early years of MMA's loan approval process. EVERENCE

to exceed 3 percent. Although Graber made it clear that he hoped the majority of MMA's start-up capital would come from gifts and participation certificates, the bylaws of the organization also allowed MMA to borrow money from a commercial bank if the need arose.[57]

At its meeting on December 14, 1945, the MMA board approved the first round of CPS loans, with the checks issued three weeks later. During the following year the board met nine times to consider loan requests, eventually approving a total of thirty-nine loans in 1946, totaling slightly more than $50,000.[58] The following year, MMA had made sixty-seven CPS loans of nearly $80,000. Between 1945 and 1955 the CPS loan program resulted in nearly 320 loans, with a total capital of some $600,000.[59]

In contrast to some of MMA's later loan programs, the collection rate on CPS loans was relatively strong. In August of 1947, Graber reported to the board that thus far "in only one case have we failed to receive the conscientious cooperation and regard for the obligation incurred which should be expected of Christians in such circumstances."[60] But when the program broadened to include more general requests from needy church members, collections proved to be far more challenging. At one point Harold Swartzendruber, who oversaw the loan program, reported that one creditor "had the same dozen milk cows mortgaged with MMA, a bank, a credit union, and a Federal Farm Credit program without seemingly being aware of any wrongdoing."[61] Sometimes, loans were granted without collateral and with relatively little information from local ministers.

Since these loans were often needed by individuals who had already been refused by local banks or relatives, the program raised difficult questions about the meaning of mutual aid. Board members strenuously insisted that MMA was not about charity; at the same time, they felt acutely the need to respond to appeals for help in the face of sickness, natural disasters, or personal tragedy. Board minutes from the early 1950s suggest that MMA staff members spent enormous time following up on these loans, often visiting creditors directly and seeking counsel from pastors or other family members as they investigated delinquent loans.[62] At one point, Swartzendruber appealed to Guy F. Hershberger to write a statement "regarding the extent to which we as a church should go in exerting 'pressure' in collection of delinquent accounts."[63]

Another early question for the board had to do with the scope of denominational eligibility. Already in February 1946, Orie Miller received requests from L. A. Miller, an Old Order Amish bishop from Arthur, Illinois, and from Elmer Swartzentruber of the Conservative Amish Conference, wondering whether ex-CPS workers from their groups would also qualify to participate in the loan program. At almost the same time, similar requests arrived from the Brethren in Christ and Lancaster Mennonite Conference church leaders. Miller, and especially Graber, were eager to expand the program and responded in the affirmative, barring any resistance from the General Conference Executive Committee. And indeed, in April 1946 the Executive Committee approved the request to broaden the program, though a committee member noted somewhat testily that "it might be well to point out that it isn't good policy to make a decision to go ahead, as MMA directors apparently did, subject to any word to the contrary which the General Conference Executive might have."[64] At its June 1946 meeting the Executive Committee agreed to expand the MMA loan program to also include the Brethren in Christ and all groups who participated in Mennonite Central Committee, which had provided general oversight to the CPS camps.

The MMA board also quickly faced pressure to expand the loan program beyond CPS workers, since it had begun to receive loan applications from other Mennonites, including service workers returning from MCC assignments as well as individuals who simply found themselves in financial need and were looking to the church for assistance. Since such loans were consistent with the mandate approved by the (Old) Mennonite Church General Conference, the board approved many of these loans. For a short time in the early 1950s, MMA promoted student loans to Mennonites pursuing graduate studies, especially in medical fields.[65] And in 1952, Graber spent a great deal of energy considering a loan to support a watchmaking factory owned by Mennonites in Tramalan, Switzerland, trying to recover their financial footing after the war.[66] In the end, the board decided not to move ahead; but the lengthy discussion provides an insight into the rather haphazard expansion the loan program took in subsequent years.[67]

By 1950, the rationale for the CPS loan program had largely faded. But the unique mandate of the new organization and the experience gained by MMA staff members opened the door to numerous other related initiatives. One idea, promoted especially by Guy Hershberger, was to encourage groups of families to settle collectively in rural locations with the idea of establishing new communities and churches. Between 1945 and 1957, MMA staff spent considerable time investigating several tracts of land—particularly in Minnesota, South Dakota, and eastern Washington—trying to persuade young CPS veterans to relocate there with the promise of financial support from the church. Although the colonization concept received considerable coverage in various Mennonite periodicals, the proposals met with general indifference. The most significant outcome of the conversations was a request from Orie Miller that MMA serve as a financial channel for handling loans overseen by MCC to support postwar Mennonite refugees from the Soviet Union in a resettlement—or "colonization"—effort in South America, primarily Paraguay.[68]

In the years that followed, it quickly became apparent that the new organization was going to be a useful framework for the creation of many other programs, all theoretically under the supervision of the Executive Committee of the (Old) Mennonite Church General Conference, but often requiring a level of expertise and executive decision-making that went far beyond what the denominational leaders could expect to oversee.

MMA emerged in 1945 against all odds, willed into being only by the stubborn efforts of a few key churchmen. Within a decade the organization had become the largest customer of the Goshen post office and the church's most dynamic and visible institution.

THREE

"Bearing One Another's Burdens"

Diversification and Growing Pains (1949–1962)

On the afternoon of May 10, 1961, Orie Miller, Harold Swartzendruber, and Ralph Hernley converged for a meeting in New York City at an imposing building on Park Avenue, just a few blocks from the Empire State Building. Miller, president of MMA, had arrived from Akron, Pennsylvania, home to the Miller, Hess & Co. shoe manufacturing business he managed alongside his work on numerous church boards. Hernley, who was in charge of the Mennonite Publishing House in Scottdale, Pennsylvania, was present in his role as an MMA board member. Swartzendruber, MMA's general manager, had made the trip the previous day from the MMA headquarters in Goshen, Indiana.

There in the offices of Cresap, McCormick and Paget (CMP) they were welcomed by the company's vice president, E. J. Bofferding. The representatives of MMA had traveled to New York City in search of help. In 1955, MMA consisted of three employees and had less than three thousand participants in its various programs. Five years later, the organization had expanded to include thirteen full-time employees, with more than twenty-three thousand members and assets totaling $1.5 million. At its board meeting in July of 1960, MMA's leaders agreed that even the most conservative estimates suggested that these numbers would double in the next five years. MMA was growing faster than its homegrown staff could manage. In October, the board decided that the time had come "to procure the services of professional management consultants to examine the organizational structure" and to make recommendations regarding "the entire MMA organization."[1] After soliciting bids from several firms, a subcommittee had settled on CMP, in part because of a favorable report from Goshen College, who had drawn on their services the previous year.

Now the representatives from MMA had come to New York to sign the contract and to meet the people who would carry out the review, scheduled for the summer of 1961. The meeting went well. Miller, Hernley, and Swartzendruber were impressed by the understanding that Bofferding brought to their unusual organization, and particularly his sensitivity to MMA's ties to the church and to the Anabaptist-Mennonite theological tradition.[2]

The relationship forged with CMP would prove to be momentous in the history of MMA. Although MMA leaders were consistently slow to adopt their long list of recommendations, CMP's counsel—provided first in 1961 and then again in 1978—marked decisive turning points in MMA's trajectory. CMP did not supplant the authority of the (Old) Mennonite Church's executive board, but its rational, policy-driven approach, shaped by modern principles of organizational efficiency, helped MMA transform itself into the organization it is today. Along the way, CMP's counsel sharpened the persistent question of how MMA would negotiate the ongoing tension between church and marketplace.

The immediate challenge, however, was transitioning from a CPS loan program into an organization envisioned by its broad mandate.

The Circuitous Path to Insurance

From the beginning it was clear that the visionaries who called MMA into existence in the summer of 1945 intended the organization to be more than merely a loan program for former CPS men. Already in 1937, the Stewardship Study Committee had identified a list of potential services that a churchwide organization might provide, including a savings and investment plan, automobile and property coverage, relief for the poor, and burial aid assistance.[3]

Of all the potential new initiatives, health and life insurance were clearly the most fraught. For many Anabaptist-Mennonite groups at midcentury, insurance was anathema—the secular opposite of the church's practice of mutual aid. Like gambling, insurance was based on a logic of calculated risks and profits that inevitably took advantage of poor people and lined the pockets of the wealthy.

The church, by contrast, understood human relationships in a very different way. If an individual suffered a loss or could not afford to pay a doctor, then assuredly someone in the congregation would step in to cover the expenses. If a farmer was sick or had a disability, community members would ensure that the corn was planted, the oats were tilled, and the wheat harvested so that the family did not go hungry. If a widow had no source of income, she could count on someone in the church to show up with a load of coal in the fall or a work crew to repair a leaking roof. Unlike insurance, mutual aid was not about calculating risks or keeping track of profits. It did not place bets on the likelihood of disaster or the health of human beings. It simply followed the scriptural injunction to "bear one another's burdens," treating others with the same sort of generosity that you yourself would like to be treated if you were facing similar circumstances.

Nevertheless, church leaders had long been aware that Mennonites in many parts of the country were secretly purchasing commercial insurance policies—including health, disability, and life insurance plans—that went well beyond the modest property damage or burial aid programs that the church had traditionally sanctioned. Some of these policies were linked to business loans—a requirement imposed by the bank who held the mortgage. Other Mennonites were purchasing commercial insurance so that they would not become a burden on their extended families or congregations; still others simply did not trust their church community to provide their families with the financial assistance they thought would be needed if they were no longer able to work. By the mid-1940s, supporters of the fledgling Mennonite Mutual Aid organization were clear: If the church was going to successfully resist the inroads of health and life insurance, it would need to develop an alternative that retained strong elements of traditional mutual aid.

In 1947, board members at MMA began to explore options that would meet the needs of members who were purchasing commercial insurance and satisfy the ethical concerns of church leaders. In the midst of these conversations, the loudest critic was one of MMA's own first employees—John M. Snyder, an accountant from Oregon whom Graber had hired in the fall of 1945 to oversee MMA's new CPS loan program.

Snyder was passionately opposed to all forms of insurance, which he described as "a device for people to buy the right to receive benefits for themselves or their own families."[4] He was adamant that any plan sponsored by the church not use actuarial projections or make benefits a right based on policies, formal membership, and premium payments. In addition to articles in the *Gospel Herald*, Snyder expressed his convictions in several long letters to Guy F. Hershberger, which he then circulated in summary form to the MMA Board.[5]

Hershberger had a different perspective. Worried that MMA was losing the initiative, in February of 1947 Hershberger wrote an essay titled "Mutual Aid for Sharing of Losses in Case of Calamity, Sickness or Death."[6] In his reflections, Hershberger reminded readers that the MMA proposal approved by the church in the spring of 1945 had included "a provision for aid in case of *property loss, sickness, or death.*" After all, Hershberger argued, this was "the major reason for favoring the new organization." Hershberger also reviewed in detail the reports from the Stewardship Study Committee between 1937 and 1943 that had led to the formation of MMA, emphasizing that the organization's mandate had always gone far beyond merely "the rehabilitation of returning CPS men." He also pointedly reminded his readers that delays in formulating a broader plan would only encourage more Mennonites to patronize commercial insurance companies, and he responded to the concerns that Snyder and others were raising by reiterating his argument that a new plan for mutual aid in times of sickness or death was no different in principle than the plans for property damage or funeral expenses already in existence. "The New Testament," he insisted, "says nothing against a mutual aid plan of the insurance type." MMA, he concluded, "is the logical organization for the inauguration of this program. . . . The time for action has arrived."[7]

Unconvinced, on April 12, 1947, Snyder responded to Hershberger's arguments in a lengthy memorandum to the MMA board. In his manifesto, Snyder expressed four basic concerns: 1) insurance does not have any basis in the New Testament; 2) insurance does not foster dependence on God; 3) mutual aid forms of insurance will weaken the church's witness; and, finally, 4) the New Testament principles of Christian stewardship, rightly practiced, make the "business proposition" of insurance unnecessary. To bolster his case, Snyder cited a litany of resolutions that regional Mennonite conferences had taken in the late nineteenth century against insurance plans, and he closed with a resounding defense of the traditional spirit of generous and spontaneous sharing whenever needs might arise.[8]

The debate between Hershberger and Snyder prompted responses from other *Gospel Herald* readers and sparked a long discussion within the MMA board at its April 1947 meeting. Though most board members were persuaded by Hershberger's arguments, the group nevertheless called for a survey of the leadership of all congregations affiliated with the (Old) Mennonite Church General Conference. In the summer of 1947 MMA staff sent a questionnaire to 434 active bishops and ministers throughout the church, inquiring about their perceived need for a program that would provide aid in three distinct areas: coverage against property loss; payment of hospital, medical, and surgical expenses; and "help for survivors following the death of the persons enrolled." Of the 187 leaders who responded (43 percent), a strong majority expressed support for all three types of plans.[9]

Vindicated, Hershberger insisted that the survey provided a mandate for the MMA board to move forward with plans to: 1) "share property losses"; 2) create "a group savings fund . . . for the payment of hospital, medical, and surgical expenses;" and 3) "assist survivors following the death of the person enrolled"—in short, property insurance, health insurance, and life insurance. Such programs, Hershberger argued, would be established "on a sound spiritual and financial basis" that would avoid "the extremes of inadequate and unsystematic saving for sharing losses, on the one hand, and the selfish, unchristian, commercial spirit associated with many worldly organizations" on the other.

At its biennial meeting in the fall of 1947, the General Conference gave its blessing to the MMA proposal to move forward with new programs. At the same time, however—heeding criticism from Snyder and others—it appointed a "Life Insurance Study Committee" to give further thought to the most controversial form of insurance.[10] In August, Snyder resigned from his position with MMA, as a principled protest against the direction he saw the organization moving.[11]

The debate in the church over life insurance would continue for another decade. But the August 1947 decision by church leaders to affirm various forms of mutual aid beyond the CPS loan program—even ones that looked suspiciously similar to property, health, and life insurance—cleared the way for MMA to launch a host of new projects.

New Burial Aid Plan Created

The MMA board wasted no time, assigning C. L. Graber the task of creating the necessary legal framework. At a meeting in May of 1949, the board approved a plan for a new corporation, modeled after the Ontario Mennonite Benefit Association, which it called the "Mennonite Mutual Relief Association."[12] The focus of the new organization—a churchwide Burial Aid plan—should not have been controversial, especially in light of the fact that several district conferences had long affirmed similar plans. Nevertheless, that fall the (Old) Mennonite Church General Conference approved the proposal only after the language of "death benefit"—which had overtones of an insurance payout— was revised in the final draft to read "burial expenses."[13] In reality, the plan was deceptively modest, since the new corporation that emerged—now identified as "Mennonite Aid, Inc." (MAI)—would ultimately transform the entire identity of MMA.

On August 23, the same day that members of the General Conference approved the concept, the MAI board convened in Harrisonburg, Virginia, for its first meeting, where it announced the formation of a Burial Aid plan with benefits set at $500. The board charged Graber and Ralph Hernley with the task of announcing the new program in the *Gospel Herald*, albeit with instructions that "the philosophy behind such [publicity] should be 'informative' rather than 'promotional.'"[14]

At the same meeting the MAI board also asked MMA staff to expand the program to include a "hospitalization and surgical" plan—a significant extension beyond the noncontroversial Burial Aid program. Several weeks later, Samuel Wenger—a Mennonite attorney from eastern Pennsylvania overseeing the incorporation of MAI—reported that a Lancaster County court had approved the MAI charter as a not-for-profit corporation, with a constitution and bylaws that envisioned a broad scope of activities.[15]

Almost immediately the newly-established MAI ran into complications with both the church and the law. In his enthusiasm, Graber had sent information

MMA created its first subsidiary, Mennonite Aid, Inc., to offer Burial Aid and a Hospital-Surgical plan. The first MAI board meeting in 1950 included: (sitting, left to right) Orie Miller, H. Clair Amstutz, Ralph Hernley, Milton Good, C. L. Graber and staff member Aaron Herr; (standing left to right) Albert Weaver, Carl Kreider, and Harry Wenger.

about the proposed Burial Aid plan to members of both Lancaster and Franconia conferences, who were not formally part of the (Old) Mennonite Church's General Conference. Bishops from these conferences quickly complained to MMA president Orie Miller that their members "should not have been solicited without conference approval." Concerns were also raised that the MAI flyers had been distributed to members in the Virginia conference. Although Virginia was a member of the General Conference, its own conference regulations were in tension with the new plan. Ever the wise administrator, Miller apologized and instructed Graber that going forward he should respond to inquiries with information about the program "but not argument, as our assignment is not propaganda but administrative." Since the General Conference had approved the MAI, "we need not defend MAI principles."[16]

The program also quickly ran into legal complications in the state of Indiana. Although the MAI charter of incorporation in Pennsylvania covered a broad range of potential services, Graber, writing from the organization's headquarters in Indiana, reported that Indiana state law would grant MAI permission to provide death benefits, but not accident or property insurance, and definitely not hospitalization coverage. Wenger, MMA's attorney, would later describe MAI's status in Indiana as "a-legal" and expressed concern that the Indiana insurance department would issue a "cease and desist" order if they knew the details of MAI's intended operations.[17]

Undeterred, at its November 29, 1949, meeting the MAI board temporarily set aside the legal questions of operating in Indiana, and continued to move forward with the framework of a Hospital and Surgical plan. At that gathering, the board sketched the outlines of a healthcare plan whose basic principles would shape the organization for the next forty years. "It was the feeling of the Board," the minutes noted, "that poor risks be taken along with the others since this represents genuine 'mutual aid.'"[18] Although it could not envision the full consequences of that decision, MMA's identity in the church in the decades that followed was inextricably linked to this radical commitment to include all qualified members, regardless of preexisting health conditions.

By Christmas, Graber had prepared and distributed a prospectus that enthusiastically described the benefits of both the Burial Aid and the Hospital-Surgical plans. The MAI burial plan was simple and straightforward. Those who enrolled and paid an annual "assessment" (the board studiously avoided the term *premium*) would be assured of a $500 payment upon their death that was intended to cover basic funeral expenses.[19] The Hospital and Surgical plan was more complicated. Based explicitly on the Mennonite Benefit Association

Ray and Lillian Bair married June 8, 1948, soon becoming the fifth customers to buy "burial aid," an early form of MMA life insurance. The couple later published *God's Managers*, a budgeting guide widely used among church members.

of Ontario, it was intended as a classic mutual aid program in the sense that the quarterly assessments to participants were adjusted according to the actual cost of claims and overhead from the previous quarter. It also set aside no financial reserves, surely a matter of great concern for any outsider with knowledge of the insurance industry. And initially, the plan had no screening of members and only a six-month waiting period to qualify for surgical benefits. Congregations that joined as a group did not need to fill out individual application forms, and could avoid the waiting period.[20] H. Clair Amstutz, a Mennonite physician from Goshen, served as the program's medical consultant.

Both MAI plans met with an immediate and enthusiastic response, despite the fact that the staff did not pursue any promotional campaigns other than news articles in church periodicals. Within two years, 1,888 adults were enrolled in the Hospital-Surgical plan and 513 in the Burial Aid plan. At the end of 1957, the hospital-surgical plan was serving 13,799 adults and 9,874 dependents, with 1,623 people enrolled in the burial aid plan. By 1961, those numbers had basically doubled once again.[21]

In contrast to the Burial Aid plan, the MAI board quickly encountered a host of unanticipated complications with the Hospital-Surgical program. Already in 1951, for example, the board needed to clarify to its members that reimbursements would be restricted to "real, licensed" doctors. The next year the board debated whether the MAI plan would cover orthodontia (no), ingrown toenails (yes), or the maternity costs for an unmarried eighteen-year-old (yes). The board also quickly needed to wrestle with the dilemma raised by individuals who were clearly taking advantage of the program—submitting dubious claims or waiting to join the plan until the moment when they were facing an illness.[22] By early 1952, the board responded with a reasonable adjustment to the principle of unlimited mutual aid: individuals with preexisting conditions would only be accepted into the Hospital-Surgical plan if at least half the congregation's members also joined the plan at the same time, and the waiting period for surgery was extended from six months to a year.[23]

Despite these challenges, MAI's board members remained resolute in their conviction that the basic ideals of the program would not be compromised. In 1952, Swartzendruber reported in a letter to MAI members that the assessment had risen from $15 to $25 per member in light of higher claims, but also reminded participants that "we have paid claims in cases where we had no legal liability but we were directed to help share the burden because of the circumstances and thus carried out our Christian responsibility for the Brotherhood."[24] At its fourth annual board meeting on January 8, 1954, MAI board president M. R. Good, who brought extensive experience from his time overseeing the Mennonite Benefit Association of Ontario, argued that the primary challenge MAI faced was maintaining features which should contrast it with commercial organizations of a similar nature. "'What do ye do more than others?'" he asked rhetorically. "Is anything distinctively Christian in it?"[25] At the same meeting, the board developed a list of considerations by which individual members who suffered significant losses might be eligible for additional financial support through a "Catastrophe Aid" program that they envisioned could be funded by donations and a $1 annual assessment on each policy.[26]

The MAI board also quickly recognized the imperative of urging members of the Hospital-Surgical plan to bear greater responsibility for their own role in controlling costs. Already in 1952, H. Clair Amstutz, the plan's medical consultant, emphasized the importance of health education—both physical and mental—to the success of the program and introduced the term "preventative medicine" to a board that knew little about medical matters and even less about the technical language of actuarial tables or "risk pools."[27] In 1955, W. J. Dye, a hospital administrator from La Junta, Colorado, warned the MAI board of significant changes that were taking place in the medical world.[28] In the past fifty years, he reported, life expectancy in the United States had grown from forty to seventy; during the same period the cost of medical care had risen precipitously. Increasingly, the medical field was moving from a model of "repair" to one of "prevention," with a shift in emphasis from "care for the poor"—which focused on charity in the last stages of life—to the establishment of community centers that stressed "wholistic health."[29]

In 1954 the board addressed another difficult question that had far-reaching consequences for the MMA organization as a whole: could participation in the MAI programs extend beyond members of the (Old) Mennonite Church? The issue arose partly in response to requests for coverage from spouses of Mennonites who had not officially joined the Mennonite church. But the bigger test case was a request for participation from administrators of the *Hilfsplan*—a property plan in Kansas whose members were part of the General Conference Mennonite Church. In 1955, after much debate, the MAI board agreed to open its plans to "any member of any group cooperating with Mennonite Central Committee."[30]

Overshadowing all these challenges, however, was the fact that the Hospital-Surgical plan had no legal status outside of Pennsylvania, which meant that it was operating outside the regulatory framework of Indiana state law, largely without reserves, and with only a rudimentary understanding of its actuarial risks.

Floyd and Margorie Yoder, Wellman, Iowa, were early adopters of MMA's health plans, and it continued to be the only health insurance they ever used. MERLIN MILLER

The Early MMA Office and Staff

Standing at the intersection of all this was the growing MMA staff—an unusually gifted set of individuals who clearly thought of their work as a calling. Initially, the primary focus in the two-room office at 1413 South 8th Street was raising capital, processing loans, and gaining experience with the details of accounting and record keeping. But only a few years after its founding, MMA had been transformed from an ad hoc loan office with two part-time employees into a beehive of activity, as MMA's leaders struggled to establish clear workflow procedures and create appropriate lines of supervision and accountability, while staff strained to keep up with the new programs that the board agreed to pursue.

Ostensibly overseeing this rapid, sometimes helter-skelter, expansion was C. L. Graber. Graber's primary task on behalf of MMA in the last half of the 1940s was public relations and raising capital. Gregarious and worldly-wise, Graber knew dozens of key Mennonite leaders and business people in Iowa, Illinois, Ohio, Pennsylvania, and Virginia. These contacts were crucial to raising funds on behalf of MCC for the Refugee Resettlement program that MMA was helping to finance, even as he served as the primary salesperson for the MAI Burial Aid and Surgical-Hospital programs.

Late in 1949, Graber made a key hire when he convinced Aaron Herr to oversee the new MAI program. Although painfully shy, Herr had a preternatural gift for numbers and a scrupulously detailed approach to accounting.[31] Though never trained as an actuary, he quickly recognized the need for such skills as the MAI program took form. He did so with remarkable aptitude, keeping the board apprised of changing trends in medical expenses and adjusting premiums accordingly.

More than anyone else, however, it was Harold S. Swartzendruber, Graber's young son-in-law, who shouldered the greatest part of the organizational operations generated by the rapid expansion of MMA in the first decades of its existence. Like Graber, Swartzendruber grew up in a Mennonite family in eastern Iowa. In January 1946, while working in a CPS camp in Michigan, Swartzendruber came to the attention of Orie Miller, who persuaded him to move to Akron as his bookkeeper and assistant. In 1947, Swartzendruber joined MMA as a part-time assistant bookkeeper while completing studies at Goshen College. In 1951, Swartzendruber became assistant manager of the young organization, and in 1954 he replaced Graber as the general manager, though it was Orie Miller, president of MMA, who actually directed the organization through frequent phone calls and almost daily correspondence. Under Miller's watchful tutelage, Swartzendruber labored tirelessly to turn the visions of Hershberger and Graber into reality. His fingerprints were everywhere—ordering office equipment, generating balance sheets, visiting holders of delinquent debts, preparing detailed reports for the MMA board meetings, ensuring quorums for the perfunctory meetings of various subsidiary companies, organizing travel schedules, and taking minutes, all the while tending to mountains of correspondence.

Late in 1953, MMA negotiated the purchase of a nearby home at 1202 South 8th Street, which had recently been refurbished to accommodate several apartments. The office space at 1413 South 8th Street had become far too small to accommodate the growing organization, and Graber was tired of cleaning dust and slabs of plaster from desks on Monday morning after a weekend of "carousing" by the college boys living in the apartments above.[32] The MMA staff moved into the new office in February of 1954. In addition to Swartzendruber, by the fall of 1955 three full-time staff members devoted their attention to the day-to-day operations of the Burial Aid and Hospital-Surgical program: Ray Sala served as the plan's field representative; Aaron Herr focused on the details of membership, claims, and assessments; and Carl Yoder served as the plan's accountant.

A Cutting-Edge Foundation (1952)

Even as the Burial Aid and Hospital-Surgical plans were gaining traction, Hershberger, Graber, and Miller were eager to introduce additional programs based on the expansive mandate the church had granted to the MMA board. One concern shared by many church leaders was the challenge of securing adequate capital for the rapid expansion of Mennonite institutions. Some organizations like the Mennonite Board of Missions and Charity could count on regular financial support from congregations. But others—such as the colleges, Mennonite Central Committee, and Mennonite Publishing House—relied heavily on contributions from individual church members. The American economy was growing rapidly in the years immediately following the war, and people of wealth who supported these Mennonite institutions were increasingly interested in structuring their charitable contributions in ways that minimized tax obligations.

Charitable foundations had long been an important part of American philanthropy. But they generally were associated with extremely wealthy families like the Rockefellers and Carnegies. By the early 1950s, new legal structures were emerging that made it possible for small business owners and ordinary individuals to also benefit from incentives for charitable giving built into the

Albert and Frieda Entz
began donating crops from
their farm in Elbing, Kans.,
to Mennonite Foundation
soon after it was established,
a tradition their family continued. JIM STUCKY

Internal Revenue Service tax code. When MMA established the Mennonite Foundation in December of 1952, the corporation was at the cutting edge of a new frontier in American philanthropy.

According to Harold Swartzendruber, the origins of the Mennonite Foundation could be traced to an exchange between his father, Edwin E. Swartzendruber, and Graber in the fall of 1951 when Edwin was in Goshen for a visit. The previous year had been quite profitable for Swartzendruber's elevator business in Manson, Iowa, and he was eager to make a significant contribution to a building fund for his home church. The problem, however, was that the congregation did not yet have a building committee—or even much interest in a building project. So, somewhat naively, Swartzendruber asked Graber, who served as the business manager of Goshen College, if he could make a contribution to the college in exchange for a charitable gift receipt. Then, at some later date, he explained, he would ask Goshen College to redirect the gift to the congregation in Manson. Not surprisingly, Graber responded with a resounding, "No!" But the exchange led Graber to sense a new opportunity for MMA.[33]

In his trips to solicit funds on behalf of the college, Graber frequently encountered similar instances of individuals or businesses who wanted to make a charitable gift within a given calendar year for tax purposes, but were not yet ready to channel the money to an ultimate destination. When Graber learned that Wittenberg College, a Lutheran school in Ohio, had created a plan to address these concerns, he sent Swartzendruber to investigate. He returned with valuable information about a Lutheran foundation that had received IRS approval to support charitable giving to various church-related institutions.

In October of 1952 Graber persuaded the MMA board to approve the creation of a "Mennonite Foundation," a decision that church leaders affirmed a month later.[34] Thus, when the State of Indiana approved Mennonite Foundation as a not-for-profit corporation on December 30, 1952, with a mandate to "act as a depository for gifts by individuals and corporations which would be deductible in calculating Federal Income taxes," MMA added another subsidiary to its growing family of organizations.[35] Oversight of the daily operations fell to Harold Swartzendruber.[36]

Although the foundation would go on to manage enormous sums of money, initial interest in the program was slow. During the first decade an average of $30,000 new dollars came into the foundation annually, with some $20,000 dispersed each year to various charitable causes—almost certainly Mennonite institutions, though this information could not be disclosed. Despite advertisements in the *Gospel Herald* and flyers distributed along with MAI assessment notices, by 1960 the foundation had accumulated only $75,000 in assets.

Two significant developments marked a turning point for the eventual success of the Mennonite Foundation. The first came in 1959, when Orie Miller—always a sensitive reader of the context of his time—persuaded (Old) Mennonite Church leaders to allow MMA to provide church members with estate and retirement planning services. Five years later, Miller successfully recruited John Rudy, a young research-engineer-turned-pastor, as a part-time staff person with the Mennonite Foundation. Rudy accepted the assignment

Harold Swartzendruber ran the organization's operations for decades, turning the early MMA vision into reality.

at a fortuitous moment, since Mennonites, especially in the eastern part of the United States, were just beginning a long pattern of selling highly-appreciated farmland to housing developers. At the same time, a growing number of Mennonite-owned businesses were realizing large profits in various construction, meat packing, and manufacturing industries.[37] In both instances newly wealthy Mennonites were seeking assistance in managing their tax liabilities, while also looking for ways to support church-related causes. The rapid growth of Mennonite schools, church camps, retirement centers, and historical societies during the second half of the twentieth century—along with numerous church building or remodeling projects undertaken during the same period—was made possible in no small part by the existence of the Mennonite Foundation.

Automobile Aid and the Liability Challenge (1955)

Just as MMA administrators created the Mennonite Foundation as a church-based response to a practical financial need, other MMA programs also emerged to provide church members with alternatives to readily available commercial products.

In 1953, based on a favorable report from the (Old) Mennonite Church's Insurance and Investment Study Committee, Orie Miller directed Swartzendruber to develop a churchwide collision-comprehensive plan for automobile insurance.[38] Swartzendruber quickly turned for help to John D. Burkholder, Jr., the director of a successful Mennonite auto aid plan in Virginia. Together the two men drew up a constitution and bylaws for a new Mennonite Automobile Aid corporation which the MMA board approved in October 1954.[39] Although MMA had no previous experience in automobile insurance, Swartzendruber was confident that the plan would benefit from the experience that MMA staff members were developing in bookkeeping, billing, and financial management through their work with the Burial Aid and Hospital-Surgical plans.

From the beginning, the most challenging aspect of the automobile plan was not handling the premiums or payouts but rather ethical concerns related to liability insurance. Fire or storm insurance plans do not need to address the question of liability—Mother Nature cannot be held legally responsible for the destruction caused by a tornado or flood. But in car accidents a human being is almost always at fault, or "liable," for the damages done to property, another car, or the occupants of the car. If everyone would immediately acknowledge their responsibility in causing an accident, the matter could be readily resolved.

But when disagreements ensued over the question of liability—as was quite often the case in car accidents—a court needed to adjudicate the matter.

Given its long-standing position against initiating lawsuits, however, the (Old) Mennonite Church found itself in a difficult position when it came to automobile liability coverage. To illustrate the problem, Swartzendruber frequently repeated a story related to him by Wayne S. Martin, a founder of the Goodville Mutual Casualty Company, about a Pennsylvania Mennonite who had taken out car insurance with a commercial company. The man had run off the road and hit a sign advertising fresh produce in front of a farmhouse. Clearly he was at fault. His insurance company covered the costs of repairing his damaged car, but the driver was shocked to read in the paper soon thereafter that he was named in a lawsuit for damages against the owner of the farm— who happened to be the bishop of his own congregation. The farmer's sign, as it turned out, had been illegally posted on the highway right-of-way. So the insurance company was exercising its legal right, in the name of car owner, to sue to recover the damages it had paid.[40]

Though some found the logic morally troubling, the MMA board proposed that they resolve the conundrum of liability insurance by establishing a partnership with the Goodville Mutual Casualty Company. Goodville Mutual had been founded in 1926 by a group of Lancaster Mennonites. Though not an official organization of the Lancaster Mennonite Conference, most members of the board and management team were Mennonites, and policyholders shared a tacit assumption that Goodville was a "Mennonite" company. Significantly, Goodville's auto aid plan provided liability coverage. However, it assured its members that it would do everything possible to resolve disputes outside the court system. By the early 1950s, Goodville had expanded to serve members of the Mennonite Church throughout Pennsylvania, and it had recently been chartered in the state of Virginia as well, where it provided liability coverage for the Virginia Mennonite Conference automobile aid plan.

Following the Virginia model, MMA's newly-created Mennonite Automobile Aid covered the collision-comprehensive portion of the plan, while strongly recommending to its members that they turn to Goodville for the more controversial liability insurance.

Like the MAI program, the new Mennonite Automobile Aid plan was incorporated as a not-for profit association in Pennsylvania. Almost immediately after it opened for business in January of 1955, the program proved to be very attractive. Within five years it had enrolled 3,500 vehicles and built up a reserve of more than $40,000. In the spring of 1957 the MAA board agreed that it would need to adjust premiums to account for the fact that teenage drivers, who accounted for 17 percent of its membership, were responsible for more than 30 percent of the claims.[41] The larger MMA board also continued to wrestle with the ethics of the Goodville solution to liability coverage. "If we believe that liability and property damage insurance is wrong," argued Carl Kreider, dean of Goshen College and a long-time MMA board member, "then it is also wrong for us to ask an organization outside the church but composed of church members to do what our church organizations do not want to do themselves."[42]

Nevertheless, the MAA program went forward, strengthened by Goodville's readiness to extend its services into other states with high concentrations of Mennonites, provided that MMA assist with the costs of Goodville's expansion.[43] Over time, MMA's relationship with Goodville would become exceedingly complicated; but for many years the two companies enjoyed a symbiotic working relationship that benefited both and served their customers well.[44]

By the mid-1950s, the basic contours of MMA were taking shape. In the course of little more than a decade, the organization had developed a successful loan program, a Burial Aid plan, a Hospital-Surgical plan that operated on the principles of mutual aid, a legal structure that encouraged charitable giving, and an automobile insurance plan. Each of these programs attempted to bridge the divide between the sacred and the secular, between the church community of faith and the realities of everyday life. Each remained anchored in the theological convictions and expectations of the Anabaptist-Mennonite community while also responding actively to a changing economic context and the demands of the marketplace.

Menno Travel Service Tacked On

As if there were not already enough activities packed into the small office, MMA also housed a branch office of a travel agency known as Menno Travel Service (MTS). More than any other subsidiary organization, MTS reflected the peculiar blend of personal interests, entrepreneurial spirit, and churchly connections that came together in the person of Orie Miller. In 1947, concerned that Mennonite Central Committee was paying thousands of dollars to travel agencies in New York to handle passports and boat tickets for its overseas relief workers, Miller asked Swartzendruber, who was then serving as Miller's personal assistant and as MCC's shipping agent, to explore the possibility of dealing directly with passenger boats and airlines. After a series of exploratory meetings in New York City, Swartzendruber garnered the needed contacts and credentials, whereupon Miller drafted articles of incorporation and bylaws that established a travel agency with himself as president and Swartzendruber as vice president. At the time of the 1948 Mennonite World Conference—an international gathering that took place in Goshen, Indiana, and Newton, Kansas—Miller established a temporary branch MTS office in Goshen, with MMA office staff assisting in the travel details related to the event. By 1953 Swartzendruber, now working in Goshen as the assistant manager of MMA, had become a licensed travel agent and began sending regular reports to the MMA board regarding his part-time work for MTS.[45] Although it was never very clear how the travel agency fit within the larger goals of the organization, MTS retained a connection to MMA through the late 1970s.

A New Program to Finance a Construction Boom—Mennonite Church Buildings (1956)

MMA's direct oversight of Menno Travel Service was relatively short-lived. But it illustrates the readiness of church leaders like Orie Miller to use the MMA structure as a vehicle for addressing a range of organizational needs, even if they stretched the definition of mutual aid. Miller had something similar in mind with the creation in 1956 of yet another MMA subsidiary—Mennonite Church Buildings (MCB).

For many years the Mennonite Board of Education had supervised an entity known as the Mennonite Educational Finance Corporation as a vehicle for raising money to fund large building projects on the growing campuses of Mennonite colleges.[46] Church leaders, however, recognized that colleges were not the only entities needing loans for large building projects.[47] So, on April 24, 1956, at the request of the Mennonite Board of Education, MMA incorporated a new organization called Mennonite Church Buildings with a mandate to raise capital, negotiate interest rates, oversee loan payments, and amortize expenses for the church's schools, hospitals, and other institutions.[48] At its first meeting in July 1956, the newly-created MCB board established the goal of raising $200,000 for capital projects, which the Board of Education estimated would need to extend to $580,000 over the next three years.

Initially, MCB issued thirty-year debenture notes promising a 4 percent return, though it clearly hoped that supporters of the fund would forgive the loan. "Our Christian beliefs and doctrine," read the brochure in the rather stilted language of the time, "indicate that we must consider more than the financial returns from an investment and surely an investment in the Lord's work is putting our beliefs into practice. . . . [Will you] accept the challenge of making material means serve spiritual ends?"[49] In the coming decades, MCB would also extend its loan services to a host of Mennonite congregations and hospitals undergoing building projects. The program, however, was chronically undercapitalized and loan requests consistently outpaced available funds.

A Savings Plan Experiment (1956)

In an effort to resolve the problems of the underfunded MCB initiative, the MMA board also approved a suggestion from Orie Miller to promote a savings program so that individual church members could invest their savings in projects that benefited the church. Since the MMA bylaws of incorporation did not permit it to function as a commercial bank, Swartzendruber proposed that the savings program Miller envisioned be called a "thrift accumulation" plan. Participants would send deposits at regular intervals, which MMA would hold for seventy months before the money would be available for withdrawal at an interest rate of 3 percent.[50] The concept, promoted almost entirely in the form of a hastily printed brochure, never elicited much of a response. After several years, the Thrift Accumulation program simply disappeared, though broader conversations about providing other kinds of banking services—a credit union, for example, or a trust company—would remain high on the MMA board's agenda for many years to come.

Menno Insurance Services Expands (1957)

Before the decade came to an end, the MMA board approved the creation of still one more subsidiary company. Shortly after the formation of the Automobile Aid plan in 1954, it became clear that MMA could expand that program to Mennonites nationally only if it was accompanied by the liability coverage provided by the Goodville Mutual Casualty Company. When MMA asked Goodville to extend its services into other states with large concentrations of Mennonites, Harold Swartzendruber and Ray Sala obtained licenses that qualified them to serve as Goodville agents in Indiana working out of the MMA offices. As a longer-term solution, in 1957 the MMA board created a new entity—Mennonite Insurance Service—that could serve as an agent for companies issuing casualty insurance.[51] Incorporated in the state of Indiana, MIS, Inc. was structured as a stock company wholly owned by MMA, even though its sole purpose initially was to represent the liability insurance coverage provided by Goodville Mutual Casualty Company for Indiana Mennonites who purchased auto insurance from MAA. The creation of MIS points to the creative spirit that characterized the relationship between MMA and Goodville, but also to the legal complexities associated with the heavily regulated insurance world.

Creating Mennonite Retirement Trust (1963)

By the mid-1950s the general utility of MMA as a framework for addressing a wide range of financial needs within the church had become apparent to denominational leaders. Just as the Mennonite Foundation was addressing the growing interest in financial planning with the goal of helping church members think more carefully about retirement, leaders of various Mennonite institutions—particularly Mennonite Board of Missions, Mennonite Publishing House, and Goshen College—began to recognize the need to offer their employees a retirement plan. At the same time, the (Old) Mennonite Church General Conference was raising questions about the financial security of ministers as they moved into retirement. In 1959, church leaders convened a conference of all the major church boards to review their policies regarding compensation, but especially to discuss the possibility of establishing a church-wide retirement plan for employees of church institutions. In April of 1961, the MMA board agreed to develop a plan.

Working with the actuarial firm Arthur Stedry Hansen in Chicago, Swartzendruber hammered out the details of a plan that met with IRS approval in June 1963 and began operations on July 1. Church employees could contribute up to 10 percent of their annual salary into the plan. The earnings on those contributions were tax deferred until the funds were withdrawn for retirement, and they remained vested with the employee.[52] Presumably, the church-related institution would also contribute to the retirement fund. Within a year, the MRT program had 421 participants. A little more than a decade later the plan had grown to include 2,171 participants with a fund balance of $2.4 million. Although MMA staff always included MRT in its annual board reports, legally the program was sponsored by the (Old) Mennonite Church General Board, with MMA serving as its trustee, administrator, and investment manager.[53]

Sharing Risks and Counsel: Association of Mennonite Aid Societies

Within the larger context of Mennonite mutual aid societies, MMA was clearly a newcomer in 1945. But whereas most of the other societies were local or, at best, regional organizations, with relatively small memberships, MMA was the first churchwide mutual aid society. Moreover, its membership extended well beyond the (Old) Mennonite Church, to include the General Conference Mennonite Church, Mennonite Brethren; Conservative Mennonite, Brethren in Christ, and many other smaller Anabaptist-Mennonite groups. With the rapid growth of the MMA organization and the proliferation of its programs, tensions began to emerge with local mutual aid societies that had traditionally specialized in automobile, fire and storm damage, or burial aid plans. For many of these groups, already undercapitalized and increasingly unable to match policies offered by commercial insurance companies, it was not clear whether MMA's sudden appearance was a competitive threat or the salvation of the principle of mutual aid.

In 1954 MCC agreed to convene a meeting of all the mutual aid societies in the United States and Canada to address the issues. On July 14 to 15, 1955, almost exactly ten years after the incorporation of MMA, some forty people representing twenty-eight mutual aid societies gathered at the Atlantic Hotel in downtown Chicago to discuss the future of Mennonite mutual aid.[54] Melvin Gingerich opened the gathering with an overview of all the existing mutual aid organizations in North America. Then followed a series of detailed reports on each of the various mutual aid initiatives. The meeting was a resounding

This planning committee pulled together mutual aid societies so they could help their members when catastrophic disasters hit without major losses to their organizations. Back row, from left: William Snyder, Jacob Wedel, Elvin Sauder, and Howard Schmidt. Front row, from left: Samuel Wenger, Harold Swartzendruber, Howard Raid.

success. Representatives of small mutual societies discovered new allies in the challenges they faced and were enriched by the collegial spirit of the gathering, which created a context for forging new collaborations.

In his survey of property aid programs, for example, Howard Raid, a professor at Bluffton College and a pioneer in the mutual aid movement, called attention to the growing need for small mutual aid societies to plan for catastrophic losses, especially since many of them did not have adequate reserves or any form of reinsurance. In making the case for a cooperative "reinsurance program," Raid noted with special concern the geographical concentration of many mutual aid societies, which exposed them to large losses in the event of a flood or tornado. According to Raid, thirteen of the sixteen Mennonite mutual societies he contacted expressed an interest in forming a cooperative reinsurance program.[55] The conference concluded by electing a continuation committee as well as a Risk Resharing Committee.

The following year, the group gathered again in Chicago—this time to outline a constitution for the newly-formed Association of Mennonite Aid Societies (AMAS). In addition, they discussed a proposal from the Risk Resharing Committee that the groups form a reinsurance pool to cover their plans against catastrophic losses. In 1957 the group approved the constitution and bylaws of AMAS and agreed to form a risk sharing organization called Mennonite Indemnity, Inc. (MII).

Incorporated on October 22, 1957, in Pennsylvania with a capitalization of $150,000, MII was a stock insurance company, under the auspices of MCC, that provided protection to its members against catastrophic losses.[56] During the early years of the new company, only twelve mutual aid societies signed on as members, undertaking the complicated challenge of aligning their practices in terms of enrolling risks or handling claims. As the largest group, MMA took the lead in raising the capital required for the MII reserve fund; MCC and Goodville administered the program. The significance of MII was underscored in the spring of 1965 when a major tornado struck northern Indiana, home to thousands of Mennonites and related groups. Neither of the two local property aid societies—Indiana-Michigan Aid and the Conservative Mutual Aid Plan— were members of MII, and neither had reserves nearly large enough to cover their losses. The experience was chastening, and shortly thereafter membership in MII dramatically increased. When, in the spring of 1990, the town of Hesston, Kansas, and several other Mennonite communities in the area were devastated by a series of tornadoes, the MII plan—which now included twenty-four groups—enabled a rapid response to the claims.

In addition to the success of the MII program, AMAS meetings proved to be a significant venue for the exchange of ideas and information among the various Mennonite mutual aid societies. For nearly forty years, until its dissolution in 2005, the annual program nurtured a sustained dialogue among Anabaptist-Mennonite leaders regarding the theology of mutual aid, while also providing a mix of inspiration, industry insights, and counsel on issues related to legal questions, new technology, or technical details associated with processing claims.[57] In a real sense, AMAS—with MMA as its dominant member—was the leading advocate for mutual aid on behalf of the dozens of small mutual aid societies as they struggled to adapt to the rapidly changing economic realities of post-WWII America.

A Resolution to the Life Insurance Debate

By the mid 1950s, it was clear that Mennonite Aid, Inc. (MAI)—that is, the Burial Aid and Hospital-Surgical plan—had become the signature program of the Mennonite Mutual Aid organization. But for Guy F. Hershberger and the other visionaries who helped to bring the program into existence, MAI was still lacking a major component: it had no means of providing financial assistance to families after the death of a parent or primary breadwinner—what Hershberger and other Mennonites called "Survivors' Aid," but what the rest of the world understood to be "life insurance."

In traditional rural Mennonite communities, care for widows and orphans was understood to be the responsibility of extended families and the local congregation, with the deacon playing a major role in coordinating the distribution of needed support. The history of Mennonite widows has not yet attracted the careful attention of historians; but plenty of anecdotal stories suggest that family and congregational support for its most impoverished members rarely played out as well in practice as the ideal may have sounded, especially as traditional ties of community weakened with the advance of urbanization and industrialization.[58] At the same time, as household incomes rose following World War II, so too did expectations regarding financial security. Life insurance promised upwardly mobile families the assurance of an additional measure of economic protection in the event of a sudden loss of income through injury or death.[59]

Yet even though it was clear that many church members were secretly taking out policies, the ethical arguments against life insurance remained largely unchallenged. Indeed, many regional conference regulations still included life insurance among the sins that served as a test of church membership.

Compounding the emerging debate over life insurance was a second issue. From its beginning in 1949, the MAI Hospital-Surgical plan had been operating in a kind of legal limbo, at least in Indiana. MAI had been incorporated in Pennsylvania, the only state that allowed churches to create healthcare plans for their members that were not regulated by the State Department of Insurance. For this reason, MAI's official mailing address was Akron, Pennsylvania, home of MMA president, Orie Miller, even though all its activities were carried out in the MMA offices in Goshen. This had seemed like a great solution in that the Pennsylvania charter enabled MMA to provide healthcare benefits in the form of true mutual aid—e.g., operating without reserves, adjusting assessments according to claims, and the freedom to grant additional support in special cases to needy members. Technically, however, the Hospital-Surgical plan had no legal status in Indiana, since its activities there should have come under the regulatory purview of state agencies.[60]

If MMA was now going to further expand its services to include a "Survivor's Aid" plan, it would not only need to explain to its own constituents how a life insurance program preserved the elements of mutual aid expected by the church, but it would also need to convince state officials in Indiana and elsewhere that the program they envisioned should be exempt from standard insurance regulations.

Of the two challenges, convincing the church proved to be the easiest.

One More Study Committee

Traditional Mennonite arguments against life insurance often started with pragmatic concerns. A tract published by Mennonite Publishing House in 1910, for example, described life insurance as the terrain of scam artists and scoundrels, claiming that no fewer than 2,225 insurance companies had failed in the previous decade, leaving their policyholders bereft of any benefits.[61] Other Mennonite leaders argued that life insurance discouraged the poor from becoming responsible managers—policyholders were captivated by unrealistic dreams of a large payout.

But the most compelling argument against life insurance for Mennonites was that the practice seemed to place a dollar value on the life of a human being. At least property and health insurance paid claims on actual expenses incurred; life insurance, by contrast, seemed to suggest that a payment was being rendered in exchange for the life of the policyholder.[62] Church leaders at the 1947 biennial meeting of the (Old) Mennonite Church General Conference had approved MMA's Burial Aid and Hospital-Surgical plan, but they dodged the question of Survivor's Aid by doing what they so often did when confronted with a controversial issue—they appointed a study committee. The mandate of the Life Insurance Study Committee, as framed by the church's General Problems Committee, was to propose "an intelligent, workable, and Scriptural solution of the life insurance problem as it is posed before us in industries and in appeals to security in old age."[63] For the next six years, the committee deliberated, offering interim reports to the General Conference in 1949 and 1951 before submitting its final recommendations in 1953.[64]

In that recommendation the five-member group, now renamed the Insurance and Investment Study Committee, summarized their work in a methodical manner.[65] They began by noting that the context for ethical discernment regarding life insurance had changed considerably during the past fifty years. Government regulations had curbed the worst abuses associated with the industry, and industrialization and urbanization made new forms of mutual aid necessary. In a bold step, the committee affirmed that the meaning of "mutual aid in the Biblical way" needed to be interpreted anew for each generation. The report then elaborated a series of basic biblical and theological principles relevant to the "economic relations of the Christian, including insurance and investments." The principles they highlighted offer a helpful window into the theological worldview of (Old) Mennonite church leaders at midcentury:[66]

1. Christians must seek first the Kingdom of God—wealth is only a means for serving this end.
2. Scripture teaches "ownership of private property, industry, thrift," and the principle of self-reliance.
3. Stewardship means that everything the Christian has—be that "property," "ability to work," or "earning powers"—belongs to God.
4. Love of neighbor compels the Christian to share freely and to conduct business affairs honorably.
5. Christians should not be unequally yoked—i.e., "in partnership or corporate relationships"—with "unchristian economic and business policies directed by others."
6. The New Testament teaches "the principle of organized, cooperative, mutual aid within the brotherhood."
7. The New Testament also makes it clear that "changing social and economic situations justify the adoption of new methods and new forms of cooperative mutual aid within the brotherhood."
8. The appropriate test of any mutual aid program is not "the form of its organization or of its operation, but rather its purpose, its objectives, and the spirit with which it is carried out."

9. All programs—government as well as private—must be judged by the "standards set for organized mutual aid within the brotherhood."

10. Unless a government-administered program of insurance [i.e., Social Security] is in conflict with Scripture principles, "the principle of submission to the requirements of the state would argue for cooperation."

11. Regardless of one's understanding of cooperative mutual aid or insurance, the Christian's trust is ultimately in God alone.

With these carefully worded principles—which emphasized the reality of cultural change and elevated scriptural principles above a more literalist, rule-based approach to Christian ethics—the authors of the report were clearly setting the stage for a favorable recommendation regarding simple term life insurance. But they did so in a typically guarded and highly-nuanced fashion. Indeed, in the next section of their report, committee members emphasized that the primary responsibility of care for the needy rested with the family and the church. But they immediately went on to argue that "modern mutual aid *or insurance plans* . . . are not necessarily a violation of Scriptural principle."[67] Specifically, the report affirmed that Social Security, worker's compensation, and auto liability insurance "were not objectionable." Buried in a host of noncontroversial recommendations was a request that MMA bring to the next session of the General Conference "a plan for the assistance of disabled persons and the rehabilitation of dependent survivors [i.e., "life insurance"], by means of periodic payments over an extended period of time."[68]

On August 25, 1955, the (Old) Mennonite Church General Conference adopted virtually all of these principles in a much shorter "Statement of Position on Insurance."[69] Although the statement explicitly recognized that regional conferences and congregations ultimately had "the prerogative and responsibility in matters of discipline," church leaders were clearly breaking with a century of tradition when they called on church members to judge various forms of insurance "by the spirit and purpose which underlie participation in it." They closed the statement by encouraging regional conferences and congregations "to participate in the mutual aid plans of the brotherhood [i.e., MMA] in preference to commercial plans."[70]

Rehabilitating Widows and Survivors (1960)

Even with this endorsement from the General Conference, MMA was slow to implement a life insurance plan. In 1956, the MMA board created a Widows and Survivors Rehabilitation Sub-Committee to work out the practical details for the new plan. Their goal was to create a program that could "ease the financial burden arising from the untimely death of the breadwinner (either man or woman) if this occurs at the time of their lives when they have survivors who are dependent on them."[71] The committee also hoped that the charter for the new plan would be recognized in all states where Mennonites were living, and that the new program could merge with the Burial Aid and Hospital-Surgical plans as a unified entity.

The vision quickly became more complicated than they had anticipated.

The committee soon learned that a charter for a new insurance company in Indiana would require a minimum of four hundred subscribers, each with a policy worth at least $1,000. The company would also need to have the word *insurance* in its name, and it would need to demonstrate cash reserves of at least $60,000. In their deliberations, the committee concluded that "the objection to the name including the word insurance is no longer valid," noting that a fire aid plan in Lancaster County had adopted the name "Mennonite Fire Insurance Association," in order to conform with a similar requirement in Pennsylvania law. However, the committee continued, "the word 'Life' in the name would be very objectionable."[72]

Over the next year, Charles Ainlay, a Lutheran attorney who served as MMA's legal counsel, worked directly with representatives of the Insurance Department of Indiana to iron out the technical details. In August 1959, the state granted tentative approval for the creation of Mennonite Aid Insurance, Inc. (MAII). Swartzendruber and the MMA office staff hastily drew up a brochure advertising the plan, which they sent to all MAI members.[73] A year later, on August 18, 1960, Swartzendruber reported to the board that the MMA office had indeed received the requisite four hundred applications and secured the $60,000 in government bonds needed as a reserve.

On October 13, 1960, the (Old) Mennonite Church's first official life insurance program went into effect with 410 policies.[74] Although the insurance plan was incorporated as Mennonite Aid Insurance, Inc., MMA's administrators avoided calling attention to the word *insurance* by identifying the program as "Survivor's Aid" in their promotional literature or by its acronym, MAII.

A New Building . . . and Organizational Restructuring

Amid the flurry of activity generated by the subsidiary companies, it quickly became apparent that the office space in the house on 1202 South 8th Street was not keeping pace with MMA's rapid growth. The MMA staff, now eight people, had taken over the entire home, including the second floor apartment rooms. In 1957, only a few years after moving into the new offices, Swartzendruber noted that the heavy weight of the addressograph plates used for mailings, along with the thousands of files and the new NCR bookkeeping machine, had strained the floor joists so much that it was becoming impossible to open the interior doors. After a flurry of correspondence with Miller, Graber arranged the purchase of several lots just off Main Street directly west of Goshen College, and hired Orus Eash, a Mennonite architect from Fort Wayne, to draw up blueprints for a new split-level building.[75]

MMA's staff was thrilled when they moved into a new building at 111 Marilyn Avenue in the spring of 1958. In contrast to the tiny rooms in remodeled homes where they had previously worked, the new building, located in the shadow of Goshen General Hospital, offered 7,500 square feet of well-furnished office space, and was designed to accommodate growth well into the future. During the next decade, the MMA board routinely granted Swartzendruber's requests for new office equipment; and with the rapid growth of the Hospital-Surgical plan, they also affirmed his appeals for additional staff. At the time of the move, MMA had nine employees; by 1964 that number had tripled to twenty-seven.[76]

The new building captured well the spirit of the organization. From the moment of its inception, the organization had been in a mode of continuous growth. Between 1945 and 1960, MMA staff were called upon to support the work of at least six new legal entities, many of which quickly expanded. Each of these subsidiary organizations had its own board, with a legal obligation to meet regularly, tend to its fiduciary responsibilities, and receive an annual audit. The minutes of these meetings, however, suggest that many of the boards played only a perfunctory role in the actual operations of the organization. The real work unfolded in the bustling MMA offices, with Harold Swartzendruber, Aaron Herr, and a growing number of staff members attempting to maintain oversight of hundreds of details within the maze of organizational complexity. In the midst of it all, Orie Miller maintained a remarkable grasp of the overall picture as he and Swartzendruber communicated almost daily by phone or mail. But as Miller began to talk about pulling back from his role as president of MMA, it became increasingly clear to the MMA board that some sort of structural reorganization was badly needed.

Organization Review

One sign of the pressing need for an organizational review was the growing evidence of interpersonal tensions within the MMA office. In April of 1960, for example, Ray Sala, director of field services, submitted his resignation to Miller, expressing his deep frustration with Swartzendruber for his lack of communication.[77] Guy F. Hershberger echoed Sala's concerns, writing to Miller on April 25, 1960, that Swartzendruber's "gifts in the financial and accounting phase of the work," are wasted "by having him continue in personnel and general management where his gifts apparently do not lie."[78] Miller scrambled for a solution. Both Ralph Hernley, general manager of the Mennonite Publishing House in Scottdale, Pennsylvania, and William J. Dye, a successful administrator at the Mennonite hospital in La Junta, Colorado, rejected his suggestion that they might step in alongside of Swartzendruber.

Tensions took on an even more personal note the following summer when Swartzendruber summarily fired Paul Hershberger, son of Guy F. Hershberger, who had been hired only a few months earlier to promote MMA activity in church periodicals. In filling out a form for MAA auto insurance, Hershberger refused to state unequivocally that he would never drink alcohol. His sudden dismissal left the MMA office staff in turmoil. On October 23, 1961, Mildred Witmer, a member of the secretarial staff sent a stiff letter to the board asking that "a statement be made to the group by the manager or a Board member regarding the dismissal of Paul Hershberger. . . . It is not entirely clear," she continued, "what work and/or conduct was considered unsatisfactory. Aside from the suspicion of unfairness to Paul, one wonders when and by what means one's own job is placed in jeopardy." Aaron Herr followed two days later with a similar letter to the board: ". . . where is the redemptive love we talk about in Sunday School? The action can be taken as a threat to the job security of all employees of MMA. Are our private lives to be measured by standards which no one has spelled out?" Then Herr broadened his concerns: "Do staff meetings have any meaning or value if the questions of whether or not they are held, and the subjects for discussion, and the actions resulting from such discussions are purely arbitrary matters for the general manager to decide?"[79]

In the summer of 1960, the board responded by asking Swartzendruber to seek proposals and bids from several consulting firms in Chicago for a thoroughgoing review of MMA's organization—its legal status, work flow, finances, job descriptions, and staffing. The following spring they settled on Cresap, McCormick and Paget, the New York company with offices in Chicago that had made a name for itself as a leading management consultant firm skilled at creating organizational efficiencies and reducing operating costs.

Early in 1961 CMP staff members conducted a thorough review of MMA's history and its relation to the Mennonite Church, along with its organizational structure, workflow, and internal culture. CMP representatives asked church leaders and employees to fill out questionnaires. They spent hours interviewing employees, officers, and board members. They examined budgets, financial reports, and board minutes. And they closely reviewed MMA's office procedures and workflow. The thirty-eight-page preliminary report, which the MMA board received on August 18, 1961, at a special meeting in Chicago, reflected a remarkably astute understanding of the organization—respectful of its religious commitments and sympathetic to its commitment to the principles of mutual aid. However, the report was also quite critical.[80]

In the first place, CMP suggested that the church's philosophical position on mutual aid was not sufficiently clear. On the one hand, new staff members had become accustomed to use the distinctive vocabulary of the church—speaking, for example, of "assistance" rather than "coverage," "assessments" rather than "premiums," "membership agreements" rather than "policies," "representatives" rather than "agents," and "association" or "membership" rather than "company."[81] And yet the report also noted "a wide divergence of opinion, even among members of the various boards, regarding the extent to which such services should develop and the needs of the Church membership for such services."

Second, CMP observed that MMA's control over its subsidiaries was only nominal, consisting mostly of efforts by Swartzendruber, who usually served as secretary of the various boards, to communicate among them. CMP further observed that the objectives of the various mutual aid programs were not clearly stated, making it difficult for the MMA board to evaluate success. Although the presidents of each subsidiary served on an advisory board to MMA, the MMA board itself "relies on its faith in individuals to achieve control, rather than by developed controlling policies." Some of the people CMP interviewed went so far as to say that it was the subsidiaries that controlled MMA.[82] Moreover, each of the boards looked to the other for some of its basic functions resulting in a "fragmentation of real control over the operations of each activity, a lack of coordinated objectives, and no clear pattern of relationship of the president of each corporation to the General Manager." Assumptions regarding Swartzendruber's authority in relating to organizations outside of MMA—like Mennonite Indemnity, Inc., Goodville Mutual, and AMAS—were particularly unclear. The "entire organizational structure of MMA," the CMP report continued, was "so complex that it is almost certain to generate confusion and friction."

And there were still other operational concerns. The organization had "insufficient expertise to interpret statistical data." In the absence of a second tier of managers, Swartzendruber acted both as chief executive and as a glorified mail clerk, performing a host of detailed administrative tasks.[83] Little attention had been given to the development of a field services organization. And the organization had no coherent plan for the future.

> [R]ecent growth and expansion have been the product of circumstance, rather than an organized and planned growth. Without specific objectives, and without plans designed to achieve these objectives, the total mutual aid functions of the Church are left without proper operating guidance and may develop in a manner dictated by circumstance rather than solely in accord with approved Church precepts.[84]

Finally, MMA staff had little overall control of its investment activities, occasionally "shifting funds between units by the parent Board without direct approval by the subsidiary, . . . nor have they developed investment competence for handling routinely the investment problems of each corporation."[85]

In short, the report gave the impression of an ad hoc jumble of programs and priorities, held together loosely by the all-seeing eye of Orie Miller and the frenetic efforts of Harold Swartzendruber, but ultimately a house of cards that could not be sustained for much longer in its present form. The CMP consultants did not suggest the slightest hint of malfeasance or scandal. To the contrary. The general impression was that of a well-intentioned, hardworking group of people who were simply ill-equipped to effectively manage the complex organization that MMA had become.

One senses from the minutes that the MMA board was stunned by the magnitude of the challenge. The CMP report had recommended fundamental changes to the MMA organization, changes which likely needed to begin at the top. In a quiet move, Orie Miller began the process in 1962 by stepping back from his role as president of MMA, turning the position over to Abe Hallman, a trusted confidant and long-time general manager of Miller Hess shoe manufacturing.

After a board meeting in the fall of 1962, Hallman created a subcommittee to implement the recommendations.[86] In the ensuing months, MMA reconstituted its board to include seventeen members, with many of the subsidiary boards reconfigured as subcommittees of the MMA parent board. Swartzendruber retained his role as general manager, but now with the added title of executive secretary and the expectation that he would supervise a second tier of managers.

At the same time, however, the board seemingly ignored—or choose not to implement—several other specific recommendations. It was not clear, for example, whether they followed CMP's counsel to "appoint board members who are qualified by expertise" rather than their standing in the church. The MMA board did not merge Mennonite Automobile Aid with Goodville Mutual as CMP recommended; they were very slow to "create a specialized investment program to handle investments for all units;" and they struggled for the next thirty years to develop a coordinated sales and field services team.

To be fair, at the same time that the board was trying to absorb the full implications of the CMP recommendations, a crisis over the legality of MMA's most visible program—the MAI Burial Aid and Hospital-Surgical plan—forcibly directed its attention to other, even more pressing, matters. As it turned out, efforts to gain formal recognition of the new Survivors' Aid program had alerted the Indiana Department of Insurance to the activities of MMA's Hospital-Surgical plan. Now, suddenly, the threat of a "cease and desist" order galvanized the attention of the MMA board and staff, focusing their energies on a struggle for the very survival of the organization's signature program and the principle of mutual aid.

Conclusion

The visionary Mennonite leaders who called MMA into existence in the fall of 1945 had sensed a pressing need to help ordinary people address the growing complexity of finances in ways that were consistent with their theological values. Like everyone else, Mennonites at midcentury wanted a sense of financial security. If their property was destroyed by fire, their car rendered useless by an accident, or their savings threatened by an unexpected illness or sudden death, church members wanted the assurance that they could regain their economic foothold in spite of the calamity. To be sure, most still looked to their congregations as an important source of economic as well as spiritual support. In the face of a tragedy, they could count on friends and neighbors to provide assistance. But the world was becoming more complicated. Properties were rapidly increasing in value; cars required liability insurance; medical and funeral costs were steadily rising; and widows and the elderly faced the real possibility of impoverishment, even when their congregational deacons offered gestures of charity.

Mennonite Mutual Aid emerged in response to these genuine human needs. From the beginning, its leaders were conscious about not replacing the congregation as the primary source of mutual aid; yet the reality was that congregations were often either unwilling or unable to respond adequately to the financial needs of their members. The first fifteen years of its history were filled with numerous experiments, sometimes executed in clumsy ways, but carried out by a staff possessing a remarkable mix of entrepreneurial skill, dedication, creativity, and homespun practicality. In keeping with Orie Miller's admonition, MMA sought to follow "where the people go," while also maintaining the principle of mutual aid—generously sharing material possessions with those in need—in a structured fashion that could draw on resources across the church in a systematic way.

FOUR

MMA Comes of Age

Fraternal Benefits, Insurance, and Investments (1961–1978)

*G*ood morning, radicals!" Had the Atlantic Hotel staff members in downtown Chicago overheard those words on the morning of November 11, 1966, they might have had good reason to do a double take. Nothing in the outward appearance of the sixty-five delegates who had crowded into the hotel's main meeting room that fall morning would have suggested a gathering of "radicals." The group, overwhelmingly male, represented five major Mennonite denominations and twenty-two district conferences—fourteen from the Mennonite Church,[1] five from the General Conference Mennonite Church, three from the Mennonite Brethren, and one each from the Evangelical Mennonite Church and the Brethren in Christ Church. Some were farmers, likely uncomfortable in their suits and ties; some were retirees, serving their church's mutual aid programs as lay volunteers; many were pastors or church employees; and several were administrators of various Mennonite healthcare plans or financial service organizations. They had gathered from across the country to participate in the first delegate meeting of the Mennonite Mutual Aid Association (MMAA). Few in the group that morning would have described themselves as radicals. Yet Howard Raid, a pioneer in the Mennonite mutual aid movement, insisted that this was the right term. "By worldly concepts," he continued enthusiastically, "you are radicals!"[2]

In the meetings that followed, delegates listened attentively as various MMA leaders—among them Harold Swartzendruber, Guy F. Hershberger, and Howard Raid—described their role as representatives of the church in a newly-organized "fraternal benefits" association that would preserve the principle of mutual aid while offering all the benefits of a commercial insurance company. Those present at the meeting reported that the excitement in the room was palpable. Although all the faces at the podium were familiar, the creation of the Mennonite Mutual Aid Association marked a new era in the history of MMA that was indeed radical.

Breakneck Growth and Legal Challenges

Between 1945 and 1961, MMA had grown at a breakneck pace. By the early 1960s MMA offered church members not only a Hospital-Surgical plan—which was rapidly expanding—but also a Burial Aid plan, comprehensive automobile coverage, a retirement savings program for church-related employees, a means for structuring charitable giving through the Mennonite Foundation, and, most recently, a life insurance program, euphemistically called Survivors' Aid or Survivors' Rehabilitation. Fewer people in the pews would likely have heard about MMA's Mennonite Church Buildings loan program or the Thrift Accumulation savings plan; and almost no one knew what services the organization called Mennonite Indemnity, Inc. offered. But by the mid-1960s MMA was clearly a viable and visible arm of the church, an acronym that appeared frequently in church papers even if the organizational chart was confoundingly complicated.

Still, despite the outward appearance of success, the challenges facing the organization in the early 1960s were enormous. In 1961, the organizational review of MMA by Cresap, McCormick and Paget had highlighted a host of organizational deficiencies.[3] Even more pressing, MMA faced enormous legal challenges regarding its most successful program—the Hospital-Surgical healthcare plan—as Indiana regulators began to question how, unbeknownst to them, the organization had been operating a health insurance plan that was chartered in Pennsylvania, run by administrators with virtually no training in actuarial science, had few reserves, and granted more benefits to some members in the plan than to others, according to individual needs and circumstances.

The consultants' recommendations called for a dramatic shift in MMA's identity, moving it from a church program—operating on the basis of informal authority and under the tight control of the Mennonite Church's General

The first meeting of MMA's fraternal association included delegates from the following churches: Brethren in Christ, Evangelical Mennonite, General Conference
Mennonite, Mennonite Brethren, and (Old) Mennonite.

Conference—into something that looked much more like a modern insurance
and financial services company. The transition would not be easy. Addressing
that challenge eventually called for skills that went beyond the capacity of the
first generation of leaders.

GROWING CHALLENGES

In 1961, the biggest priority facing MMA was to implement the fledgling
Survivor's Aid (or life insurance) program. The plan was beset with
complications from the beginning. Already in the spring of 1961, Aaron
Herr, a key MMA staff member, complained that the new program was not
pulling its weight in terms of office expenses. "If the [Survivor's Aid] program
is financially sound, as I have no doubt it is," Herr wrote in a letter of formal
protest to Orie Miller, "it can afford to pay its fair share of the costs. Certainly
the MAI hospital-surgical subscribers should not, without their knowledge
and consent, be compelled to contribute to the support of other programs in
which they may have no interest nor desire to participate."[4] Herr went on to
note that the new Survivor's Aid program was not being charged anything for
field services or for medical adviser services, and only token amounts for office
expenses, including staff time. Struggling young organizations might be given
a loan, he concluded, but MMA should not hide the true costs of its programs
"by manipulating figures."[5]

Another challenge came from the church. In June 1962, Arthur A. Smucker,
a professor of chemistry at Goshen College, wrote a scathing letter reviving
the traditional concerns regarding life insurance. MMA, he wrote, implied
that the new Survivors' Aid plan was based on the biblical injunction to share

each other's burdens. Yet "I utterly fail to see how your plan even begins to meet these concepts, or differs from any commercial life insurance program which, far from being a sharing of burdens, is basically self-centered." In a truly biblical model, he continued, "the assessment would be in proportion to financial status, while the benefits would be in proportion to need." If such a plan proved to be impractical "we would do better to have no such program."[6]

LEGAL NO-MAN'S-LAND

But by far the most complicated issues related to the new Survivors' Aid program were of a legal and regulatory nature. In the first place, the charter of the new Mennonite Aid Insurance, Inc. (MAII) was restricted to Indiana. If the plan was to operate legally in Pennsylvania it would need to have $200,000 in reserve and five hundred confirmed policies. Moreover, Neal Dubson, MMA's insurance consultant, warned Swartzendruber that borrowing from other MMA accounts to meet the reserve, as Swartzendruber had done for the Indiana charter, would not fly in Pennsylvania. Commingling funds among various corporations, Dubson wrote, "was not only inadvisable but an infringement of the law."[7]

Under pressure from the MAII board, Swartzendruber struggled to comply with the Pennsylvania regulations. But even though the Insurance Department of Pennsylvania did finally grant MAII permission to operate in the fall of 1961, a year later the program was barely viable. On August 28, 1962, Ralph Hernley, president of the MAII board, wrote to Abe Hallman, who had recently replaced Orie Miller as president of MMA, that little had been done to service the Survivors' Aid plan, "making it hard for me to convince people to stay in the program."[8]

To make matters even worse, Indiana regulators began to raise significant concerns about the popular MAI program, especially the Hospital-Surgical plan. From its inception, Swartzendruber had been aware that the Hospital-Surgical plan was operating in a kind of legal no-man's-land. MAI was chartered in Pennsylvania; Indiana regulators had approved only the Burial Aid part of the program, not the Hospital-Surgical. Thus, when MMA sought an Indiana charter for a fully accredited mutual insurance company, Charles Ainlay, MMA's legal representative, had intentionally used language broad enough to include the MAI programs with the goal of bringing all three of the operations—Burial Aid, Hospital-Surgical, and the new Survivor's Aid plan—under a single corporation that would meet the regulatory requirements of the Indiana Insurance Department.

ATTEMPTED SOLUTIONS AND NEW ROADBLOCKS

But resolving one legal problem opened the door to another. Like all state insurance departments, Indiana regulations required insurance companies to determine premium rates in advance and to file these rates with the department. Policies could not be issued until the rates had been approved. Moreover, the state required minimum reserves to guarantee the solvency of the plans, and it rigorously scrutinized all investments made with the reserve funds. Furthermore, no solicitation could be carried out in other states unless agents had been formally trained and licensed to do so. And all insurance plans were subject to state and federal taxes. MMA's Hospital-Surgical plan met *none* of these requirements.

Even more problematic from the church's perspective was the state requirement that all participants be treated equally. Thus, MAI's practice of granting Catastrophe Aid to individual policyholders in the spirit of mutual aid—the sort of "benefit in proportion to need" that Arthur Smucker was looking for—was clearly illegal, a form of discrimination that arbitrarily gave more benefits to some policyholders than to others. So even as the new Survivors' Aid plan was moving forward, MMA staff members wondered whether the program would retain anything that could be identified as mutual aid.

In the fall of 1962 Swartzendruber—along with MMA staff members Neil Beachy and Lamar Reichert—met in Chicago with Edward Mullen, an insurance expert with the Arthur Stedry Hansen Consulting Actuaries firm, to discuss the future of the MAI and MAII programs. There, Mullen made a proposal that would profoundly change the trajectory of MMA's history. MMA objectives could be better achieved, he suggested, if the company was chartered as a "fraternal benefit organization." Fraternal benefits associations, he explained, were not-for-profit legal entities, organized around a specific mission, that provided services to a clearly defined membership. Fraternals were required to have a strong representative form of governance that included regular meetings of a local lodge or branch. In lieu of paying taxes, fraternal organizations set that portion of money aside for charitable purposes that would benefit their members. When the MMA delegation heard Mullen's description of a fraternal benefit association they immediately recognized its potential as a solution for the challenges that the MAI and MAII programs were facing.

On January 17, 1963, Swartzendruber received a letter from the law offices of Berman and Woodruff stating that the Indiana Insurance Code would indeed permit the formation of a fraternal benefit society, and setting out a fee structure for their assistance in accomplishing that goal. Soon thereafter

Swartzendruber initiated correspondence with the leaders of several Baptist and Lutheran fraternal organizations to learn more about their experiences.[9]

At a meeting in April 1963, MAII board members received an extremely positive report from Swartzendruber about the emerging possibilities.[10] Each participating congregation, Swartzendruber explained, would serve as the local "lodge" in the fraternal association structure. Moreover, the fraternal benefit approach would enable the new organization to provide insurance without licensed agents and in the form of mutual aid. Support for members with special needs would come from the "fraternal funds"—the repurposed taxes that were now designated for charitable purposes.

In early June, however, the plan hit a major roadblock. On June 6, 1963, Swartzendruber reported to Mullen that he and Ainlay had met with the Deputy Attorney General, the Deputy Insurance Commissioner, an actuary in the Indiana Insurance Department, and the Chief Examiner of the Insurance Department to review the articles of incorporation for the fraternal association that they envisioned. "It became obvious very early in the interview," Swartzendruber lamented, "that they had decided they did not want a fraternal insurance corporation established in the State of Indiana. They threw all types

In Lancaster, Pa., Ray Lefever lost thirty-two of his forty-two steers to "red nose" disease during Christmastime 1974. Friends and neighbors sent him replacement steers and others raised money to replace the herd.

of road blocks at us culminating with the fact the Hospital-Surgical could not in any case be included under the fraternal insurance set up in the State of Indiana."[11] The commission expressed strong disapproval that the Hospital-Surgical plan had been operating in Indiana under their radar and asked Ainlay to submit a formal description of the existing program along with a sketch of MMA's plan to merge MAI and MAII into a single organization.[12] At the end of the meeting, the officials insisted that all MAI activities currently chartered in Pennsylvania be transferred immediately to an established Indiana insurance company and threatened to impose a "cease and desist" order if MMA failed to comply. MMA, one of the officials concluded, "wanted the benefits of insurance without meeting the requirements."[13]

For many MMA old-timers the story of how these knotty legal problems were ultimately resolved has taken on the status of a miracle—or, at the very least, a clear sign of God's intervention. When all the doors are shut, God opens a window.

A FORTUITOUS VISIT FROM A STRANGER

In the late summer of 1963, only a few weeks after the disappointing meeting with state officials, Swartzendruber received an unexpected visit from a stranger. Edward J. Peters ran an actuarial consulting business and also served as the CEO of the Police and Fireman's Fraternal Insurance Co. in Indianapolis. A few weeks earlier he had stumbled across a reference to a newly-formed Mennonite mutual life insurance company in Indiana. Peters had known Mennonites from his childhood days growing up in eastern Pennsylvania. Aware that Mennonites were generally opposed to insurance, he was intrigued and asked Swartzendruber if he could stop by the Goshen office for a visit.[14]

The encounter came at a fortuitous moment. After hearing of the disappointing meeting with officials in Indianapolis, Peters, working behind the scenes, encouraged the Chief Actuary in the Department of Insurance to make an "off the record" phone call to Swartzendruber. The call shifted the entire tone of the conversation. With the coaching of Peters and the new openness of the Chief Actuary, Swartzendruber and Ainlay renewed their efforts to draft a plan for a Mennonite fraternal benefits association.

At the MMA board meeting in the spring of 1964, Peters himself was present to outline the concept in more detail. According to the new plan, the MAI Burial Aid and Hospital-Surgical plans would merge with MAII's Survivors' Aid plan to form a new organization called Mennonite Mutual Aid

Association (MMAA), which would oversee all three insurance programs. After hearing Peters' presentation, the board gave its enthusiastic approval.[15] In the following months, Peters presented the plan to the Indiana Department of Insurance and helped to negotiate preliminary approval.[16]

While all of this was unfolding, the Hospital-Surgical program itself was in the midst of thoroughgoing revisions as a result of the new federal Medicare program. In February 1965 MMA urged all eligible participants in the MAI program to transition to Medicare, though they also made it clear that MMA would provide ongoing coverage for any member who had conscientious objections to it.[17] More than 90 percent of the eligible members switched immediately to Medicare; nearly all the rest followed within the next few years. Thirty years after the introduction of Social Security, principled opposition to government-funded social welfare programs had nearly disappeared.

In the meantime, Peters continued to lend his services. In light of the requirement that the new fraternal benefit association have regular branch meetings, Peters negotiated an understanding that congregations could serve this purpose. Congregational representatives would attend biennial meetings of the national organization—the Mennonite Mutual Aid Association—where they would hear reports and offer counsel on the work of the association. In light of the fact that a fraternal benefits association was owned by its members, MMAA's seventeen board members would now be voted into office by the delegates. Swartzendruber acknowledged that this meant that the new organization would technically no longer be under the full legal control of the (Old) Mennonite Church General Conference; but he assured church leaders that "from a practical standpoint there will be little change from our present relationships . . . and our operating activities among the constituency."[18] The church would nominate nine members to serve on the MMA board, who would then need to be formally approved by the association's delegates. These nine, in turn, would appoint eight additional members.[19]

MMAA CREATED

It had taken three years, but finally on January 6, 1966, the Indiana Department of Insurance formally approved the creation of MMAA. On May 20, 1966, MAII was legally merged into MMAA. On July 1, 1966—the same day as the beginning of the federal Medicare program—MMA staff members celebrated the official beginning of the Mennonite Mutual Aid Association with the legal transfer of all the assets and liabilities of the Burial Aid and Hospital-Surgical plans.[20]

The language of the MMAA charter defined the scope of its potential members quite broadly to include "all Mennonites who are members of the churches represented in the Mennonite Central Committee together with Mennonites of such churches as the Board of Directors may from time to time determine for fraternal benefit purposes."[21] The stated mission of the organization— "to promote the Biblical concept of mutual aid sharing historically practiced among Mennonites as it relates to social, economic and spiritual needs of its members"—was equally broad, keeping the door open for additional programs in the future.

The event marked a profound moment in the history of MMA, one that would forever change the trajectory of the organization. If, at other times in MMA's history, legal regulations seemed to be in tension with the principles of mutual aid, the fraternal benefit association model offered a surprising counterexample in which the legal framework enabled and enhanced those same ideals, albeit in new ways. Now, a direct relationship with local congregations would be an essential component of MMA's identity; now MMA could offer members a full range of insurance programs, under the name of "fraternal benefits," while also providing additional financial assistance to those with special needs in the spirit of mutual aid. Moreover, the funding for those subsidies—which would also support a host of other church-related causes—would come from the program itself through the diversion of tax liabilities into the Fraternal Aid Fund. In the years that followed MMA went on to receive full legal status in Pennsylvania, Virginia, Ohio, Illinois, Iowa, Nebraska, Kansas, Oklahoma, Minnesota, South Dakota, and California—virtually every state that claimed any sizeable Mennonite population.

Implementing the New Organization: Office, Staff, and Equipment

When the MMA offices moved from 1202 South Eighth Street into the newly-constructed building at 111 Marilyn Avenue in 1958, the organization had nine staff members, including part-time workers. Ten years later, there were forty-one employees on the MMA payroll with no space left in the Marilyn Avenue offices for expansion.[22] In 1966, as MMA leaders were contemplating building an addition to accommodate the growing computer and accounting departments, administrators at Goshen General Hospital asked to purchase the Marilyn Avenue building in order to facilitate an expansion project of their own. Although the MMA board clearly felt obliged to support the needs of the local hospital, negotiations over the details of a potential sale proved to be difficult. In the fall of 1966, on the basis of a realtor's assessment, MMA agreed to sell the building and property for $91,000 and gave the hospital six months to respond.[23] But when the hospital countered with $71,360 and refused to budge on the price, MMA withdrew their offer and proceeded with their own building expansion.

The new "Butler building"—a twenty-four- by sixty-foot prefab steel enclosure named after the company that constructed it—was designed especially with a view to CMP's strong recommendation regarding the need for greater "mechanization of business systems." In early 1967, as a follow-up to their initial report, CMP consultants reported that "the greatest need for further mechanization exists in the procedures for maintaining membership records and for processing hospital-surgical and auto aid assessments, claims and reports."[24]

CUTTING-EDGE TECHNOLOGIES ALONGSIDE OLD GENDER PATTERNS

The consultants strongly encouraged MMA to create a new position of data processing operator, and to purchase an IBM computer and punch card system.[25] In October of 1967, Swartzendruber reported to the board that some sixty to seventy thousand IBM punch cards and an NCR 32 calculating machine, housed in the Butler building, now played a crucial role in the processing of claims.[26] By early 1970, MMA purchased a state-of-the-art IBM System/3 computer. The office staff soon dubbed the computer—a bright yellow machine the size of a larger freezer—the Yellow Bird, because it "sang all day long." In the coming years, MMA regularly upgraded its IBM computer,

By 1968, MMA was outgrowing its third office space, which it had built only ten years earlier on Marilyn Avenue in Goshen.

making it almost certainly the most technologically advanced organization in the Anabaptist-Mennonite world.

Even though MMA was relatively quick to adopt cutting-edge technology, the office culture itself seems to have conformed quite predictably to the larger social and gender conventions of the day, habits that were reinforced by the patriarchal assumptions of traditional Mennonite culture. Photos from the period underscore the extent to which MMA—like virtually all Anabaptist-Mennonite church institutions of the day—was dominated by males. Indeed, of the eighty-six people who served on MMA's various boards in the early 1960s, all were male. Within the office organization, staff positions corresponded completely with traditional gender roles: the entire secretarial and clerical staff was female; all of MMA's managers and administrators were male. The compensation scale also drew a sharp line between the male salaried managers and the female clerical staff who worked at an hourly rate. Thus, in the summer of 1963, MMA had twenty-one staff members—the ten male employees were all assigned to jobs classified as salaried; the eleven women, all of whom were either administrative assistants or secretaries, were paid by the hour.[27]

Not surprisingly, these gendered realities were also reflected in the language of the day. In the fall of 1968, for example, Lamar Nissley, editor of the MMA internal newsletter, the *Office Mem-Oh!*, reported that "the ladies around here all but knocked themselves out in cooking, arranging tables, decorating and serving the 'men' at the Bosses Luncheon. It was really great ladies . . . Hurrah for the Girls!"[28] At the same time, with the steady growth of technology, managers were forced to recognize their growing dependence on the women's new set of specialized skills. In a tone alternately affirming and patronizing, the *Office Mem-Oh!* asked

> What would the members of MMA think if some of the rest of us had to run the MTST, IBM Selectric, Flexowriter, Executive, Hermes, Odhner, Frieden 1151, Norelco 82, Pitney Bows 5600, P.B.LA, P.B. 1860? What would life be like around here without our beautiful, smiling, kind, hard working, efficient, understanding, thoughtful, indispensable secretaries. Hats off! The Secretaries are marching by.[29]

Compensation was another area the CMP consultants had identified as badly in need of attention. In the early 1950s, Swartzendruber had routinely negotiated his own salary, and that of MMA employees, generally by referring to the wages of employees in other Mennonite Church organizations. In the fall of 1956, the board approved a somewhat more formal wage scale in which a "single person or family head" earned twice as much ($40/week) as a "dependent wife" ($20/week) with adjustments of an additional $4/week for each dependent child and a $5/week raise after the first year (though secretaries needed to wait three years for this adjustment!). Swartzendruber and the other managers received approximately twice this amount—in 1957, for example, Swartzendruber took home $91/week, Aaron Herr, $90/week; Ray Sala, head of sales, earned $79/week. Secretaries earned $42/week.[30]

CMP consultants had strongly recommended that the organization develop a clear wage and salary policy, along with an office handbook, routine evaluations, and a personnel manager. Thus, following their report, an employee manual emerged that addressed basic policies around sick leave, vacation time, fringe benefits, and retirement.[31] At the same time, MMA staff also developed a field manual for the sales force.

Developing a wage and salary policy, however, proved more difficult. Because MMA was an institution of the Mennonite Church, the board understood MMA employees to be working for the church. The first employee manual made this clear: "We trust that you will accept the challenge of commitment for more than just a 'paycheck' but also to a stewardship of service in Christ's kingdom."[32] Thus, the board assumed that MMA employees would regard their low-paying work as a form of missionary service, rather than a job with compensation in line with the standards of commercial companies. In 1966, the board took up the challenge by creating nine different classes of jobs, each associated with a base pay. Whereas CMP had proposed a more traditional business wage scale with wider variations between the classes calculated at 25 percent for salaried employees and 7.5 percent for hourly workers, the MMA board called for a formula of 20 percent and 10 percent, seeking to push the curve closer to a straight line—that is, a more compressed egalitarian wage scale with a smaller difference between the lowest and the highest paid employee.[33]

By 1970, with nearly fifty employees and the space in the Butler building now filled, MMA had once again run out of room. In the meantime, the hospital continued to express a strong interest in purchasing the Marilyn Avenue buildings. In the spring of 1971, the board authorized the purchase of the Robertshaw Controls research building located at 1110 North Main Street on ten acres of land north of Goshen. The purchase price of $100,000 was almost exactly what the hospital then paid for the Marilyn Avenue property, though the board budgeted an additional $90,000 for interior remodeling that included a new entrance and lobby.[34]

Growing Programs; Rising Tensions

At the time of the move, MMA was a dynamic and growing organization. But the organization had many different parts, some of them still moving in different directions. According to the new organizational plan proposed by CMP, MMA's various programs would be divided into three departments. A director of Mutual Aid Services would oversee the various insurance programs along with the fraternal funds program. A newly-created Financial Services department would assume responsibility for the Mennonite Church Buildings loan program, the Mennonite Foundation, Mennonite Retirement Trust, and stewardship education. Finally, a director of Field Services would supervise marketing, sales, and customer support at both the regional conference and congregational level.

Although the plan seemed logical in theory, tensions between the Mutual Aid Services and Financial Services departments persisted, even as most of the programs in both divisions continued to grow.

MUTUAL AID PROGRAMS REIMAGINED

By the early 1970s, the various insurance plans were the most visible and profitable aspect of the organization. In 1974, the fraternal association included more than forty thousand participants. Although the majority were members

In the fall of 1971, MMA moved its forty-eight employees into the sixteen-thousand-square-foot former research center of Robertshaw Controls, 1110 North Main Street in Goshen. The building is gone, but the corporate headquarters remains on the site today.

of the (Old) Mennonite Church, 26 percent of the adult members enrolled in healthcare came from the General Conference Mennonite Church, 13 percent were Mennonite Brethren, with another 6 percent representing smaller groups such as the Brethren in Christ or the Evangelical Mennonites.[35] These groups sent representatives to the MMAA biennial meetings and were represented on the MMA board. By 1976, a plan had emerged to divide the fraternal funds among the four largest denominations in rough proportion to their membership in MMAA.

The most popular policy, held by more than half of all participants, was the Comprehensive Health Plan, which paid 80 percent of medical expenses with a $250 deductible, spread over a three-year period. The Medicare Supplemental Health Plan, designed to assist seniors with medical expenses not covered by Medicare, accounted for nearly a quarter of the membership, followed by student plans for those enrolled in Mennonite colleges. A wide range of Major

Jim Wagner of Fairview, Mich., received a scooter and other support from the Comin General Conference Mennonite Church after his stroke in 1973. He had MMA health insurance coverage during his illness and received an MMA Catastrophe Aid grant as well through his church.

Medical Health options enabled congregations to establish group plans, with MMA providing technical counsel and a reinsurance "backstop" in the event of overwhelming medical expenses.

Without question, the most distinctive aspect of MMA's approach to health insurance was its generous membership policy. Profitability among health insurance companies depends on having large numbers of healthy members whose premiums cover the claims of the minority in the pool who incur significant medical expenses. Unlike commercial insurance companies, MMA agreed to cover any individual who was part of an Anabaptist-Mennonite congregation, regardless of preexisting conditions, if at least 50 percent of their congregation was also signed up for the healthcare plan. Individual subscribers faced waiting periods before they could file a claim, but virtually no one was denied coverage, even though people sometimes signed up for health insurance only when they were facing a large medical expense. This practice contrasted sharply with most commercial insurance companies who routinely screened applicants for medical conditions and rejected those who were likely to be high risks in terms of large medical expense claims.

The Hospital-Surgical plan and subsequent healthcare plans covered only around 80 percent of actual medical costs. Most members could make up the difference out of their own pocket. But for some families, those additional costs could become overwhelming. In such cases, congregations were encouraged to help pay the difference as an expression of local mutual aid. But they could also could appeal to MMA's Catastrophe Aid fund for additional help. The Catastrophe Aid fund, now bolstered by new revenue from the fraternal funds, regularly assisted members with medical bills, helped to cover insurance premiums for needy families, provided subsidies for adoptions, and offered matching grants to congregations who supported members who were facing unusual financial needs.[36]

With the creation of the fraternal benefits association, the existence of the fraternal funds—that is, the money that ordinarily would have gone to the IRS, which was now set aside for charitable purposes—posed both an opportunity and a challenge. On the one hand, the funds exponentially increased the possibilities for practicing forms of mutual aid at both the congregational and denominational level. Yet wherever there are available resources, competing claims need to be sorted out. To whom, for example, did the fraternal fund belong—MMA or the denomination? Leaders of the Mennonite Church still clearly regarded MMA as an organization under its oversight and even control. Yet MMA was not ready to simply turn over the entire fund to denominational leaders, especially since its membership represented a broad spectrum of Anabaptist-Mennonite groups. Why, many members asked, was MMA becoming a granting agency? Why not just reduce premiums for everyone rather than designating those resources to charity? And what were the criteria for disbursements? Would the fraternal funds displace the role of congregation as the first line of mutual aid? All of these important questions needed to be addressed in the early years of MMAA, and they would continue to emerge in the decades that followed.

In 1967, the first year that the fraternal funds were available for disbursement, MMAA provided $55,000 in support of seminary scholarships, pastoral recruitment, seminars for ministers, and brochures promoting Christian stewardship. In 1969 the funds helped to launch the Congregation Health Improvement Plan (CHIP). CHIP was an outreach to small, mostly Spanish-speaking congregations that enabled members to purchase healthcare that would have otherwise been unavailable to them. The program called for each member of the congregation to pay healthcare premiums according to their ability, with the assurance that the difference would be subsidized by MMA fraternal funds.[37]

In years to come, the financial resources available from the fraternal fund led to hundreds of stories of transformed lives. In addition to direct assistance to congregational members, the fund heavily supported the Minority Ministries program of the Mennonite Church, promoted the work of church camps, subsidized scholarship and publication on stewardship-related topics, supported a host of community development grants, and underwrote two major church member profiles that included the Mennonite Brethren, General Conference Mennonites, and Brethren in Christ.[38]

PROGRESS IN PRODUCT DEVELOPMENT

In response to the Employee Retirement Income Security Act of 1974 (ERISA), MMA took a bold step in 1975 of moving into a new category of products known as annuities. Annuities are an insurance product often used to fund a steady stream of income during retirement. Swartzendruber's decision to place the new initiative within the mutual aid side of the organization benefited the fraternal fund, but the field staff was slow to promote annuities and early sales were tepid. In a report to the board six years later, La Mar Reichert reported that "in many of our programs we have not succeeded in making a solid connection with our target audience," noting that annuities "are a grim reminder that where we are not competitive, growth is very slow."[39] In later decades,

Early on, funds generated by the fraternal product sales were plowed back into churches, including the Congregation Health Improvement Plan (CHIP). Susan Lopez (center) with sister Melissa (left) and Raquel (right) received help from her church, Iglesia Menonita del Cordero, Brownsville, Tex., and the CHIP program.

however, annuities proved to be quite popular, and the program helped to fund numerous church building loans, enabling participants in the program to support church-related projects even as they were planning ahead for retirement.

In the meantime, Mennonite Automobile Aid, though never a highly visible part of the organization, witnessed steady growth throughout the 1960s and 1970s. Although the relationship with Goodville Mutual Casualty remained complicated, and occasionally contentious, leaders on both sides consistently managed to work through their differences; and policyholders were often oblivious to the fact that they were dealing with two different companies.

By contrast, the Survivor's Aid program—MMA's version of life insurance—which had been the focus of so much energy in the early 1960s, never really found a foothold within the Anabaptist-Mennonite community. In the fall of 1970, Swartzendruber reported to the board that the viability of the program was in doubt.[40] Competition from commercial life insurance companies was intense, and since the mutual aid aspect of the Survivor's Aid plan was harder to demonstrate, congregational representatives tended to also be unenthusiastic.

Financial Services

Parallel to the Mutual Aid Services department, MMA's Financial Services programs—which consisted of Mennonite Church Buildings (MCB), Mennonite Retirement Trust (MRT), and the Mennonite Foundation—also enjoyed rapid growth throughout the 1960s and early 1970s.

Mennonite Church Buildings was the program with the least activity. The plan, originally designed to provide capital for church-related building projects, had served the denomination well at a time when banks refused to extend such loans. But now that banks had relaxed their lending restrictions, MCB no longer had a clear role. For several years, MMA leaders struggled to find an appropriate way to close out the program, until they eventually discovered that MCB's tax exempt status made it an ideal holding company for MMA's buildings and properties.

MENNONITE RETIREMENT TRUST (MRT)

Rapid growth in Mennonite Retirement Trust, the retirement plan for Mennonite church workers created in 1963, testified to the ongoing expansion of Anabaptist-Mennonite institutions, particularly in education and health-related services, and growing concerns about financial security after retirement. To be sure, the federal Social Security program provided some assistance to the elderly; but it was clear to most people that they would not be able to live on Social Security payments. Support for MRT increased as church institutions began looking for ways to provide employees with more robust benefit packages. But MRT also gained popularity in congregational settings as pastors recognized the need for a retirement plan, particularly if they expected to be in full-time ministry for the bulk of their working years. MRT promised a retirement income for the participant and, depending on how the plan was structured, for a spouse and dependents as well. In 1973, ten years after the program was introduced, MRT had over two thousand participants with assets of $2.5 million.[41]

THE MENNONITE FOUNDATION . . . AND THE GROWTH OF FINANCIAL EDUCATION

The program with the most visible and dramatic growth in the 1970s was clearly the Mennonite Foundation. For the first decade after its creation in 1952, the foundation had mostly languished within the MMA structure, lacking administrative direction and clarity about its place within the organization's overall priorities. But in 1964, Orie Miller, always a gifted talent scout, hired John Rudy, a native of York, Pennsylvania, to breathe new life into the program. After two years in Civilian Public Service, Rudy had been employed in the engineering department of RCA in Lancaster, Pennsylvania. There he rapidly advanced into an administrative role with oversight of the company's finances. In 1960, after fourteen years with RCA, Rudy unexpectedly resigned his well-paid position in order to take up a pastorate at a small Mennonite congregation near Gettysburg. The decision impressed Miller. Recognizing Rudy's unique combination of administrative, financial, and pastoral gifts, Miller persuaded him to join MMA, initially in a part-time position with the Mennonite Automobile Aid program. In August of 1965, however, he and his family moved to Goshen where he became the full-time director of MMA's Financial Services department.[42]

Rudy brought with him a level of managerial experience and professionalism that was new to the organization. He excelled in public settings, where he was quick-witted, confident, and affable, equally at ease with farmers and business leaders. Rudy spoke knowledgably about economic trends, investment strategies, and personal finances, while also freely expressing his deep convictions about Christian stewardship and the ethical responsibilities that went along with wealth.

In many ways, Rudy's personality and gifts meshed well with the new economic realities of the Anabaptist-Mennonite churches as a growing number of members were entering the professions and the world of business. By 1972, 80 percent of the households in the largest Anabaptist-Mennonite groups in North America owned their own homes, a figure that would continue to rise in the coming decades.[43] When Rudy assumed responsibilities for Mennonite Foundation, he matter-of-factly described its mission as serving the church by "offering specialized assistance in matters relating to the stewardship of accumulated possessions."[44]

Other MMA staff members, however, were more ambivalent about the ethics of "accumulated possessions," worrying that Mennonite wealth posed a direct threat to the principles of community. In the July 1970 issue of *Sharing*, for example, D. Lamar Nissley observed that "an alarmingly huge number of Mennonites participate in MMA primarily as a 'good insurance buy' rather than as a tool for brotherhood. . . . Because of our spirit of muchness we have developed a kind of independent spirit that doesn't need a neighbor or brother."[45] Mennonite Church leaders expressed similar concerns. In 1975, a task force appointed by the church's Council of Faith, Life and Strategy to address the question of wealth concluded their study in a pessimistic tone.[46]

We as North American Mennonites find ourselves today in the world. Our traditional isolation from our surrounding culture is dissolving. The signs of this trend are many. One particular example is the trend toward affluence and away from simplicity of life.

As evidence they cited rising standards of living, growing disparities in wealth and income, and a preoccupation with the accumulation of wealth. The committee drew a clear connection between increased wealth and a decline in faith. "Times of affluence have signified a decline in our radical, biblical stance toward the world."[47]

I LIKE MONEY

John Rudy and the staff he assembled within the Mennonite Foundation, on the other hand, took a quite different approach. In an article titled "I Like Money!" Rudy outlined a much more positive view of wealth.[48] "Nowhere in Scripture," Rudy argued, "do I read that Jesus condemned anyone for making money, or having money." Indeed, money can be very useful in extending the Kingdom of God. What mattered most, he continued, had to do with how Christians made their money and what they chose to do with it. Rudy concluded with seven principles that characterized his basic philosophy, the essence of which he repeated in hundreds of sermons, speeches, and conversations: 1) let frugality control your consumption; 2) aspire to the tranquility of contentment; 3) cultivate the grace of letting go; 4) complete your stewardship by creating a plan to dispose of your wealth; 5) shape your investments around what you believe; 6) place your security in relationships as well as pension plans; 7) include conversations about money in the life of the congregation.[49] In his work with the Mennonite Foundation, Rudy both affirmed the hard work, frugality, and stewardship that had led Mennonites to accumulate wealth, while also vigorously encouraging wealthy individuals to "become partners in the mission of the church" by "using money to serve people."

Under his leadership the Mennonite Foundation rapidly grew. In 1966 the General Conference Mennonite Church formally recommended the Mennonite Foundation to its members. Rudy was quick to include General Conference Mennonite and Mennonite Brethren representatives on the Mennonite Foundation board. In 1968, the foundation opened an office in Hesston, Kansas, with Harold Dyck—a well-known former CEO of Hesston Corporation—as the field manager. Dyck would go on to serve in that role, as a volunteer, for nearly twenty years. In 1972, Rudy invited Harry Martens, a highly-regarded former MCC relief administrator, to open another branch office in Lancaster, Pennsylvania, where he served as the organization's first full-time Estate Planning Consultant. Within a single year, between 1968 and 1969, the assets of the foundation increased by 65 percent, breaking the $1 million mark. By 1972, Mennonite Foundation funds totaled more than $5 million.[50]

The appeal of Mennonite Foundation was not a mystery. For the first time, wealthy Mennonites could speak openly about money with a financial expert who shared their basic values, understood the impact of tax law, cared deeply about the church, and helped them leave a legacy that would endure beyond their death. For the rapidly-expanding Mennonite institutions in the second half of the twentieth century, the Mennonite Foundation was a godsend. Mennonite colleges and seminaries began to establish endowment funds, capital campaigns, and scholarship programs fueled by the financial resources the foundation had gathered.[51] Mission organizations, church camps, research projects, and service initiatives all benefited from money channeled through the foundation. Several congregations even used the Mennonite Foundation to establish local endowments to support mission work, building maintenance, or theological training.

As a natural extension of his work, Rudy recognized that middle- and lower-income Mennonites also needed to think carefully about stewardship. At his initiative, MMA launched several financial education programs that went beyond tax and inheritance law to address basic issues like budgeting, debt management, wills, and, eventually, advanced directives for end-of-life decision-making.

SOCIALLY RESPONSIBLE INVESTING

The Mennonite Foundation also focused new attention on the complex question of ethical investments. With a significant influx of capital—both in MRT and the Mennonite Foundation, but also in the reserve requirements of MMAA insurance programs—MMA was soon managing millions of dollars in assets. In 1964 MMA created its first formal investment policy, which simply clarified that the organization would not invest in "objectionable industries"— namely, tobacco, alcohol, motion pictures, armaments, and gambling.[52] But MMA administrators soon recognized that they needed to address a more complex set of questions regarding their investments. By the late 1960s, for example, as Mennonites slowly recognized just how deeply the military budget was embedded in the American economy, they began to ask new questions about how their commitment to the gospel of peace was related to their financial investments. MMA was clear that it would not invest in companies explicitly identified as defense contractors; but what about companies who had small subsidiaries who supplied basic components—nuts and bolts, for example—to defense contractors?

In 1970, economist Peter Landau published a landmark article that framed key questions around the social responsibility of investors.[53] In the essay,

Landau described efforts in the late 1960s by social activists to use shareholder proxy challenges to protest against colleges whose endowments were invested in companies that supported the policy of apartheid in South Africa. As these protests gained visibility, Milton Friedman, a well-known Chicago School economist, mounted a counterattack. Any investment strategy that put matters of social responsibility above making as much money as possible, he argued, "is a fundamentally subversive doctrine."[54] Yet federal courts had begun to issue rulings in favor of activist shareholders, and in 1970 the Securities and Exchange Commission, which regulated shareholder-company interaction, supported the rights of shareholders to express their opinions on overtly political issues.

In 1971 MMA leaders, seeking broader counsel from the church on their investment policy, sponsored a seminar at Goshen College organized by C. Norman Kraus. Kraus was a professor of theology at the college who had just created a Center for Studies in Christian Discipleship to promote precisely these sorts of conversations. Unfortunately, the outcome was not what MMA leaders hoped for. In a letter to Kraus after the event, Howard Raid expressed deep concerns that pointed to a widening cultural gap in the church between the business community and a rising generation of Mennonite ethicists. Raid opened by noting the irony that the alleged goal of the gathering—namely, to bridge the gap between college and church—had actually resulted in a conference where college students lectured business people on what they ought to do.[55] Why would people pay money and give their time to attend a seminar, Raid asked rhetorically,

> and then be confronted with almost immediate questioning of their value system and their way of life? Why didn't you have a businessman talk on investments as he sees them and the problems he confronts? Why not listen to them long enough to discuss problems that they are actually facing? . . . Frankly, I believe that the Mennonite businessman has thought of every question you can ask him about ethics, morals, etc. and has developed a working solution.[56]

Nevertheless, the seminar spurred MMA investment managers to do further research into the investment practices of other denominations, which were then reflected in a revised set of Investment Guidelines that appeared in 1972. The new guidelines continued the older practice of avoiding "objectionable industries," but added a positive commitment to invest in companies that "supported world peace" and "promoted social betterment," while also earning "reasonable returns." Furthermore, the MMA investment committee would "observe management performance" of the companies in their portfolio with regard to diversity in hiring and treatment of workers, and would "register ethical concerns" or "sell unacceptable holdings." The guidelines were to be reviewed every five years.[57]

In the coming years, tensions between MMA's fiduciary responsibilities to its investors and its commitment to adhere to the Investment Guidelines continued, with the church sending very mixed messages along the way. Delmar (Del) King, hired in 1971 as MMA's first investment manager, recalls that many church agencies who had invested in MMA funds affirmed the guidelines, but were also deeply concerned about the rate of return on their investments. During the 1973–1974 economic downturn, for example, church leaders demanded an account for the short-term market losses. It became clear, King noted, "that many people in the church were not ready to handle volatility and risk in investment."[58] A different set of questions surfaced when several denominational leaders called on MMA to provide loans to urban churches that most banks would have considered high risk. What was the fiduciary responsibility of MMA to its investors in such cases?[59]

Managing assets effectively—in ways that would comply with legal obligations to maximize returns while also remaining attentive to ethical constraints—was not always easy. Nevertheless, over time, MMA would play a pioneering role in a broader national movement toward socially responsible investing.

Field Services: Marketing and the Link to Congregations and Consumers

Of the three departments that emerged in the aftermath of CMP's recommendations, Field Services proved the most difficult to organize, particularly in the areas of marketing and distribution. Mennonites have traditionally had a deep-seated aversion to marketing, regarding it as somehow at odds with the values of humility, honesty, and plain speech. Thus, MMA's early brochures were almost studiously pedestrian in their design, crammed with text and heavily focused on information. Marketing was further complicated by the fact that each of MMA's subsidiaries related to its participants in a slightly different way, often describing its particular services with brochures, direct-mail flyers, articles in church periodicals, and promotional speakers without any sense of overall coordination or consistency regarding the MMA brand.

In 1967, MMA introduced *Sharing* magazine, both to comply with a legal requirement that fraternal benefit associations communicate regularly with their members and as a way of presenting a more unified identity to the church. The illustrated semiannual publication regularly featured personal stories—some of them quite dramatic—of individuals in the church who had benefited from an MMA insurance policy, along with profiles of MMA field staff, news from MMA's office in Goshen, and regular reports on how the fraternal funds were being spent. The stories in *Sharing* reminded church and MMA employees alike of the purpose of MMA's work. But the periodical was also clearly a marketing initiative, often presented in the form of education.[60] The first issue of *Sharing* went out to nearly twenty-one thousand addresses.[61] By the end of 1968, MMA office staff reported that sixty-three thousand copies of *Sharing* had been printed and mailed from Goshen, Indiana; Scottdale, Pennsylvania; Newton, Kansas; and Hillsboro, Kansas.[62] In 1971 MMA staff also began distributing a newsletter called *Informant* to congregational representatives and pastors, which promoted MMA programs, explained changes in policies, and encouraged applications to the Catastrophe Aid program.

At CMP's prodding, MMA leaders began to give more attention to marketing. In the summer of 1975 a marketing task force announced the completion of several filmstrips that they hoped would serve MMA representatives well in Sunday school and congregational settings.[63] One of them, "The Empty Chair," used a narrative played out by cartoon characters to warn of the health risks associated with stress, overeating, and lack of exercise. Another, promoting the Survivors' Aid program, told the story of the Pleasant View congregation in Harper, Kansas, which had experienced twenty deaths within the span of four years. "Death," a reassuring voice on the accompanying cassette tape intoned,

> is not something mysterious to be feared. Our faith in God assures us of an eternity far better than this world. But death has another side: the survivors. Those that live on must face not only the human grief of their loss, but the economic realities of carrying on, especially if the one lost was a provider.

For the first time, MMA also began to run ads in church periodicals, rather than relying on news releases alone to communicate new products. Their brochures began to take on a more professional look with a sharper edge. A 1979 brochure promoting the Survivor's Aid plan, for example, featured a stark heading that read, "If You Die, Can They [i.e., your children] Count on Your Neighbors?"

Behind these halting steps at marketing were deeper questions. MMA was committed to "going where the people go," but who, ultimately, was controlling the message? Denominational leaders? MMA division managers? Pastors? Or ordinary people in the pew who were the primary users of MMA's products and services? Was MMA in the education business, actively shaping the church's understanding and practices around stewardship and mutual aid? Or was it charged with providing what people actually wanted—that is, what the market was demanding? And what if the Mennonite market was no longer interested in traditional forms of mutual aid? Those questions, and others like them, generated a persistent undercurrent of tension among the Field Service representatives, Harold Swartzendruber, the MMA board, and denominational leaders in the 1970s. More often than not, the questions went unanswered.

The distribution side of MMA's sales and customer support was equally complicated. Historians Steve Nolt and Royden Loewen have recently documented the rapid decline in the role of the deacon, which had traditionally been the face of congregational mutual aid in North American Mennonite congregations.[64] In the 1940s more than 60 percent of (Old) Mennonite congregations had an ordained deacon; by 1965, less than 25 percent of churches had deacons, and the percentage continued to decline in the decades that followed. The key reason for the change was a growing sense that individuals should be responsible for their own financial well-being. Mennonites needing material or financial assistance in the 1960s and 1970s were turning not to deacons, but rather to loan officers and financial planners.[65] At the inaugural gathering of MMAA fraternal representatives in 1966, Guy F. Hershberger argued vigorously that congregational representatives were the church's "new diaconate."[66] In the decades that followed, these congregational representatives played multiple roles, acting simultaneously as administrators of the fraternal funds, stewardship educators, and MMA's agents and customer service representatives.

Internal Tensions: A New CMP Study and Transitions in Leadership

By all outward appearances, MMA in the mid-1970s was a dynamic and thriving institution. The various healthcare plans had grown steadily throughout the previous decade, Mennonite Automobile Aid posted regular profits, assets from the Mennonite Foundation and Mennonite Retirement Trust were growing rapidly, and MMA was known and trusted among a growing number of Mennonite-related groups. The creation of a fraternal benefits association had resolved MMA's legal status while ensuring that the cause of mutual aid would go forward through the revenues accumulated in the fraternal funds. And the staff had recently moved into more spacious accommodations.

Membership supervisor Rolene Gingerich joined congregational delegates at this MMA fraternal meeting in Chicago. She began at MMA in 1962, left to raise her children, and came back to the organization to work in accounting where she continues to work today.

Yet internally the organization was struggling. Fifteen years after the CMP review of 1961 it was clear to the board and to most insiders that MMA continued to face significant organizational challenges—some structural and some personal. Efforts in the early 1960s to reorganize MMA around the recommendations of the CMP review had only partially succeeded. More rationalized procedures and greater clarity of job descriptions had eliminated some of the inefficiencies of the older organization; but they also exposed and heightened internal tensions.

Many of the frustrations staff had noted around Harold Swartzendruber's leadership just before the 1961 organizational review had persisted. There could be no question about Swartzendruber's commitment to the organization. He was a careful accountant, a detailed minute-taker, and a strong believer in the principles of mutual aid. For nearly three decades he had served MMA faithfully as an accountant, an office manager, and as its president. But an undercurrent of tension around Swartzendruber's leadership persisted. The new organizational structure gave considerable authority to the directors of the three departments, yet Swartzendruber continued to operate in his accustomed role as General Manager, in which he often became entangled in the minutiae of office details.

Swartzendruber's relations with John Rudy—and the larger question of how the Financial Services department fit into the overall structure of the organization—were especially challenging. Although Rudy technically reported to Swartzendruber, he operated largely outside the MMA office. Moreover, the two departments—Mutual Aid and Financial Services—tended to function in quite different worlds, especially in the field where Rudy was aggressively building a network of financial advisors who had very little connection to the marketing or representatives of the Field Services division who were promoting mutual aid insurance products.

And there were tensions between the two departments over profitability. To the public, who only heard Rudy's presentations and saw the graphs showing a steady growth of assets, it appeared that the Mennonite Foundation was extremely successful. But behind the scenes the Mennonite Foundation and the Mennonite Retirement Trust struggled to meet their operating expenses. Both operations managed significant amounts of money. But the administrative fees on the money invested rarely covered their internal costs, especially when the total assets were still relatively small. As a result, the Mutual Aid Service side of the organization was often forced to subsidize the overhead expenses of the Financial Services department.[67]

Rudy was also deeply frustrated by the close identity of MMA with the Mennonite Church. As he traveled across the Anabaptist-Mennonite landscape, the questions of financial stewardship he encountered among business owners or middle-class professionals were just as real among General Conference Mennonites, Mennonite Brethren, and the Brethren in Christ as they were among members of the Mennonite Church. As a practical matter, Rudy also recognized that if the growing number of people from these groups who were actively investing in the Mennonite Foundation did not have formal representation in the foundation or on the board of MMA, they would likely retreat and spin off their own parallel organizations.[68] At one point, frustrated at the exceedingly slow pace of the Mennonite Church's Study Commission on Reorganization to address his concerns regarding greater inter-Mennonite representation, Rudy threatened to take the Mennonite Foundation out of MMA altogether, a move that the board blocked.[69]

The tensions between the two departments were structural; but Swartzendruber's leadership and operating style did little to bridge the divide. By the mid-1970s it was becoming increasingly evident to the MMA Board that the organization was in need of fundamental changes. In the spring of 1975, William Dunn, a highly-respected executive at the Mennonite hospital in Bloomington, Illinois, and representative of the General Conference Mennonite Church's Central District, became the new MMA board chair. At the fall 1976 board meeting, Dunn recommended that MMA return to the organizational consultants, CMP, for another major review of the company. He also called for a planning retreat for the board, MMA staff, and Mennonite Church leaders to "look carefully at the MMA mandate for all of its programs, to review the philosophical, theological, and conceptual basis, to discuss issues, and to

In his final role as president, Harold Swartzendruber left MMA after thirty years of service.

'dream.'"[70] In addition to the seventeen MMA board members, the meeting was to include six management staff, eight home office staff, six field staff, five denominational leaders, and six special guests—nearly fifty people in all.

On November 19–20, 1976, the group assembled at the Windsor Inn in Rosemont, Illinois. The participants spent most of their time in smaller groups sharing concerns and identifying priorities for the future. The conclusions were wide-ranging and not always consistent. Whereas MMA executives, for example, thought that holistic education on lifestyle issues and preventative health practices needed to become a more visible part of MMA's marketing, the church conference representatives explicitly argued that MMA "not be an educator but a resource to help educational agencies," and that it should "be careful not to mix education and promotion of product."[71] MMA staff called on the company to simplify its logo, to train more women and minorities for management positions, to emphasize prevention rather than Catastrophe Aid, and, above all, to improve management-staff relations through better communication and more training.[72] Altogether the group identified sixty-three concerns, which they then reduced to the ten most urgent issues. The top priorities focused on strengthening connections to congregations—congregational representatives needed more training, more sensitivity to the needs of their members, and more active involvement in the mutual aid process. Other top tier concerns included the need for more attention to financial counseling, especially with a view to helping members stay out of debt and assisting those who were planning for retirement; stronger connections to the global church; better services to young adults; simpler healthcare plans; an unemployment insurance program; improvements to the CHIP plan; and more effective marketing that would include a stronger emphasis on improved lifestyles.

If the leadership retreat in the fall of 1976 allowed MMA staff to openly express their frustrations and to claim a larger sense of ownership regarding future directions, the board's decision to reengage the consulting firm of Cresap, McCormick and Paget for another organizational review proved to be even more decisive in effecting changes. In May of 1977 CMP returned with their report, which included a recommendation that MMA restructure its management positions and called for a new job description for the top executive officer.[73]

With the benefit of hindsight, it seems clear that both the staff retreat and the CMP review were designed with a leadership transition in mind. The retreat clearly brought to light some of the internal tensions within the organization; and the CMP recommendations were especially convenient in enabling the board to remove Swartzendruber while placing the responsibility for the decision primarily on the counsel of outside experts. Nevertheless, Swartzendruber was clearly taken by surprise when he received the news of his dismissal.

According to the sanitized language of the official press release, published in the *Goshen News* and various church periodicals under the headline "Swartzendruber Quits MMA Post," it was Swartzendruber who initiated the transition. Swartzendruber's decision came "in the context of a recent organizational study undertaken by the board and allows the opportunity to freely staff for the future." After praising Swartzendruber for his "splendid career record," William Dunn noted that MMA's rapid growth had prompted the board to ask consultants "to help develop an organizational blueprint for the future and to isolate modifications which will help the organization adapt to changing needs."[74]

Swartzendruber's resignation was to take effect on May 12, 1978. He never fully recovered from the blow. In his autobiography Swartzendruber suggested that both his father-in-law, C. L. Graber, and friends in the insurance business encouraged him to lodge a lawsuit against MMA for unlawful dismissal.[75] At one point he suggested, albeit without evidence, that the board was punishing him for failing to fire John Rudy after word leaked that Rudy was allegedly looking to spin Mennonite Foundation off from MMA.[76] After his departure, Swartzendruber recalled that he had several offers for work in Mennonite-related organizations—offers he turned down because he felt "burned out and shell-shocked. I was suspicious of church institutional responsibilities."[77]

Swartzendruber's lengthy tenure with MMA was marked by a long list of significant accomplishments. More than any other leader, it was Swartzendruber who translated the vision of MMA into actual programs, tending steadfastly to countless details in an era of remarkable growth. The termination of his leadership in 1978, after nearly thirty years of employment, was understood by many as both necessary and tragic.

The Unanticipated Consequences of Institutionalization

By the late 1970s the advantages of MMAA's status as a fraternal benefit association were enormous. But the new legal structure also brought with it some subtle changes—including the question of ownership and authority—that would have lingering consequences. MMA was created as a child of the church by denominational leaders who defined its mandate and the scope of its operations. By contrast, as a fraternal benefits association, MMAA was technically owned by its individual members, represented through local congregations, who voted on the board of directors. Although Mennonite Church leaders effectively maintained their control over the organization, the new structure subtly shifted the primary focus of MMA's identity to local congregations rather than denominational leaders. Theologically, this shift made sense—Anabaptist-Mennonite understandings of mutual aid had always been rooted in face-to-face, spontaneous sharing of material aid in local settings. And it conformed fully with Orie Miller's promise to follow "where the people go." But the structure also meant that going forward, MMA would be more sensitive to the market realities and consumer wishes of local congregations than to the strictures of denominational interests or ideals.

The introduction of the fraternal funds also signaled a significant shift in traditional understandings of mutual aid. The older definition of mutual aid assumed that financial sharing would happen spontaneously, as the need arose; that it would be truly mutual in character rather than a form of charity; and that it could be sacrificial, calling on members to dip into their savings or to lower their standard of living to meet the needs of a vulnerable member. With the creation of the fraternal funds, MMA had significantly more resources at its disposal to share with its members and considerable flexibility as to how that money would be spent. But the fraternal funds came not from the charitable contributions of members, but from the state and federal government in the form of reduced tax liabilities.

If the older model of mutual aid was oriented primarily to support members in vulnerable times, the new realities of "stewardship" or "financial management" seemed to focus more on helping individuals take better control of their wealth through tax-savvy forms of charitable giving, careful retirement planning, and a clear understanding of inheritance laws. All of these actions could result in remarkably generous expressions of philanthropy. But this understanding of generosity, it seemed, was something different than a barn raising or a spontaneous collection of money to help a fellow church member meet an unexpected expense.

MMA's access to financial resources also represented a new form of power. In a denominational world where church institutions often struggled to meet their budgets, MMA emerged in the coming decades as the church agency with the deepest pockets. Even though Mennonite Foundation staff members did not have direct control over the charitable gifts the foundation distributed, church officials and college presidents keenly understood the subtle power that foundation officers wielded in their intimate conversations with wealthy individuals regarding the disposition of their estates. The growing resources of the fraternal funds—and the eventual denominational dependence on those funds—represented a form of power that was real.

MMA administrators and board members were not blind to these questions. Indeed, they addressed them repeatedly in conversations and board meetings. And they would continue to return to these same questions in the coming decades, adapting to new realities while remaining firmly rooted in the Anabaptist-Mennonite tradition out of which the organization emerged.

LOVE AND JUSTICE DIFFER

At the annual gathering of mutual aid societies in the fall of 1960, J. Lawrence Burkholder, professor of theology at Goshen College, addressed these questions in a devotional to the group that he titled "Love and Justice in Mennonite Mutual Aid."[78] Burkholder was a strong defender of mutual aid, but he challenged the idea that any institution—including those created by the church—could actually practice the sort of love that Jesus taught and modeled to his disciples. Christian love, Burkholder asserted, was not "reasonable" or "moderate"—it was limitless, uncalculating, self-sacrificial, and inexhaustible—a generosity that transcended all policies or rules.[79]

On the other hand, justice was also a virtue. "Both love and justice," Burkholder claimed, "serve the same God." Justice is needed when large numbers of people who do not live in close geographical proximity choose to organize for a common goal. The institutions they form *necessarily* operate by agreements, policies, and rules that fall short of love's ideal.[80]

Burkholder was emphatic that Mennonites should not reject institutions. "Collective life must be served collectively," he insisted. Nevertheless, "there is a certain price that has to be paid in exchange for the advantages of the organization. Impersonality, inflexibility, defense of rights and privileges—these go along with organization." "We should not reject justice," Burkholder concluded, but we should continuously critique rules, policies, procedures in the church in order to "inject love into the structures of justice."[81] Few Mennonite theologians or ethicists captured more succinctly the inner tensions that MMA faced in the 1960s and 1970s as it sought to honor the radical principles of Christian mutual aid in its various programs.

Despite all the qualities that set MMA apart from commercial insurance, Burkholder's distinction between love and justice was insightful. MMA's leaders desired to embody the radical practices of Christian love central to Christian teaching and the Anabaptist-Mennonite tradition. Yet as Burkholder observed, collective organizations—organizations that seek to connect large numbers of people across geographical distances—inevitably operate according to principles of justice. They may pursue policies and procedures that attempt to "inject love into the structures of justice," but even the purest of intentions will result in unanticipated consequences that fall short of the intended goal.

Two years after Howard Raid greeted the delegates to the first MMAA gathering at the Atlantic Hotel with the words "Good morning, radicals," the city of Chicago would be paralyzed, as riot police and protesters violently clashed outside the 1968 Democratic National Convention. By 1968, the word *radical* had taken on a quite different meaning in American culture. But even if the visionaries who started MMA would not likely have joined the protestors on the streets of Chicago, their appeal to the principles of community and compassion, their dreams of a society that protected the weak and defended the vulnerable, and their deep conviction that institutions could be redeemed in the service of these larger visions, were part of a much deeper prophetic tradition that has long been the impetus for social change.

The challenge, of course, was sorting out exactly how the ideals of Christian love and mutual aid would be translated into practice.

FIVE

The Healthcare Crisis Intrudes

(1975–1991)

*T*wenty-five years after the event, James Kratz still remembered the moment with vivid clarity. Barely two years into his role as MMA president, Kratz was on a nationwide listening tour of churches. Late in 1988, MMA had informed its members of a 40 percent increase in health insurance premiums, only the latest in a steady series of premium increases in the face of spiraling nationwide healthcare costs. Now MMA administrators were traveling the country, offering an explanation for the rate hikes and encouraging members to hold firm to the principle of mutual aid. The scene Kratz recalled took place at a congregation in California when an elderly woman—moving slowly, with the aid of a walker—came to the front of the room, waving her premium notice. In her quivering voice, the woman told her story of financial impoverishment because of healthcare costs. "How," she asked, "how can you do this to me?"[1]

The pain expressed at that meeting was personal—both for the elderly woman and for Kratz. Yet the issues that gave rise to the pain were structural. Caught in a vortex of rapidly rising healthcare costs, national economic trends, and shifting attitudes in the church toward mutual aid, MMA faced a profound crisis in the late 1970s and 1980s that challenged its identity as a church-based institution and, indeed, called into question the very viability of the organization. In 1988 alone, MMA lost more than 5 percent of its members who had been enrolled in health insurance plans, foremost among them healthy individuals who decided they could purchase comparable plans at more competitive rates from commercial health insurance companies. The loss of these healthy members—combined with its long-standing policy of accepting virtually all Anabaptist-Mennonite applicants, regardless of preexisting conditions—brought MMA perilously close to a death spiral in the late 1980s. Yet the company survived, thanks largely to the resolute determination of its leaders and the board's readiness to adjust long-standing principles and programs to meet the changing sensibilities of their members—following "where the people go."

A Context of Anxiety

The crisis of the late 1980s would almost certainly have been worse had it not been for the organizational reforms recommended by the CMP consultants in the spring of 1977, which attempted to rationalize MMA's convoluted corporate structure and to bring the church-based institution, which had outgrown its homegrown management, into the modern world. By the late 1970s deep structural changes were taking place in the American healthcare system that fundamentally altered the landscape within which MMA was operating. Complicating that story were equally profound shifts in American politics and economics, which shook public trust in government and raised doubts about the integrity of institutions in general. The reforms recommended by the MMA staff retreat in the fall of 1976 and CMP's report in the spring of 1977 came at a crucial moment; yet the challenges the MMA board and administrators faced in the late 1970s and 1980s went far deeper than the recommendations anticipated, or indeed what leaders themselves were able to fully grasp.

POLITICAL, ECONOMIC, AND RELIGIOUS UNCERTAINTY

In the mid-1970s American society was caught in a whirlwind of economic, political, and social upheaval. The optimism behind the social reforms of the 1960s—the Civil Rights Act of 1964; the introduction of Medicare and Medicaid in 1965; Lyndon Johnson's "war on poverty"—yielded in the early 1970s to the persistent realities of racism, urban violence, and the growing income gap between rich and poor. In 1974 President Richard Nixon resigned under the threat of impeachment due to his role in the Watergate scandal. That and the Vietnam War left a generation deeply skeptical about their government—and institutions in general. The deep economic recessions in 1973–1975 and again in 1981–1982, combined with double-digit inflation and unprecedentedly high interest rates, forced thousands of farmers into bankruptcy. Although the U.S.

economy improved somewhat in the mid-1980s, President Ronald Reagan's supply-side economics—which argued that reducing taxes would create new jobs and higher wages—largely benefited the wealthy. Overlaid on these economic uncertainties were growing anxieties regarding the nuclear arms race and escalating tensions between the United States and the USSR.

Against the backdrop of these unsettling realities, Mennonites in North America were also in the midst of a significant transformation. An entire generation of Mennonite young adults had been shaped by their experiences in Civilian Public Service during World War II and then, in the 1950s and 1960s, by their postwar service with Mennonite Central Committee, PAX reconstruction work, or the Teachers Abroad Program. These experiences helped to awaken Mennonites to the world beyond the ethnic enclaves of their rural communities or the borders of their own nation.

In the years following World War II, a growing percentage of Mennonites were attending college, anticipating upward economic mobility as they entered into new professions. Armed with diplomas and a new set of technical skills, this new generation of college-educated Mennonites wielded an outsized influence on the church. They were not hesitant to voice their opinions about the social concerns of the day, and they were willing to express their convictions as activists by organizing coalitions, lobbying Congress, and participating in electoral politics.[2]

Meanwhile, another sizeable group of Mennonites remained oriented to their local congregations and the rural communities of their birth, even as they too were leaving behind the sectarian identity of their grandparents. As opposition to radio and television faded in the 1960s and 1970s, tradition-oriented Mennonites were increasingly exposed to mass media, along with the consumer trends and commercial interests of modern advertising, and the populist political and religious movements of the day.

The increased affluence of both progressive and tradition-minded Mennonites found expression in larger homes, extensive church remodeling projects, a growing interest in philanthropic causes, and a new concern for financial and retirement planning. The growing wealth among Mennonites also made itself felt in a new interest in charitable giving beyond the local congregation.[3] In the context of these changes, choices regarding dress, access to technology, ethical behavior, and religious beliefs that were once framed within the context of a group were increasingly made on the basis of individual taste or in new communities defined by economic class, interest groups, consumer tastes, or political orientation.[4]

THE SHIFTING NATURE OF CHURCH AUTHORITY

Another expression of these changes could be seen in the shifting nature of authority within the church and its institutions. By the 1970s, as institutions like MMA or church-related colleges became more complex—and as a rising professional class of educated administrators assumed positions of authority within church-related institutions—leaders tended to value the counsel of experts in their fields at least as much as the opinions of the pastors and bishops. Professors at Mennonite colleges, for example, regarded themselves as thought leaders in the church, helping to renew the Anabaptist-Mennonite tradition by encouraging their students to raise questions about received truths and to actively engage the latest discoveries in science or technology. But more conservative leaders increasingly regarded church colleges and other denominational institutions as a threat. Whereas church-related institutions were once an extension of the almost tribal sense of communal identity for many Mennonites, by the 1970s those bonds of allegiance were increasingly tenuous.

In a similar way, the direct control that Anabaptist-Mennonite denominations had once wielded over their institutions was fading. Mission boards, seminaries, and service agencies now had budgets that far exceeded that of their parent denominations, and took increasing liberties in managing their own fundraising, communication, and strategic planning. The tight interlocked network of male leaders who once populated the boards of a dozen or more church institutions had now relaxed to admit women, people of color, and individuals selected on the basis of their professional expertise.[5]

By the late 1970s it was clear that the Mennonite Church was in the midst of a profound cultural shift; but the nature and consequences of those changes were only dimly understood. Best-selling books like Ron Sider's *Rich Christians in an Age of Hunger* (1975), Doris Janzen Longacre's *More-with-Less Cookbook* (1976), and Don Kraybill's *The Upside-Down Kingdom* (1978), expressed a clear sense of anxiety about the degree to which North American Mennonites—and Christians in general—had accommodated themselves to wealth, affluence, and power, both institutional and individual.[6] Like all good prophetic literature, each appealed to convictions already deeply embedded in the tradition that called the church back to radical faithfulness. At the same time, all of these books sought to reformulate the ideals of a past Anabaptist-Mennonite identity into language and practices that were relevant to the contemporary cultural context.

EARLIER VOICES ON WEALTH AND AFFLUENCE

But these were not the only voices in the church addressing the question of affluence and wealth. Although their books were not bestsellers, a cluster of much earlier authors probably had an even deeper impact on Mennonite attitudes toward wealth in the second half of the twentieth century through their sustained focus on the theme of stewardship. The pioneer of this movement was Milo Kauffman, long-time president of Hesston College, who left that role in 1951 to become a traveling evangelist within the Mennonite Church for the cause of Christian stewardship. In 1953 Kauffman prepared a series of lectures, later published as *The Challenge of Christian Stewardship* (1955), which he went on to present in more than 250 churches in the United States and Canada.[7]

Kauffman's infectious passion for biblical stewardship prompted a colleague at Hesston College, business manager Daniel Kauffman, to accept a position in 1961 as the Mennonite Church's first secretary of stewardship. In that role, Daniel Kauffman traveled throughout the church admonishing members to be more thoughtful about the resources of time, talent, and money that God had entrusted to them, and he encouraged ordinary members to include church institutions such as the mission board, the publishing house, and colleges in their wills.[8]

Kauffman, in turn, was a close friend and colleague of John Rudy, who explicitly built on these foundations in his own efforts to promote stewardship in his work with the Mennonite Foundation. Through Rudy, MMA would emerge as the heir to this long tradition of stewardship education, eventually taking on the identity of the "stewardship agency of the Mennonite Church."

All of these perspectives on wealth were part of the cultural and religious landscape of Anabaptist-Mennonite communities in the early 1980s. Although MMA's programs and personnel tended to identify with the themes of stewardship, the ideals and concerns of the more radical voices were always part of the conversation in MMA boardrooms, committees, and office cubicles. MMA was at its best when its programs and policies reflected some element of both of these ethical traditions.

New Leadership in Anxious Economic Times

The same MMA news release that reported Harold Swartzendruber's "resignation" in the spring of 1978 also announced that Dwight Stoltzfus, director of MMA's Field Services department, had accepted the role of MMA president.[9]

In 1978 the country had entered a period of rising energy costs, high interest rates, growing unemployment, and a sharp decline in consumer spending, which led the economy into a deep recession that lasted nearly four years. For a time, interest rates skyrocketed as high as 18 percent and compelled all financial advisors, including those who managed MMA's portfolio of funds, to rethink traditional investment strategies.

Stoltzfus was not a banker. He was a man of the people—a successful farmer with a down-home, amiable style of communication, a strong sense for the practical side of business, and a deep love of the church. A 1941 graduate of Goshen College, Stoltzfus was part of a generation of Mennonite institutional leaders for whom the church was the primary frame of reference for virtually every aspect of life. While managing a dairy farm east of Goshen, he had served on the loan committee for the local Farm Bureau Credit Union and as treasurer of the Indiana-Michigan Mennonite Conference. For nearly thirteen years, from 1958 to 1971, Stoltzfus was a member of the MMA board of directors, witnessing the dramatic growth of the Burial Aid and Hospital-Surgical plans as well as the transformation of MMA's identity in 1966 when it officially became a fraternal benefit association. In September of 1971, he accepted an invitation from Harold Swartzendruber to join the MMA staff as the director of Field Services, a task that brought him intimately in touch with the impact of MMA's programs at the congregational level. Thus, when the board asked him to step into a new role as president, Stoltzfus brought a deep understanding of the ideals that had given rise to the mutual aid movement, and two decades of experience with the organization.[10]

Stoltzfus, who clearly regarded the work of MMA as an extension of the church, was never fully at ease with the business aspects of the organization. The actuaries who served under him recall how uncomfortable Stoltzfus was with the concept of reserves—the pool of money insurance companies were required to hold in reserve in order to ensure that policies could be honored if the program folded.[11] MMA, he argued, should not be in the business of making a profit, and he was embarrassed by the large sums of money that the organization reported in its assets column. In 1986, reflecting back on his tenure as president, Stoltzfus asserted: "I have deliberately avoided, the last 10 or 15 years, talking about how our monetary resources have increased. . . . The measure of our success is not how many dollars we recycle. It's how many people we help."[12]

Unlike other church leaders at the time, Stoltzfus did not lament the move in the Mennonite Church away from denominational and regional conference authority toward congregationalism. Indeed, he celebrated the fact that congregations "have developed a greater self-identity in the last 20 years. . . . I am

Dwight Stoltzfus began his term as president in 1978. He reorganized MMA's internal structure, increased the number of local congregational representatives, supported the creation of ShareNet, a new MMA's health plan for businesses, and increased stewardship education in the church.

a firm believer in local initiative. I've nudged MMA that direction as often as I could."[13] A central feature of that commitment was the network of congregational volunteers who represented MMA products to their local congregations, advocated on behalf of individuals needing assistance from the Sharing Fund, and promoted the principles of mutual aid and Christian stewardship in their local settings.[14] During Stoltzfus's tenure, the number of congregation representatives increased from several hundred to more than a thousand, "not because it was the perfect system, but because it reflects local initiative in ways the central agency system does not."[15]

Stoltzfus was also a strong promoter of the MMAA Group Health Plan, a congregation-based program that offered immediate and full coverage to all participants, regardless of preexisting health conditions, if at least 50 percent of the congregation agreed to enroll.[16] He worked hard to support these congregations, whose self-insured programs settled the ordinary healthcare costs of members, while MMA provided reinsurance for major medical expenses. And he took pride in the emergence of ShareNet, a health insurance plan, modeled on the same basic principle, that MMA designed for Mennonite-related businesses. As medical costs and premiums began to rise sharply in the early 1980s, Stoltzfus worried that the new realities would not "overshadow spontaneous and intentional mutuality—the lifeblood of our churches and families."[17]

Implementing Reforms: Competing Visions?

The two reviews that MMA undertook just before Stoltzfus's presidency—the 1976 board retreat followed by the CMP organizational assessment in 1977—pointed in quite different directions for the future of the organization. The first gathering focused primarily on how the organization could better serve the church and its changing needs. The long list of initiatives that emerged from the planning session clearly accepted the language of insurance and the need for organizational reforms, but participants also asked challenging questions about MMA's theological foundations: what would distinguish MMA from commercial products in the future? How could MMA adjust to the movement toward congregationalism? And, more crucially, how could MMA better support the broadening mission of the church in the areas of urban economic development, environmental concerns, mental health, and racial equality? Included among the top ten list of priorities, for example, was a pressing need to "train women and minority persons for management level responsibilities."[18]

The CMP study, by contrast, offered a critical assessment of MMA's organizational culture. Consultants noted, for example, that the composition of the MMA board was still dominated by trusted church leaders rather than individuals with specific skills or competencies. The organization's wage/salary scale

MMA staff and space needs continued to grow with major additions in the late 1970s and early 1980s. The new office space added in the early 1980s was initiated to accommodate growing technology equipment and staff.

was out of touch with market realities. The organization was slow to adapt to changes in market realities. MMA still had an allergic reaction to the concept of marketing, and it seemed oddly reluctant to engage in strategic planning.[19] Many of the concerns expressed by the CMP report in 1977 echoed the same themes they had noted in 1961.

ORGANIZATIONAL RESTRUCTURING

In the spring of 1978, when Stoltzfus took office, it was clear that he had a mandate for organizational reform.[20] Following the CMP recommendation, he immediately created a new position of Director of Office Services, which had primary responsibility for overseeing internal office logistics as well as communication, sales, and customer service. James Kratz stepped into the role. Lamar Reichart continued as director of Mutual Aid Services, as did John Rudy as director of Financial Services.[21]

Stoltzfus also moved to restructure board committees and, in an effort to encourage greater continuity, increased board member terms from eight to twelve years.[22] A year later, again following a strong recommendation from CMP, the board drafted the organization's first formal mission statement[23] and began to give significantly more attention to long-range planning and goal setting. Beginning in 1979, Stoltzfus presented an annual budget to the board, broken down for each of the seven subsidiary companies, along with a list of priorities, goals for the coming year, and five-year projections. The board also spent considerable time debating the nuances of a revised wage and salary scale, trying to balance industry standards—in which the president and upper management earned many times more than the lowest paid staff members—with the expectations of the Mennonite Church Executive Board, which was attempting to standardize compensation for all church-related employees.

Also in keeping with the CMP recommendations, MMA overhauled its primary health insurance plan. The Medical Expense Sharing Plan (MESP), introduced in April of 1979, offered more options for deductibles, covered mental health, and provided higher lifetime benefits. It also quietly introduced a form of underwriting by adjusting premiums according to age and geography.

A growing staff and modernized organizational structure also called for another expansion of office space. When MMA moved to the Robertshaw Controls building in 1971, it invested considerable resources in remodeling the structure. But MMA staff had continued to grow. At the beginning of Stoltzfus's tenure in 1978, MMA had 78 employees; five years later that number had nearly doubled to 147 employees. Stoltzfus worried in 1979 that investing in a major new addition might seem extravagant. But only a few years later a Facilities Task Force reported that personnel would likely increase by at least 65 additional people in the next five years and that space needs would nearly double.[24] So in 1983 the board appropriated funds for another round of design work.[25]

MMA was always on the cutting edge of technology in the Mennonite world and the remodeled facilities were explicitly designed to accommodate growing technology. During the previous decade, following the recommendations of the first CMP consultation, MMA had officially entered the computer age. At the end of 1967, the company leased its first computer—a card processing system from IBM that enabled staff to print billings, track the receipt of income, print claims checks, and produce its first statistical reports.[26] But the pace of technology kept increasing rapidly and by 1976 MMA needed to employ two full-time programmers. Recognizing that MMA's existing computers were still inadequate for generating automated claims or supporting the new Medical Expense Sharing Plan, Jim Kratz, director of Administrative Services, oversaw an extensive consultation process in 1979 that advised MMA to develop its own software for the new health plan rather than relying primarily on purchased products. In the fall of 1979 MMA purchased an IBM Model 15D. By 1986, Byron Weber-Becker, project coordinator for MMA's Systems Development, reported that MMA employed eighteen people in computer-related positions, and that its computers enabled the organization to accurately distinguish among the thirty-eight John Millers in its membership pool of eighty thousand names.[27]

Nurturing Connections to Congregations

Even as Stoltzfus moved forward with the CMP list of recommendations, he was also attentive to the concerns voiced at the staff retreat regarding closer connections to the church. Stoltzfus was convinced that if love of neighbor was not going to be reduced completely to a transaction based on policies and money, mutual aid would need to remain anchored in the local congregation. In the early 1980s, the board identified "maximizing congregational involvement" as its primary corporate goal. Its second priority, closely related, was to "develop a coordinated MMA field strategy" that would bring the mutual aid programs together with the work of Mennonite Foundation and put an end to the chasm that existed between the two departments in the field. Stoltzfus worked tirelessly to address both concerns. The first priority was to greatly expand the network of congregational representatives and to provide them with adequate support from MMA staff. In order to do this, Stoltzfus increased the number of regional offices from four to twelve. Each MMA regional field officer was responsible to be in regular communication with the congregational representatives, who served as the primary point of sale for MMA products and the key link in MMA's education programs.

CLEARER BRAND IDENTITY AND MARKETING

The CMP report had noted the absence of a coherent marketing strategy as a major deficit in MMA's business operations. So early in 1980 Stoltzfus asked John Rudy to lead a Marketing Task Force to recommend how MMA could use "marketing methods for doing a better job of meeting the needs of our Mennonite brothers and sisters."[28] Noting that MMA employees seemed to have a strong preference for the language of education rather than marketing, a consultant to the task force put his finger on a persistent set of unresolved questions. What, he asked, "are you trying to teach your market? . . . Is [stewardship] evangelism an end or is it a means to an end?"[29] One very practical question had to do with product nomenclature. Among other things,

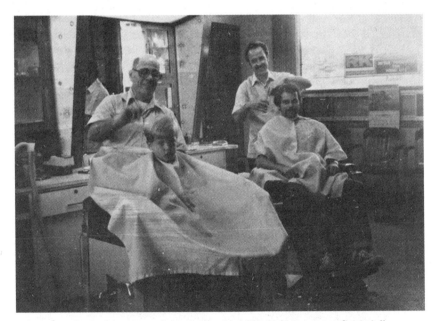

When a medical crisis occurred, many members like Rich Carr were financially helped by their MMA health plan and fellow church members. After a farming accident, Carr was blessed when a member of his North Lima Mennonite Church, Ohio, organized a "cut-a-thon" in his barbershop. He cut hair all day and donated proceeds to help Carr pay his share of medical bills.

the consultant recommended that MMA be "more conventional" in how they identified products by using "industry terms . . . like life insurance," for example, instead of "biblical terms," which he associated with "Survivor's Aid."

The task force affirmed the recommendation, but still could not quite bring itself to fully embrace marketing. "MMA's educational programs should provide biblical instruction and practical information that lead Mennonite brothers and sisters to greater faithfulness and definite decisions," it concluded, before adding almost as an afterthought "including participation in those MMA plans which meet their mutual aid and stewardship needs."[30] In 1982 Lester Jantzen took the role of Promotion Manager, but it would take at least another decade before a staff member could be associated directly with "marketing."

Although the changes did not happen quickly, the commitment to bring a greater coherence to the various MMA-related entities—particularly the Mutual Aid and Financial Services departments—showed steady progress. In 1982, MMA created a new logo that was intended to serve as a single branding image for the entire MMA family of products. The previous MMA logo was a very straightforward line drawing of overlapping symbols, accompanied by a small booklet that carefully explained the meaning behind all six elements— circle, triangle, cross, acronym, people, and church building. The new logo, by contrast, was more abstract. It depicted four rounded triangular forms of different heights, seemingly representing a nuclear family, highlighted in white

The first leader of Mennonite Foundation, John Rudy (speaking), would create the early stewardship education programs at MMA.

within a dark circle. According to the MMA description that accompanied the rollout of the new design, the image "can suggest that each person we serve is a member of a family," though the family could also be a church or "the MMA family."[31] In 1984 a newly-established members services division, led by Phyllis Mishler, promised to respond to customer inquiries—whether in person, by phone, or by mail—promptly and constructively. Years later, MMA members still recalled Mishler's calm voice on the toll-free telephone number and her concise, accurate explanations of MMA products.

STEWARDSHIP EDUCATION EXPANDS

Despite the ongoing unclarity about the line between marketing and education, MMA continued to aggressively promote the theme of stewardship as both a theological concept and a way of life. The primary vehicle of stewardship education was *Sharing* magazine, which in the late 1970s began to supplement its human interest stories with a growing number of articles on topics directly related to healthy lifestyles—diet, safe driving, accident prevention, stress reduction.[32] But MMA also made its first foray into multimedia marketing in the summer of 1978, with the distribution of several filmstrips, each accompanied by a cassette tape, that focused on practical stewardship.[33] In 1980, MMA—working directly with the Mennonite Church General Board—funded a special project on Money and Economic Concerns, which included a "Stewardship Sabbatical" for Dan Kauffman to speak in churches, conferences, and retreats, and named John Rudy as the denominational Stewardship Minister. The coordinated stewardship message encouraged all members to "adopt modest standards of living," be good stewards of resources, practice "firstfruits" tithing, volunteer their time in service, and include the church in their wills.[34] Reflecting back on the effort, Rudy observed that lifestyle was the most difficult topic to address: "You can't use generous giving to redeem careless spending. . . . You don't set your lifestyle on what you can afford."[35]

In 1982 Stoltzfus attempted to solidify the message of the Money and Economic Concerns campaign by promoting an annual churchwide Mutual Aid Sunday. That same year MMA created a Stewardship Resource Center that featured a series of short publications on car safety, exercise, stress management, alternative medicine, patient advocacy, and end-of-life conversations. Stoltzfus also appointed former Hesston College president Laban Peachey as MMA's Stewardship Minister, and charged him with the task of keeping the theme visible to pastors and congregations. Peachey traveled extensively in the following year, meeting with pastors, hosting appreciation gatherings for

MMA congregational representatives, and promoting the gospel of stewardship in churches and regional conferences. Behind all of these efforts was the goal of aligning MMA more closely with its grassroots members, and particularly with the congregational representatives who were the face of MMA in the local community.

ETHICAL INVESTMENTS AND THE INTRODUCTION OF PAX WORLD MUTUAL FUNDS

Between 1960 and 1980 assets in the Mennonite Foundation grew from $150,000 to $26 million. Combined with the money held in the Mennonite Retirement Trust, Mennonite Church Building fund, and the reserve funds required of the various insurance plans, MMA was managing nearly $56 million in 1980.[36] Like all companies charged with the responsibility of overseeing these funds, MMA had a fiduciary responsibility to invest the money entrusted to them in ways that represented the strongest financial interests of their clients—presumably some mix of carefully selected stocks and bonds that would maximize returns on these assets, ideally growing them faster than the market average. But MMA was also committed to a policy of investing the money in ways that reflected the biblical and theological convictions of the Anabaptist-Mennonite tradition and the members of the various church groups whom it served. Balancing these two objectives was not easy. The 1980 MMA Investment Guidelines explicitly acknowledged the tensions between "legal requirements and biblical principles." Ultimately, however, the guidelines clarified that MMA's fiduciary commitments had the final word—MMA's ethical investment strategies could not result in lower market performance unless participants in the plan explicitly agreed or the fund was supplemented with additional contributions.[37]

In the fall of 1982, MMA's investment manager, Delmar King, brought together a group of Anabaptist-Mennonite business leaders and theologians to review the existing Investment Guidelines by examining ten specific test cases. The conversation underscored the complexity of the issues. In the end, the group recommended that MMA only invest in companies who sell "5% or less of their products to the military." But they also openly acknowledged that the Mennonite scientists they consulted offered contradictory counsel on the merits of nuclear power, that no clear standard existed to evaluate a company's treatment of women or minorities, and that complete divestment from South Africa might also adversely affect the economic well-being of that country's most vulnerable people.[38]

Del King, investment manager, oversaw the formation of the ethical investment guidelines for MMA. SUELYN LEE

In 1984 the Financial Services Committee of the MMA board formally adopted the ethical criteria that would shape MMA's future investment programs. The statement attempted to shift the focus from moral dilemmas to positive affirmations: MMA would seek out companies that promoted peace, health and stewardship, responsible management, quality of life, and church-related initiatives.[39] Pursuing these goals would require careful research and a readiness to express those commitments as activist shareholders.

Three years later, MMA board member Willis Sommer, collaborating with Greg Weaver from the Mennonite Foundation and Del King, representing MMA's investment management team, convened another group of theologians, ethicists, and business people to review the guidelines. The hardest issue for the Investment Guideline Review task force was a question of strategy— should MMA divest from multinational companies operating in South Africa or should it remain invested and encourage social reform around the institution of apartheid through proxy statements? At its fall meeting, the Task Force "could not reach a consensus position on a policy statement partly because of not being able to agree on a theology of investments." Weaver reported that a group of five Mennonite theologians he consulted tended to favor divestment, but "all five . . . made it clear that MMA need not bother trying to attain moral purity in this matter." He also summarized an argument made by the Interfaith Center on Corporate Responsibility that encouraged churches to sponsor proxy resolutions, noting that "votes of more than 5% in favor of social issues resolutions are on the rise . . . and have a significant impact on corporate management."[40]

The debate that ensued when the task force reconvened in 1988 was vigorous. The dominant voices seemed to agree that "withdrawal from investing in an industry or company removes our power of influence over that company," arguing that MMA should find allies to cosponsor proxy resolutions that would encourage corporations to change their practices. Although the August 1988 MMA board meeting eventually affirmed the strategy of remaining invested in corporations located in South Africa, one board member, Richard Reimer, a professor of economics at the College of Wooster, wrote a sharp dissent. "I would urge in as strong a manner as I possibly can," Reimer wrote, "that MMA management and the Board Investment Committee, when formulating its investment policy, always take into consideration the impact of its policies on those who are poor and powerless."[41] In the years that followed, MMA staff members would participate in a wide range of proxy initiatives around issues related to working conditions, race and gender discrimination, and pornography.[42]

The conversation around investment guidelines focused only on the criteria by which MMA would invest the funds entrusted to its care as an organization. But individual investors—ordinary church members, for example, who wanted to invest in an Individual Retirement Account or a mutual fund—had few options for engaging these same questions. So many MMA members were pleased to learn in the spring of 1985 that they could participate through MMA in the PAX World Fund—a no-load (i.e., no sales charges when shares are purchased or sold) mutual fund managed according to ethical and social criteria. PAX World Fund, which had been in operation since 1971, met all the criteria of MMA's ethical investments. By the fall of 1988, more than four hundred MMA members were participating in the fund, with investments that exceeded $2 million.[43] The experience with PAX World Fund set the stage for MMA's own entry into the mutual fund market six years later when it introduced the Praxis Mutual Funds.

Central Focus of the 1980s: The Healthcare Crisis

In the fall of 1983, David Hostetler, the news editor of the *Gospel Herald*, asked several MMA administrators to reflect on the future—what would the organization look like in ten years? The responses were insightful. Dwight Stoltzfus hoped that MMA would place "a greater emphasis on the needs of the poor" and would reexamine "our instincts toward self-preservation and self-interest." Kent Stucky, MMA's legal counsel and manager of the Mennonite Foundation, anticipated more reflection on whether MMA is a "church agency" or a "commercial enterprise." John Rudy, Larry Newswanger, and Ron Litwiller all hoped that Mennonite congregations would take a larger responsibility for practicing mutual aid in their own settings.[44] None of the executives identified healthcare costs as a primary concern. Yet in the decade that followed, escalating health insurance premiums, driven by soaring medical expenses, would propel MMA into a whirlwind of unanticipated challenges, calling into question deeply held principles and threatening the very existence of the fraternal benefit association.[45] Although the warning signs of an impending crisis were evident in the 1970s, it was not until the following decade that these forces converged into a tsunami that crashed into American public awareness as the "healthcare crisis."

The numbers, though abstract, tell an astounding tale. In 1970, Americans spent a total of $74.6 billion on medical care (public and private); a decade later, Americans were spending approximately $245 billion annually, and by 1990 that figure had jumped to $760 billion, with no signs of letting up.[46] On a per capita basis, health spending increased from $1,797 in 1970 to $4,760 in 1990.[47] Closer to home, average monthly healthcare claims of MMA members rose from $39 in 1984 to $106 in 1992.[48]

The roots of the healthcare crisis—which still has not been resolved—and the sources behind these spiraling costs, merit closer attention.

TRANSFORMATIONS IN HEALTHCARE

One of the most obvious explanations for the explosion of medical expenses can be attributed to a host of costly new innovations in medical technology.[49] Some of these technologies—advances in the treatment of infants born prematurely, for example, or new protocols for the treatment of cancer, joint replacements, or bypass surgery following heart attacks—clearly contributed to rising life expectancy in the United States and could only be welcomed. But they also raised new and difficult questions about the quality of life, the cost-effectiveness of experimental treatments, and the rapidly growing percentage of healthcare costs spent on prolonging the final weeks or months of life.

A second, closely related, explanation for the rapid increase in healthcare costs was the fact that more people had access to employer-paid health insurance than had previously been the case, and that most health insurance plans in the United States operated by the principle of "third party" payments which disguised the actual cost of treatment from the patient, making it more difficult for individuals to do comparison shopping for health plans. In 1965, the government also entered the healthcare market with Medicare for the elderly

and Medicaid for the poor. These programs immediately met with intense resistance from healthcare providers, who described them as "socialized medicine." In the face of these lobbying pressures, the Medicare/Medicaid programs
were designed on a "cost-plus" basis—that is, the actual cost of services plus
margin of profit for the provider—which also shielded costs from the competitive marketplace. By 1980, the majority of Americans with healthcare were
covered either by their employer or through the Medicare/Medicaid system,
with federal, state, and local governments paying 41 percent of total medical
care bills and private business paying 31 percent. Some critics argued that these
trends encouraged an indiscriminate use of medical services—"If insurance is
paying, why not use the emergency room?"[50]

A third factor in the explosive increase in medical costs was linked to the
economic interests of hospitals and physicians. Since the mid-1970s, the number of hospitals in the United States has been rapidly declining, largely as a result of a healthier population, consolidation of services, and a greater emphasis
on outpatient care. But hospitals continued to be paid on a cost-plus basis. In
a similar fashion, doctors were paid according to "reasonable and customary"
charges—meaning that they could bill whatever they wanted as long as other
physicians in the area were charging roughly the same amount. As more and
more Americans came to be covered by health insurance, doctors ceased to
compete with each other and could easily increase their fees without fear of
losing patients. During the 1980s, hospitals were operating at higher profit
margins than had previously been the case and physician's incomes were rising
much faster than inflation.

Finally, a fourth explanation was the exponential growth of litigation in
the area of healthcare. For every malpractice suit filed in the United States in
1970, three hundred were filed in 1990. The cost of malpractice insurance rose
accordingly. Those costs were passed along to physicians and insurance companies who, in turn, passed them along to patients. As a hedge against potential
malpractice suits, many physicians also began adding procedures and tests that
further increased costs.

By the early 1980s all of these factors joined together in a kind of perfect
storm of escalating healthcare costs.

Within MMA these trends were amplified by the fact that the organization
did not exclude people with preexisting conditions from its insurance pool if
at least 50 percent of their congregation participated in a healthcare plan. This,
after all, was a basic principle of mutual aid. Moreover, in contrast to many
other health insurance companies, MMA generally did not dispute claims

made by members. In 1987, Laban Peachey reported that MMA was paying nearly 25 percent more in claims than other insurance companies because "we try to carry out our mission of mutual aid by not excluding anyone, and by making decisions with more compassion and understanding." But the financial consequence of these forms of mutual aid was evident in the rapidly increasing premiums MMA was forced to charge. "How do we help persons in need," Peachey continued, "but also keep our premiums lower than insurers who are selective in whom they cover?"[51]

Even as Peachey asked that question, MMA's members were already giving their answer. By the late 1980s, thousands of MMA members—many of them among the healthiest in the insurance pool—canceled their policies in favor of less expensive health insurance options elsewhere.[52] The departure of healthy people from the program, of course, made the insurance pool even more overrepresented by people who were not able to buy insurance anywhere else. This, in turn, drove premium costs even higher, which only further exacerbated the problem.

The healthcare crisis of the late 1980s posed fundamental questions to MMA and to the larger Anabaptist-Mennonite community. On the one hand, the church was clear that healthcare was a basic right. On the other hand, it was not at all clear that MMA members were willing to support the inclusion of so many unhealthy people if it meant that their premiums cost significantly more than market rates, which were also rising. In light of the fact that thousands of members were canceling their healthcare insurance in search of cheaper plans elsewhere, what did it mean for MMA to follow "where the people go?"[53]

Transition to James Kratz

This was the unenviable context that faced James Kratz in the spring of 1986 when he accepted the invitation to succeed Dwight Stoltzfus as MMA's president. Like his predecessors, Kratz was deeply rooted in the church. Raised in a Mennonite community in Souderton, Pennsylvania, Kratz attended both Hesston College and Goshen College, before continuing his studies at Goshen Biblical Seminary. After a short stint with an accounting firm in Goshen, he and his wife, Dorothy, embarked on a seven-year assignment with Mennonite Board of Missions in Argentina. Kratz then served as the administrator of Mennonite Board of Missions Latin American programs for several years before moving to MMA in the role of office manager. Kratz quickly proved himself to be a gifted organizer and congenial administrator, overseeing the rapid expansion of MMA's computer services as well as the personnel department.

When he joined MMA in 1974, the company had 59 employees; when he became president in 1986, the staff had grown to 173.

Kratz had a reputation as a warm and humble person, with a relaxed sense of humor. Colleagues appreciated the fact that he worked out of a modest office, used a manual typewriter, and took the time to learn the names of every MMA employee.[54] His deep pastoral sensibilities, his commitment to the principles of mutual aid, and his love for the church were unmistakable.[55] In his first report to the MMA board on May 9, 1986, Kratz reflected on the spiritual awakening that prompted sixteenth-century Anabaptists to share their material possessions. "The question must be raised," he wrote, "whether mutual aid and sharing and caring can be institutionally-sponsored and motivated in the midst of material well-being and prosperity, or whether they are a result of spiritual renewal and awakening." He then went on to name a theme that would be central to his leadership: "The church created MMA . . . we are part of the church . . . we serve the church." MMA might borrow tools from commercial business for its mission and market, but mutual aid, Kratz insisted repeatedly, began in local, face-to-face settings. MMA's role was to help congregations carry out that mission.[56]

Thus, it was all the more painful that Kratz was the public face of MMA precisely at a period when the organization was facing intense pressure to

The last of the organization's pastor CEOs, James Kratz took over as president in 1986, overseeing the organization's response to its health plan crisis.

resolve the challenge of rising insurance premiums, which put the health and financial well-being of ordinary families at risk. As MMA adjusted its policies and programs—including a highly-controversial decision to tighten the screening of new members in its healthcare plans for preexisting conditions—it was Kratz who bore the brunt of the angry accusations that MMA had failed in its commitment to practice mutual aid.

The source of the problem, however, was not Kratz; nor was it rising costs. Rather, MMA members were simply no longer willing to pay the increasingly high price of "bearing one another's burdens" in the traditional way. Reports from MMA regional counselors in mid-September of 1988 confirmed the growing awareness that fewer and fewer members were ready to contribute sacrificially to pay for the healthcare needs of their very ill fellow members if cheaper commercial insurance was available. Representatives from the Bergen-Friesen Agency in Nebraska, for example, reported that "younger people don't have a concept of the MMA philosophy. They simply want the lowest price."[57] Kratz and the MMA board were particularly haunted by the fact that a substantial number of people in MMA's health insurance programs would not be able to find coverage elsewhere if MMA were to discontinue their programs. Indeed, finding an ongoing way to provide healthcare coverage for these "uninsurables" was a driving force to keep the program viable.[58]

MMA's Response to the Healthcare Crisis

MMA leaders struggled to know how best to respond to these changes. Already in 1981, noting that MMA's claims payments were consistently forcing increases in premiums, Ronald Litwiller, director of Mutual Aid Services, and Jerry Troyer, director of Health Services, took their concerns to the annual meeting of the Mennonite Health Association (MHA), a gathering of Mennonite medical professionals. MHA leaders agreed to form a Joint Study Steering Committee that pulled together a set of papers on the "Ethical and Stewardship Dimensions of Rising Health Care Costs." The essays became the focus of three regional conversations among providers and users of healthcare—with public sessions held in Pennsylvania, Indiana, and Kansas, as well as at the July 1983 meeting of the Mennonite Medical Association. Still, the increases in the early 1980s had been relatively gradual, giving MMA and its members time to adjust.[59]

By the time Kratz assumed leadership the situation was more ominous. A survey of MMA members in the summer of 1987 made it clear that the majority of members clearly did not understand why their premiums were increasing so fast and that many regarded MMA "as just another insurance option." "It will not be possible to help mutual aid happen," the report concluded "with only 43% who say they will stay even if our premiums go up."[60]

During the first half of 1988 alone, MMA lost more than 1,500 members and $3.6 million from its healthcare plans, money that came directly from its reserves. About the same number shifted their coverage from a low deductible to a high deductible plan. In 1989 MMA announced rate increases of 60 percent in the Medical Expense Sharing Plan. In April 1989, Jerry Troyer reported that at least 20 percent of the self-funded congregational groups—faced with a 49 percent increase in premiums—were likely to leave MMA, which "has a greater than 50% chance of putting us into a price spiral."[61]

In the fall of 1988 Kratz called on the key leaders in MMA's healthcare department—John Bowman, Sid Richard, Stan Schrock, Jerry Troyer—to form a Health Care Strategy Task Force. At a three-day retreat at Goshen College the group compiled a twenty-page report that laid out the problems facing MMA in stark detail. The report cautiously recommended that MMA remain in the health insurance business, but it also included a list of actions, some already in play, that the organization would need to adopt if it was to remain viable.

1. MOVE TOWARD INCREASED UNDERWRITING

Without question, the most far-reaching conclusion of the 1988 report was the acknowledgment that MMA's health insurance plans would need to introduce more aggressive forms of underwriting—that is, a screening process that would either refuse insurance to people with high health risks or impose longer waiting periods and higher premiums for applicants with preexisting health problems. Most health insurance companies had always practiced some type of underwriting by excluding sick applicants, charging them higher premiums, or adding exclusion riders that qualified what expenses would be covered. But as healthcare markets became more competitive, some commercial insurance companies had also begun a practice known as "skimming and dumping." The scheme started when insurance companies would not accept new applicants to an existing pool of insured customers. Then they would open a new block with lower prices, but with heavy underwriting restrictions, encouraging the healthy people from the old block to gravitate into the new plan. The next step was to raise the rates to pay for claims from the disproportionate number of sicker people in the old block so that many could not afford to remain in the plan—the healthy were skimmed; the sick were dumped. Another tactic was to do underwriting at the time of a claim, scrutinizing the fine print to see if the applicant failed to disclose a preexisting condition at the time of the application. If they found a lack of disclosure, the insurance company could deny coverage.

MMA resolutely refused to engage in "skimming and dumping." But the pressure to compete on prices meant that their health plans would need to include some form of underwriting. The actuarial consultants stated the problem very bluntly: "MMA health plans are staring down the barrel of a loaded gun. You have two choices: a) get broader membership, including those of good risk; or b) give up on poor risks, find a way to cut them out of the present pool, and institute strict underwriting to get a more select pool."[62] MMA was not willing to accept the logic of the second option; but it did introduce a growing number of criteria that sought to shift a larger part of healthcare costs back to those who used it the most.

Underwriting was not completely new to MMA. Already in 1979 the Medical Expense Sharing Plan advertised "rates consistent with actual costs for your age group"—code language for the fact that younger people, who were far less likely to need medical care, would pay a lower premium than elderly people. The MESP also adjusted premiums by geographic region, recognizing differences in what the medical community considered to be "fair and reasonable" prices; and it introduced higher deductibles as a way of keeping a check on increases in premiums. John Rudy framed the shift toward higher deductibles in terms of Christian stewardship. MESP, he argued, "provides us an opportunity to take care of ourselves before we call for help. We don't let someone else pay what we can pay ourselves. . . . In the MESP, mutual aid begins after self aid. Help arrives after the deductible."[63]

By 1987, however, it had become clear that more drastic measures were needed if the healthcare plans were to remain viable. On April 15, 1987, Karl Sommers, Jerry Troyer, and Laban Peachey circulated a memo titled "Price Competitiveness / Underwriting Recommendation" that suggested the time had come for a more fundamental shift in MMA's approach. "In the past," the memo stated, "we interpreted our mission being to help as many people as possible with medical problems. However, in the process we brought in a disproportionate share of people with medical problems at standard rates." This problem was compounded by the fact that some congregations have "violated principles of fairness and equity (II Cor. 8:13) when they enroll a disproportionate number of high risk-high cost members in MMA plans." MMA had also followed a claim payment process that made "generous settlements with members rather than control benefit costs."[64] The memo couched its key recommendation in complex language: MMA should "implement improvements in our risk selection practices designed to assess individuals who join or change coverage their fair share of cost relative to the risk they bring to the sharing pool." It's important to note that the memo did *not* call for permanent exclusion or a blanket denial of coverage for certain medical conditions—a common practice in the insurance industry. But "fair share of cost relative to the risk they bring" clearly meant underwriting.

In more concrete terms, the recommendation would mean a denial of claims for any injury or illness incurred prior to the policy; no coverage for people who had exhausted their lifetime benefits; a waiting period of three years for major illnesses; and higher premiums for persons "rated above standard morbidity." A similar set of criteria would apply to the small business and self-funded groups. The recommendations meant the end of what had been a signature feature of the MMA's health plan—namely, that anyone who was part of a congregation with 50 percent member participation could join the pool, regardless of preexisting conditions. The new approach would require the technical skills of a medical underwriter and a medical doctor to help actuaries assess risks and set premiums. The plan was to be introduced in phases, with the first phase to be implemented no later than January 1, 1988. Sommers, Troyer, and Peachey recognized that "a small number of persons in our constituency will perceive this as not being mutual aid anymore" but there was no other way forward.[65]

2. COST CONTAINMENT

At roughly the same time, administrators were also exploring options to contain the rising healthcare costs of those already enrolled.[66] During a one year period in 1987–1988, Kratz reported that MMA paid an average of $90,000 for each of eight premature babies, infants who likely would have died a decade earlier. At the opposite end of life, he noted, about half of the average cost of healthcare for an entire lifetime was spent on the last six months of a person's life.[67] The challenge, of course, is how families—or insurance companies—could put a price tag on attempts to save the life of a baby or, for that matter, on the additional weeks or months that new pharmaceuticals or medical technology seemed to promise a dying person.

In 1985 MMA convened a Health Care Ethics Review Committee to promote frank conversations on topics related to death and dying and "to help formulate decision-making guidelines."[68] Between May 1986 and spring of 1987, the committee convened hearings in seven different Anabaptist-Mennonite communities, each framed by an essay titled "New Ethical Dilemmas in Health Care," written by Willard Krabill, a Goshen physician and health educator who was emerging as a major voice in healthcare ethics.[69] These conversations prompted MMA leaders to consider how they might develop an option in which policyholders, in exchange for a lower premium, would commit to using palliative care for life-threatening illnesses rather than curative care. Not finding a way to secure approval for such a policy with state insurance departments, MMA abandoned the idea.

In another approach to cost containment, the editors of *Sharing* magazine encouraged MMA members to be more aggressive in communicating with their physicians, seeing themselves as active consumers of healthcare rather than as passive recipients. Articles such as "How Do I Talk to My Doctor?"[70] or "How to Choose a Good Doctor," or "Five Ways to Control Medical Care Costs," called on MMA members to use only essential medical services, to avoid tobacco, alcohol, and healthcare fads, and to take greater responsibility for maintaining a healthy lifestyle. "For most of us," wrote R. Clair Weaver, "it is in this area of self-responsibility where we can maintain the best control over our medical care costs."[71] At one point, Vyron Schmidt, MMA vice president of Congregational Services, strongly promoted a concept developed by the Mennonite Nursing Association called "nurse in the congregation."[72] Such a person, he argued, could provide basic consultation for health-related issues that might keep people from needless visits to the emergency room, or provide end-of-life counsel, or encourage preventative care. Although Schmidt was able to identify funds in the fraternal grants to cover the costs of a facilitator, the idea never blossomed.

MMA was surprisingly slow to pursue partnerships with Preferred Provider Organizations (PPOs)—plans that restricted coverage to care from pre-approved healthcare providers with whom the insurer had negotiated reduced prices. In 1986, however, MMA did introduce the TeamCare Health Plan to replace the Medical Expense Sharing Plan. TeamCare Health eliminated low deductibles and offered a monthly payment plan option. But its major innovation was to involve MMA staff more directly in the healthcare process.[73] Thus, the new plan strongly encouraged patients to seek second opinions; it required an audit of all claims over $20,000 to ensure that the charges were consistent with standard practice; and it introduced a Health Claims Specialist to pre-approve and monitor major medical procedures.[74] In contrast to the lifetime ceiling on coverage of $500,000 offered by MESP, TeamCare Health Plan promised lifetime coverage of $1 million.[75]

MMA grants supported congregational wellness efforts, such as Diamond Street Mennonite Church's Wholistic Health Center. Their Philadelphia neighborhood had few medical care options for mothers like Roslynn and her children.

Finally, in an even more direct effort to contain spiraling costs, in 1989 MMA administrators appointed a task force to explore the question of organ transplants—extremely expensive procedures that were becoming increasingly successful in giving dying patients a new lease on life. The final report of the Organ Transplant Task Force, issued on July 17, 1990, helpfully summarized the issues at stake, but gave very little useful guidance to MMA administrators charged with the task of developing policy. The report concluded that MMA should cover the costs of kidney and cornea transplants, since positive results for these procedures were well established, that all transplants should be pre-certified, and that in all cases other than kidneys and corneas MMA should limit its payment to 60 to 80 percent —which seemed to suggest that transplants were an option only for the wealthy.[76] Later MMA documents would be much more explicit about the unspoken reality that was only implicit in the Organ Transplant Task Force report—namely, that all humans, regardless of advances in medical technology, are going to die at some point.

3. RENEWED EMPHASIS ON PREVENTATIVE HEALTHCARE: WELLNESS

Even before the full extent of rising healthcare costs became evident, MMA administrators were emphasizing the importance of preventative measures that would promote holistic health and well-being. In the mid-1980s this theme found expression in a comprehensive Wellness Program.[77] Directed by Ann Raber, the program included a series of easy-to-read publications, combined with regional seminars and congregational training sessions on topics related

Wellness education grew in the 1980s. Maria Schumacher, Andrea Hilty, and Keri Luginbill made warm fuzzies when "Emma Mae," the MMA "wellness reporter," visited Grace Mennonite Church, Pandora, Ohio.

to holistic health. Within two years, Raber reported that she had trained nearly four hundred local wellness program leaders in the United States and Canada. Over the following decade the program addressed topics around mental health and suicide,[78] called attention to the health risks associated with stress,[79] introduced the language of "self-care,"[80] and underscored the importance of exercise and nutrition. In a 1987 editorial in *Sharing*, Kratz cautioned against the tendency to blame rising healthcare costs only on doctors, hospitals, the government, insurance companies, and drug manufacturers. "We are also part of the problem," he insisted, "unless we take charge of our health and health care." Kratz admonished his readers to be "good stewards of our bodies" and to "use MMA's Wellness Program in congregations." In 1989, MMA summarized these themes in small handbook for congregations, copies of which MMA sent to every church in its database.[81]

It is difficult to measure the outcomes of these educational efforts to promote wellness or to shift the primary responsibility for spiraling healthcare costs from the medical world to the individual consumer. But MMA was clearly at the leading edge of a larger effort to reframe healthcare in terms of promoting wellness rather than merely treating illness and disease.

4. MOBILIZING THE MUTUAL AID SHARING FUND

As a fraternal benefit association MMA also had the option of distributing fraternal funds back to its members most in need of additional assistance. By

Getting ready for a ride with brother Brad, Wes Traeholt (right) recovered from a serious farm accident in 1984 near Lustre, Montana. He received support from his church, Evangelical Mennonite Brethren Church, and a grant from MMA's Catastrophe Aid fund.

the late 1970s, MMA had become the nation's seventh largest fraternal benefit association and was dispersing nearly $1 million annually.[82] In 1979, MMA brought all of its fraternal programs into the Fraternal Activities Department and identified five basic priorities for the money.[83] The greatest portion by far went to the Mutual Aid Sharing Fund whose programs were intended to support mutual aid to needy members at the congregational level, particularly in the area of healthcare costs. Another significant portion of the funds—up to 25 percent—was allocated to the educational programs carried out by MMA staff.[84] In the early 1980s, these funds supported the work of John Rudy (Stewardship Minister), Laban Peachey (Mutual Aid Minister), Marvin Nafziger (Health Promotion), Carl Westerbeek (Defensive Driving Instruction), and Ann Raber (Wellness). The rest of the fraternal funds were divided among Congregational Project Grants, Inter-Mennonite Grants, and Denominational Grants (i.e. money distributed to the Mennonite Church, the General Conference Mennonite Church, and the Mennonite Brethren Church in proportion to the number of their members participating in health insurance programs).[85]

Local congregations benefited most directly from the Mutual Aid Sharing Fund. The fund supported Catastrophe Aid (assistance to healthcare plan members who were unable to afford their coinsurance payments), Premium Assistance (which paid one-third of those members' health insurance premium, with the congregation and the members each providing one-third); and the CHIP program that provided premium subsidies to low-income congregations who participated in MMA's group plans.

In 1985, MMA was receiving 240 requests for Catastrophe Aid funding every month. That year the Mutual Aid Sharing Plan distributed $555,600 to 1,350 people. Three years later, the overall fraternal fund budget, now overseen by Vyron Schmidt, vice president of Congregational Services, had reached $1.7 million, with the majority of disbursements going to support healthcare expenses at the congregational level.[86] *Sharing* magazine featured dozens of stories of individuals caught in difficult circumstances who were helped by their congregations and money from the Sharing Fund.

5. PROFESSIONALIZATION OF FIELD REPRESENTATIVES

The magnitude and complexity of the healthcare crisis in the 1980s clearly stretched the capacity of MMA congregational representatives, who were often at the front line of responding to policyholders angry or distraught over rising premiums. Early in 1985 marketing research by the MMA Distribution and Services department made it clear that this system of congregational volunteers, supported by twelve regional representatives—affectionately known as the "twelve apostles"—was not functioning very well, especially in the context of rapid changes in healthcare. "There is also strong support," the survey concluded, "for MMA to take a more assertive role in promoting its programs and services."[87] By the end of the year, Kratz announced that MMA would take a new approach to distribution and service by shifting to a system of trained "mutual aid counselors," perhaps as many as fifty altogether, who would be paid on a part-time basis to serve members and resource congregational representatives.[88] Local mutual aid committees would appoint these new, more professional counselors in consultation with their district conferences and with MMA. Under the new plan, the congregational representatives remained in place, as did the regional managers. But the primary task of the congregational volunteers—now renamed "advocates"—would be to promote MMA's fraternal and educational programs.[89] Mutual aid counselors trained and paid by MMA would be the ones to explain the intricacies of the changing healthcare plans and assist members in financial planning and retirement strategies.[90]

The transition was not easy, especially since some congregations—who were already frustrated with MMA for rising premiums—regarded it as an effort by MMA to distance itself from criticism. Though some congregational representatives lamented the loss of the small finder's fee they received when they helped new people sign up for an insurance product, most were happy with the change. The world of health insurance and financial management had simply become too complex, the stakes too high, to continue with an all-volunteer network of representatives.

6. CHURCHWIDE COMMUNICATION

Finally, as the healthcare crisis deepened in the late 1980s Kratz recognized that a more direct and coordinated system of communication with congregations and individual members was essential.

In the summer of 1988 a Communication Task Force—consisting of Jerry Troyer, Barth Hague, and Vyron Schmidt—outlined a plan that they called "Operation Contact." The initiative began with a feature article by James Kratz, published in the August 1988 issue of the *Gospel Herald*, that directly addressed the reality of escalating healthcare costs.[91] After reviewing the reasons behind the rise in medical expenses, Kratz assured readers that MMA had sufficient reserves to cover their recent operating losses; but he also was clear that the trends were ominous. Among MMA's various efforts to control costs, Kratz noted a move toward "stricter guidelines which assign a specific cost to the risk a person brings to the health plan"—a very indirect way of describing "underwriting." He closed by encouraging readers to take more responsibility for managing their own healthcare costs and by remaining loyal to MMA. "The broader our base of support, the greater is our ability to control costs and to share the burden."[92]

In a second phase of "Operation Contact" MMA board members, administrators, and managers hosted eight regional gatherings between November 28 and December 6, meeting directly with MMA policyholders to explain rate increases, reinforce the principle of mutual aid, and encourage continued membership in MMA healthcare plans.[93] The Communications Department also prepared an elaborate 1989 Rate Information Kit that tried to explain the realities regarding healthcare costs and the rationale for yet another hike in premiums.[94]

All of the communications sought to emphasize several key points. In the face of enormous headwinds, MMA was still committed to the principle of inclusion, despite the new underwriting policies. The messages also stressed MMA's long-term commitment to each member in their healthcare plans. In contrast to commercial insurance companies, it refused to target its most expensive members with drastic rate increases in order to create a pool of only healthy policyholders—"skimming and dumping are simply not the way we want to work."[95]

In the context of the hard economic choices that families were making around healthcare, it is unclear just how effective the communication strategy was.[96] But the overall strategy was effective. Following losses of nearly $4 million in 1988, the Mutual Aid Services department showed a surprising gain of $5.8 million in 1989 and of $3.6 million the following year, which not only helped to restore depleted reserves but also confidence that the program still had a future.

Conclusion

In the fall of 1982 the Mennonite Church General Board composed a summary of its recent "in-depth review of MMA."[97] Representatives of the board commended MMA for its work; but the overall tone of the response hinted at a concern that MMA was straying from its identity as a church-related agency. "Can a business the size of MMA promote mutual aid at a local level or does the very size of MMA deter such aid?" the report asked rhetorically. Board members asked why MMA did not provide low interest loans to church programs, noting that charging market rates "seems inconsistent with our brotherly understanding of mutual aid. General Board hopes that mutual aid, and not profit, will be the primary policy." They also critiqued MMA's wage policy, noting that it was "somewhat out of step with the other agencies and congregations" and encouraged the organization to "use some careful restraint in salary increases even though funding for such might be easily available." The report concluded with a critique veiled as an encouragement: "MMA needs to avoid a corporate mentality in its own operation by practicing mutual aid in line with its teaching. . . . we trust that MMA will keep its programs in harmony with the faith and practices of the Anabaptist Mennonite tradition."[98]

Eight years later, James Lapp, the executive secretary of the Mennonite Church General Board sounded a very different note. In an article published in both *Sharing* and the *Gospel Herald*, Lapp shifted the focus decisively to the church. The Mennonite church, he wrote is "at a moment of truth with regard to mutual aid." The biggest crisis facing MMA, Lapp argued, is not healthcare coverage. Rather "it is a crisis of the soul and identity as Mennonite people." "When there is an erosion in these core values of the Mennonite Church," Lapp continued, then MMA becomes simply one more organization that needs to compete with secular agencies in order to exist. . . . The church needs to realize that mutual aid is not a euphemism for inexpensive programs of care. Mutual aid is fundamental theological belief of the church."[99]

In the end, he concluded, history "will judge MMA not by its sale of products but by the degree to which it has helped embody and keep alive a vision for mutual aid in our congregations."[100]

As the decade of the 1980s came to a close, MMA found itself at a crossroads. Fifteen years earlier the organization had successfully negotiated a challenging transition, marked by a major internal review and the departure of Harold Swartzendruber. By the mid-1970s it was clear that the company could no longer be run like a small family business. The changing demands of the marketplace, the growing complexities of health insurance, the rapid growth of the Mennonite Foundation, and the entanglements of new regulations called for a new managerial style and organizational structure. Harold Swartzendruber had brought many entrepreneurial gifts to the expanding young organization; Dwight Stoltzfus and James Kratz served as a needed bridge generation, helping MMA move from a cluster of discrete enterprises to a modern organization—guided by strategic plans, increasingly reliant on new technology, and better suited to survive in a competitive environment.

But Stoltzfus and Kratz were the last of the "pastor CEOs." They served MMA during a time of profound economic and cultural transformation, marked most dramatically by tectonic shifts in the world of healthcare and the changing character of the Mennonite church. Now, new realities called once again for a new type of organization and a new type of leader. In 1991, Kratz had intimated to colleagues that he planned to retire in 1993. But a small group of friends quietly suggested that it might be better for him and the organization if he would move those plans forward a year.[101] Kratz graciously agreed, and announced that he would resign as MMA's president and CEO in January 1992. "MMA's strongest asset," Kratz reflected in a final interview, "is its link to the church. That is where we find our direction and correction. . . . As Mennonites have become more individualistic, MMA's message of caring and sharing becomes even more important. We are caretakers of something greater than ourselves."[102]

SIX

"Best of Business; Best of Church"

(1992–2005)

t the forty-second annual meeting of the Mennonite Health Assembly in April 1994, Jane White, executive editor of *Health Affairs*, a close observer of healthcare legislation, and a member of the First Mennonite Church of Hyattsville, Maryland, had some stern words for MMA and Mennonite Central Committee regarding their lobbying efforts in Washington, D.C., on the issue of healthcare reform. "Your lack of coordination," she admonished those representing the organizations, "will end up defeating both of your goals." "How we handle health care reform will tell us much about who we are as a church," White continued. "My hope is that we do not capitulate to the divisive tactics that I see daily in Washington."[1]

In the fall of 1992, Bill Clinton had won the U.S. presidential election campaigning on a promise of healthcare reform. The proposal that emerged, however, quickly became the focus of enormous public controversy, one that soon extended into a debate between two of the Mennonite church's most visible organizations: MMA and MCC, represented by its Washington Office.[2] On the surface, both MMA and MCC were united in their support for universal coverage. But behind the scenes their specific concerns diverged significantly. According to the details of the proposed Health Security Act (HSA), MMA would no longer be able to offer health insurance. So even as MMA supported the principle of universal coverage, it also was actively seeking an amendment to the bill that would allow MMA to continue operating as a fraternal benefit association, meaning that it would serve only Anabaptist-Mennonite groups. The primary concerns of the Washington Office of MCC, on the other hand, focused on access to healthcare for everyone, regardless of religious affiliation. And they advocated for a single-payer model.

In the heat of the debate, MMA found itself accused of simply seeking institutional self-preservation—turning its back on the Christian principles of the Anabaptist-Mennonite tradition. The critique stung, not only because it seemed to misrepresent MMA's repeated public support for universal health-care, but also because it suggested that defending a church-based approach to healthcare was somehow capitulating to a crass "business" model that called into question MMA's theological integrity.

The debate captured well a tension that MMA administrators had been actively and self-consciously trying to balance throughout the entire existence of the organization. What did it mean to be not just a church-related institu-tion, but a church-related business? During the past decade, Dwight Stoltzfus and James Kratz had agonized over the challenge of preserving the principle of mutual aid in the face of rapidly escalating healthcare costs. All along the way, the organization faced competing, even contradictory, expectations from Mennonite church members who alternately demanded that MMA be run as an efficient business—offering competitive services at discounted rates—while also seeing it as an extension of a compassionate church that would support uninsured members regardless of their preexisting conditions and regardless of the financial consequences to the organization.

The Best of Business and the Best of Church

Such was the highly-charged environment in which Howard Brenneman began his work in January 1992 as MMA's president and CEO. Trained as a businessman, yet deeply committed to the church, Brenneman brought a bold, confident faith to his work that was anchored in real life experience in the rough-and-tumble of the business world. More than any other previous CEO, Brenneman was ready to go "where the people go." His favorite phrase, repeated so often that it became something of a mantra, was the conviction that MMA could be "the best of business and the best of church."

Born in Tofield, Alberta, Howard Brenneman grew up on a farm outside Hesston, Kansas, where he was steeped in the world of midwestern Mennonites. Immediately after high school, he began working part time in the accounting

As president, Howard Brenneman changed the organization's culture to embrace its professional business side as well as its work in the church.

department of Hesston Manufacturing Company, an enterprise started by Lyle Yost in 1947 that was quickly expanding into a dynamic innovator of various farm-related implements.[3] In 1975, at the age of thirty-four, Brenneman became the company's president and COO, and he continued in corporate leadership even after the Italian conglomerate Fiat bought a controlling stake in the company in 1979.[4] During the farm crisis of the 1980s, however, when livestock prices plunged and farmers stopped buying hay and forage equipment, Fiat restructured the company. In 1986, Brenneman ended his tenure with Fiat and spent the next five years doing private consulting, including some work for MMA.[5]

In August 1991, with Kratz's retirement on the horizon, the MMA Executive Search Committee invited Brenneman to interview for the CEO position. He agreed, conferring with the committee in Chicago while on his way to a Mennonite Board of Education meeting.[6] Shortly thereafter, the search committee put his name forward as their top candidate.

When Brenneman assumed office on January 1, 1992, the character of the Mennonite Church was very different than it had been some fifty years earlier when MMA was first conceived. By the early 1990s all the pioneers in the field of mutual aid—among them Howard Raid, H. Ralph Hernley, C. L. Graber, Guy F. Hershberger, and Orie O. Miller—had passed from the scene. The Mennonite Church General Conference, once led by a powerful Executive Committee, had far less authority in the 1990s than it did in 1945. As the century drew to a close, all of the church's institutions—missions, publishing, education, service, and mutual aid—had their own boards, each with its own fundraising strategy, marketing campaigns, and brand identities that were increasingly independent of the denomination itself. Moreover, in 1992 the primary attention of denominational administrators was turning to the complex challenge of integrating and merging the Mennonite Church and the General Conference Mennonite Church, a task that consumed enormous resources of creative energy, time, and money.

Into this context Brenneman brought a new style of leadership. He was not afraid to speak openly of MMA's need to make profits—not as an end in itself, but as "coal for the engine," as he put it—that would ultimately enable MMA to better serve the church. He was pragmatic about the organization's need to "provide competitive products at competitive prices."[7] Under his leadership, the character of MMA was reoriented around fundamental business principles like strategic planning, creative marketing, aggressive growth, and the diversification of products and services, even as its ties to the church remained unmistakably clear. His slogan—"the best of business and the best of church"—quickly became ingrained into MMA's organizational culture.

Best of Business . . .

From the beginning, Brenneman regarded MMA as having highly talented staff, even if those gifts had not yet been fully expressed. His task, as he understood it, was to unleash the creativity of employees by giving them the freedom to exercise their talents in new ways. Thus, Brenneman set ambitious goals for the organization, while also granting senior leaders considerable latitude for determining exactly how they were going to achieve those goals. He put Karl Sommers, who had previously managed the actuarial department, in charge of planning and product development, and asked him to represent MMA's interests in Washington, D.C., in tracking the legislative battles around Clinton's Health Care Reform initiative. He assured Steve Garboden, who had developed considerable expertise as a healthcare analyst, that MMA would remain in the health insurance market. He gave Barth Hague liberty to develop a robust Marketing department; he supported heavy investments in computer technology; and he strongly promoted new products in the Financial Services department that would attract additional assets to manage, without which, he argued, there would be no resources for the fraternal funds and other forms of financial assistance that were essential to MMA's identity and mission.[8]

In 1995 Brenneman introduced a ten-year strategic plan, "From Success to Significance," that outlined a series of priorities for the coming decade. To be sure, the concept of strategic planning was not new. Dwight Stoltzfus, following the mandate from CMP consultants in 1977, had introduced five-year goals, individual performance evaluations, and annual departmental reviews. But "From Success to Significance" marked a new level of focus, detail, and public accountability for virtually every business aspect of MMA. Following a model popular among business consultants at the time, Brenneman and his staff drafted an imaginary report, written in the present tense, that listed MMA's accomplishments ten years in the future. The report described in great detail where MMA leaders envisioned the company, then worked backward, mapping out exactly what it would take to achieve those goals.[9]

In broad strokes, the 1995 strategic plan called for greater attention to marketing, a more diversified product line, quantitative measures to track growth, and a new model of MMA's relationship with the church.

MARKETING DILEMMAS

Brenneman's most immediate priority was to restore confidence among MMA's remaining members that the company had a bright future. Although the organization had lost nearly $4 million in 1988 during the worst of the healthcare crisis, MMA had taken significant steps to turn those losses around. Indeed, Brenneman began his tenure building on recent significant gains in the fraternal benefits programs, including healthcare.[10]

He and his team recognized that MMA needed to communicate more effectively with their core markets and to expand those markets to include other Anabaptist-Mennonite groups that might be attracted to MMA's products. Marketing, of course, had long been a delicate point for MMA. Previous CEOs had regarded the practice as a necessary evil. A 1977 MMA Statement on Marketing insisted that MMA's publicity should avoid any hint of competition with local Mennonite insurance salespeople, and called for the primary focus of all MMA communications to be on the principle of mutual aid rather than on MMA products.[11] Five years later a renewed effort to define marketing resulted in a policy that again consciously choose the language of *communication* and *education* over *advertising*.[12]

Brenneman, by contrast, was unabashed in his conviction that MMA needed to be more sensitive to the marketplace. "We need to listen to our customers and discover their needs," Brenneman stated confidently in an interview before his move to Goshen. "Then we need to put programs together that satisfy those needs and put them in the marketplace quickly and in an innovative way."[13] In his mind, the theme of mutual aid was meaningful only if MMA's products and services could also hold their own in a highly competitive marketplace.

A key person in the new marketing plan was Barth Hague, whom Brenneman promoted from Communications Manager to Director of Marketing. Hague— along with Steve Bowers, a former journalist at the *Goshen News* who joined the MMA communications team in 1988—began to conduct regular market surveys, polling MMA members, former members, and potential members about customer satisfaction, theological convictions, financial circumstances, and new or improved products that they might be looking for.[14] By the 1990s, most American industries, seeking new ways of differentiating themselves in a crowded marketplace, had identified customer service as a crucial component in retaining consumer loyalty. With a cultural lag typical of many Mennonite institutions, MMA now sought to catch up with the new attentiveness to customer needs by hiring additional support staff trained in the art of customer-centered communication skills.

Effective marketing also called for clear, simple, and consistent messages. MMA had always struggled to create a coherent identity that would encompass its various subsidiary companies. Most of the subsidiaries, for example, had their own letterhead, and several maintained their own database of mailing addresses.[15] In 1993, at the recommendation of the marketing department, MMA once again changed its logo, replacing the rounded triangular family outlines from 1982 with a simpler design that they hoped would generate a clearer sense of brand recognition across the organization. The new logo was now entirely abstract, consisting of a white triangle inscribed on a black square. Several horizontal lines ran behind and in front of the triangle, connoting a sense of motion.

Because the new marketing initiative consciously sought to extend its reach beyond traditional Mennonite communities to include other Anabaptist-related denominations, the marketing department also replaced the language of "Mennonite Mutual Aid" with the more generic "MMA."[16] Although newcomers to the organization might have struggled to understand the meaning of the acronym, the shift signaled Brenneman's clear intention to both extend MMA's market beyond Mennonites and to diversify the company beyond mutual aid to include a wide range of financial products and services.

The occasion of MMA's fiftieth anniversary in 1995 marked another key moment in the evolution of a more sophisticated marketing strategy. At the Mennonite Church's binational assembly in Wichita, Kansas, MMA created a display called "Imagine the Future," which sought to make it clear that MMA understood itself to be anchored in a much deeper story, rooted in the teachings of Jesus, the story of the early church, and the long arc of Anabaptist-Mennonite history. A video that accompanied the exhibit included cameos by mutual aid luminaries like Howard Raid, Carl Kreider, John Rudy, Dan Kauffman, and others. Clara Hershberger, for example, wife of Guy F. Hershberger, reminded viewers that change had been part of the character of MMA from the very beginning, recalling the line from Orie Miller that "just as the world is changing, the church must change; and as far as our conscience allows, we must go along and work with it." John Rudy, with characteristic congeniality, told viewers, "When it comes to the management of investment funds, we have always said that monies entrusted to us have got to be invested in harmony with what we believe. . . . [and] adhering to these ethical guidelines has not harmed our investment returns." Howard Raid described mutual aid as "an expression of the spiritual power of the love of God in our hearts."[17]

In addition to the exhibit, MMA also used the fiftieth anniversary moment to convene a group of scholars to reflect more systematically on the history and theology of MMA. The symposium and the volume of interdisciplinary essays that resulted from the gathering, titled *Building Communities of Compassion*, paid homage to J. Winfield Fretz, an early leader of the mutual aid movement.[18]

OUTREACH BEYOND THE MENNONITE MARKET

Brenneman recognized that if MMA was to grow as fast as the strategic plan envisioned, the organization would need to expand the scope of its membership. This would not have been a problem, of course, for an ordinary commercial insurance company. But as a fraternal benefit society, MMA was required by law to define its membership according to clear criteria. Noting that historians described sixteenth-century Anabaptism as a diverse movement encompassing a variety of expressions, Brenneman pushed for a more expansive definition of membership that would include all groups who shared Anabaptist-Mennonite values even if—like the Quakers—they may not be able to trace a direct historical link to the Radical Reformation of the sixteenth century. Throughout the 1990s Brenneman worked hard to expand MMA's umbrella to include Anabaptist-related groups across a broad theological spectrum. To be sure, not all of these groups officially identified MMA as the preferred financial institution for their membership. But the more relaxed definition of MMA membership accurately reflected a growing diversity within virtually all Anabaptist-Mennonite groups, as the sharp boundaries of the past became more porous. In the spring of 2002, the MMA board broadened its

MMA expanded its relationships with more church networks and denominations, which allowed more people like Shawn and Katrina McConaughey, from Boise Friends Church, to participate.

membership to include—at least in principle—members from the Brethren in Christ, Missionary Church, Conservative Mennonite Conference, and Evangelical Mennonite Church. "With this move," Brenneman noted, "more Anabaptist members will have a direct voice in MMA."[19]

At the same time, however, the shift raised a series of questions that all church-related institutions were facing. Was the distinctive theological character of MMA—its margin of difference—anchored primarily in the qualities of its products and services? the denominational identity of its leadership? or by the market that the institution served?[20]

NEW INITIATIVES IN HEALTH INSURANCE

The healthcare crisis of the 1980s revealed that the principle of mutual aid, which had animated the founding of MMA in 1945, was no longer a central priority for church members—or, at the very least, that the church's commitment to support the health needs of all its members had real limits. Nevertheless, health insurance remained a major portion of MMA's identity and income. So the first order of business was a review and overhaul of the organization's various health insurance plans. The simplest product, requiring the least attention, was MMA's Medicare Supplement plan—an insurance policy designed to help older adults close the gap between Medicare's coverage and their actual medical costs. MMA's pool of insured older adults tended to be somewhat healthier than the general population. And since the demographics were skewing toward a rising number of older people, this plan was comparatively stable. In the decades that followed, Medicare Supplement would continue to be a steady source of revenue as MMA solidified its reserves and expanded its programs.

MMA's traditional healthcare plan—the Medical Expense Sharing Plan— functioned very similarly to other standard health insurance plans, offering a wide range of options for deductibles before the plan kicked in to cover 80 percent of medical expenses. The new TeamCare health insurance plan continued those basic principles, including underwriting, but now focused especially on

Nurses by training, Renee Miller (left) and Carolyn Lichti worked with members who had significant health issues to help them manage expenses. STEVE ECHOLS

controlling costs. Brenneman, for example, negotiated cost reductions through the use of Preferred Provider Organizations that included hospitals in key Mennonite communities. The TeamCare plan also required members to seek preapproval for major medical procedures, and MMA staff members closely tracked the billing and healthcare decisions of the small percentage of policyholders whose medical costs accounted for the majority of claims. The introduction of TeamCare brought MMA's main healthcare plan into closer alignment with other companies and clearly helped to slow accelerating costs.[21]

A third significant aspect of MMA health insurance in the 1990s, albeit one with an uncertain future, were various group plans designed for congregations, small businesses, or church-related institutions that pooled the health insurance risks of a defined group. The congregational plans had once been at the heart of the mutual aid principle since they ensured that a substantial group of healthy members would absorb the costs of high-risk individuals who were guaranteed inclusion. During the 1980s, many of these plans consolidated with larger regional pools in order to share their risks more broadly. The local groups were self-insured for small claims, but could draw on the resources of the regional pool for larger claims and on MMA for administrative assistance and as a backstop for catastrophic coverage. By the early 1990s, however, many of these plans were in danger of collapsing, usually because a critical mass of participants had found health insurance through their work or had opted for cheaper premiums with commercial insurance companies. The plans that persisted survived by adopting the principles of the TeamCare approach.

The real growth of the group plans in the 1990s—now organized under the heading of ShareNet—was in small businesses and in church-related institutions, reflecting the larger trend of employees seeking healthcare insurance through their employers. According to the regulations governing a fraternal benefit association, if the owner of a business qualified for MMA membership, the business could secure health insurance for all its employees, even if they were not members of an Anabaptist-Mennonite church. The same was true for church-related institutions such as colleges, hospitals, nursing homes, or mission agencies. In the fall of 1994, MMA also introduced a new group insurance plan for pastors—the Congregational Employee Plan—that waived many of the underwriting restrictions of its other policies in an effort to ensure access to health insurance for church leaders who might not otherwise qualify anywhere else. All of these plans required sophisticated actuarial analysis; and, like all insurance plans, they could function only if they included a high percentage of relatively healthy members.

When healthcare costs, which had stabilized in the mid-1990s, began to rapidly escalate again later in the decade, MMA promoted the newly-created Medical Savings Accounts, which allowed policyholders to direct pretax income into a savings account that was restricted to medical expenses.[22]

Even though MMA found ways to keep its healthcare plans afloat in the 1990s, profound challenges remained. A new life insurance plan, introduced in 1996, never found traction.[23] Although MMA generally did not lose money with the ShareNet plans, the pools were rarely large enough to adequately control for risks, and the plans constantly struggled with groups dropping out if, in any given year, they could find a cheaper offer from a competing company. The growing complexity of health insurance and the ongoing uncertainty in the national debate over the future role of the government made it clear that MMA would need to develop other products and services if it was to remain viable. Thus, Brenneman's attention turned to the financial services side of the organization, and particularly to the interest that the growing demographic of older MMA members were expressing in financial planning, retirement, and philanthropy.

DIVERSIFICATION—PRAXIS MUTUAL FUNDS AND THE FORMATION OF A TRUST COMPANY

In 1994, MMA took a bold step by entering the world of mutual fund investments with the introduction the MMA Praxis Mutual Funds. Individuals who buy shares of a mutual fund pool their money with other investors hoping that a diversified set of stocks or bonds, overseen by a knowledgeable portfolio manager, will be a safer investment than speculating on a limited number of specific investments. From the beginning, the distinctive aspect of MMA Praxis Mutual Funds was its commitment to what became known as Socially Responsible Investing (SRI)—investing only in companies whose products and practices were consistent with a set of ethical criteria that the investor could affirm.

MMA had long been committed to ethical screens for its own investments.[24] Since the mid-1980s, MMA's fund managers had adhered to a set of Investment Guidelines, reviewed every five years, that defined the principles guiding its investment choices. It was one thing for MMA to invest its own assets according to clear ethical criteria. But a growing number of MMA's members were also looking for similar options for their investments in personal retirement funds or college savings accounts. Given the success of the Pax World Fund and the broader interest in the emerging SRI

Deepening and broadening MMA's expertise in socially responsible investing, Mark Regier raised the profile of the organization's faith-oriented investment approach. Mark (third from left) was part of a delegation who visited Juarez, Mexico, to meet with Johnson & Johnson about sustainable wages for workers.

movement, MMA leaders began to explore the possibility of creating their own mutual fund.

MMA officially launched the MMA Praxis Mutual Funds on December 30, 1993. Praxis offered clients two options of socially screened investments: intermediate income (bonds) and a growth fund (stocks). J. B. Miller, a young banker from Florida who joined MMA's Financial Services division in 1990, became the first president of Praxis. Keith Yoder joined as the stock fund manager and Del King as the intermediate income manager. Both of the funds started with an initial investment of $10 million from MMA, and hoped to provide new investors with returns comparable to the Standard & Poor's 500 index.

The year 1994 was a challenging time to be entering a highly competitive field. Understanding the market well enough to identify companies that showed potential for growth, while balancing risks with appropriate caution, was hard enough. But managers of MMA Praxis were also committed to screening those investments according to the SRI criteria, which called for a great deal of additional research. If whole industries were going to be excluded from the mutual fund portfolio—defense contractors, for example, or casinos, or manufacturers of alcohol and tobacco—the returns were likely not going to reflect the same fluctuations as the major market indexes.[25] Between 1994 and 2000, the stock market was also heavily influenced by the "dot-com boom"—a period of excessive speculation in technology companies whose products catered to the seemingly-infinite promise of the Internet. Initially, Yoder was skeptical about the ability of tech stocks to fulfill the promise of fast growth embedded in their high prices, preferring a more cautious value investing approach.[26] So in the late 1990s, performance of the Praxis growth fund lagged significantly behind the bull market. When the tech bubble burst in the spring of 2000, MMA's strategy was vindicated as the market once again favored established companies that generated real profits. But many early investors remembered the sluggish performance of the Praxis stock fund during the boom years of the late 1990s, and continued to express skepticism long after the fund had recovered.

Over time, MMA Praxis Mutual Funds became well known as a pioneer in the world of Socially Responsible Investing. Building on the foundation of J. B. Miller, John Liechty, who assumed leadership of MMA's Investment Services in 1997, and Mark Regier, previously a seminary student with a background in marketing, collaborated to make SRI a central feature of MMA's identity. In addition to the research needed to screen investments, Liechty and Regier correctly sensed that their approach to values-driven investing would bring positive publicity to MMA at a time when the dominant image of Wall Street was selfishness and greed. Regier nurtured relationships with a wide range of other investment firms who were also screening for values. He soon became an enthusiastic participant on behalf of MMA in the Forum for Sustainable and Responsible Investment, particularly in the International Working Group, and later represented MMA in the Interfaith Center for Corporate Responsibility.

Although the SRI component of the Praxis Fund family could generate internal debates, the program brought significant assets to the organization. It also elevated MMA's profile in the broader investment world, and, most importantly, it enabled MMA to diversify its financial services in a way that was consistent with its identity and commitments as a faith-based organization.[27]

TRUST COMPANY

Another crucial component of MMA's expanding financial services department was the formation of a trust company. Trust companies act on behalf of a person or business to administer assets "entrusted" to them. A trust company, for example, might serve as the executor of an estate, or handle the sale of a family business, or oversee investments and disbursement of funds set aside for minors. Located at the intersection of banking services, tax law, charitable giving, and inheritance law, trust companies are complex entities, operating under the watchful scrutiny of a host of federal and state regulators. For MMA, establishing a trust company seemed like a natural progression from its long experience with Mennonite Foundation and the financial advising services that it had offered its members for decades.

MMA celebrated the 2001 opening of its trust company with an all-staff photo.

Once again, Brenneman turned to J. B. Miller to start the complex process. The first step was to establish a federal savings and loan bank charter through the Office of Thrift Supervision. This would allow MMA to offer a full range of trust and investment services, including estate administration, IRA rollovers, and customized investment management. As that process was moving forward, Brenneman hired Rod Diller, who brought extensive experience in the trust department of a local Goshen bank, as a senior vice president to complete the process and to lead the newly-established company.

On June 1, 2001, MMA formally established the MMA Trust Company, Inc. In the following years, the trust company played a crucial role in integrating the Mennonite Foundation, financial advising services, and a host of other related activities as a more coherent part of the larger MMA mission. Like the MMA Praxis Mutual Fund, the Trust Company also brought more assets to MMA; and it helped to diversify the organization at a time when the future of health insurance was uncertain. But it also signaled a move into a more complex financial world that reflected the changing reality of the Anabaptist-Mennonite community—going "where the people go."

IMPROVED SALES AND DISTRIBUTION SYSTEM

Early in MMA's history, the organization relied heavily on local pastors and then on volunteer congregational representatives to represent its products and to assist members with the paperwork associated with claims. In the mid-1980s, however, as insurance policies became more complex and states were becoming increasingly strict in their licensing requirements for insurance representatives, MMA began a shift away from congregational volunteers toward a more professionalized model of sales and distribution.

Brenneman embraced this new model of distribution, believing that the volume of sales would increase if MMA policies were sold by licensed agents and that it was good for MMA to compete in the open market alongside other commercial products. In the early 1990s he aggressively expanded the new approach, as MMA entered into a series of complex agreements with numerous independent agencies in various Mennonite-Anabaptist communities. By 1996, MMA was working with 160 counselors scattered across the country, who were all fully licensed as insurance agents and financial representatives. In theory at least, these independent sales agents faithfully represented MMA products within the context of a larger faith-driven understanding of mutual

MMA increased its relationships with professional representatives in the field. In April 1996, this counselor training class included, left to right (front row): Terry Hoke (Pa.), Charlene Haines (Ohio), Sylvia Sutherland (Va.), Amanda Soper (Pa.), (back row) Kevin Wiens (Kans.), Duane Wohlgemuth (Kans.), Brian Bertsche (Ohio), Carey Goossen (Okla.), and Bob Martin (Pa.). EVERENCE

aid and stewardship. In practice, however, the representation was often uneven, with many sales representatives seeing MMA products as potentially useful when meeting with Mennonite clients, but not necessarily as part of a larger commitment to Christian stewardship. To be fair, the agencies were not always clear how they were accountable to MMA, since they related at various points with congregational advocates, MMA field representatives, Mennonite Foundation representatives, and a variety of trust and investment advisors at the MMA home office. But in the context of a rapidly-changing and competitive marketplace, the new model was consistent with a larger trend in MMA toward greater professionalization.

Best of Church . . .

RELATIONS WITH A NEWLY-STRUCTURED MENNONITE CHURCH

Although Brenneman was most comfortable in his role as a business executive, his commitment to keep MMA closely related to the church always remained firmly in focus. Some aspects of this relationship were woven into MMA's very organizational structure. As an agency of the Mennonite Church, for example, MMA executives reported regularly to denominational leaders; they made highly visible appearances at the church's biennial assemblies; and the organization was subject to periodic in-depth reviews by the denomination's executive committee. In addition, Mennonite Church leaders nominated a majority of the MMA board members, and the denomination regularly claimed MMA as an extension of its own mission and witness.

Yet beneath these structural links, the nature of MMA's relation to the church was rapidly changing during the last decades of the twentieth century. By the late 1990s, for example, MMA's assets dwarfed those of other church agencies, most of which were struggling to meet their budgets. The Mennonite Foundation had come to play a crucial role in transferring wealth to church-related institutions like missions and education.[28] And subsidies from MMA's fraternal funds had become a significant percentage of the denomination's revenue. At the same time, several major studies on churchwide giving suggested that support for the church's institutions—and denominational loyalty in general—was ebbing, especially among younger people.

SUPPORT FOR DENOMINATIONAL INTEGRATION

Partly in response to these concerns, leaders of the two largest Mennonite groups in North America—the Mennonite Church (MC) and the General

Conference Mennonite Church (GC)—took steps in the late 1990s to merge their two bodies into a new denomination, a process in which MMA was to play a major role.

The story of that merger was dominated by the difficult challenge of integrating the institutions and distinctive cultures of the two denominations in a fair and efficient way.[29] During that delicate process, MMA provided crucial support by extending significant financial subsidies for the associated legal and administrative costs and by offering the services of Karl Sommers to oversee the process as a half-time consultant to MC-GC church leaders.[30] From 1997 to 2001, Sommers played a key role in the merger, helping institutional leaders, pastors, organizational consultants, and lawyers address a host of difficult questions about how the parallel denominational agencies might be integrated.[31] MMA itself was spared much of the pain associated with the integration process, since there was no clear parallel organization within the General Conference Mennonite church. But it was not a simple matter to clarify details of polity, governance, and authority within the new structure. In 2001, the process officially culminated in the creation of Mennonite Church USA (MC USA), with MMA now defined as "the stewardship agency of MC USA."

THE CARVER MODEL INTRODUCED TO THE BOARD

As Sommers and the executive committee of the newly-created MC USA attempted to unravel the details associated with the merger, it became clear that there were other organizational issues—structural and cultural—that also needed to be addressed, particularly regarding the role of the Executive Board in the new denomination. In June of 2000, the MC USA Executive Board voted to adopt a model made popular in the 1990s through the work of John Carver, known as "policy governance." A few months later the MMA board did the same and Sommers became a credentialed consultant of the Policy Governance Academy and the leading advocate for the new approach.

The theory of Policy Governance is deceptively simple. Organizations function best, Carver argued, when their boards focus less on management and more on the "owners" of the organization they are called to represent, seeking to translate owner expectations into measurable results. They do this by being extremely clear about the organization's purpose and outcomes (what Carver called "ends"). Healthy boards make expectations of behavior among board members very explicit ("governance process"); they are clear about the delegation of authority (the "board-CEO connection"); and they make a sharp distinction between *operations*, which are the responsibility of the CEO, and *governance*, which resides with the board. The board stays out of the details of how the CEO achieves the results, except to define the means that are explicitly unacceptable ("executive limitations"). Because board members frequently change and because clearly established procedures can prevent communication breakdowns and unhealthy maneuvering, Policy Governance requires boards to spell out in painstaking detail their understanding of each of these four elements. So from 2001 to 2004, the MMA board labored to define their ends, their governance process, the nature of the board-CEO linkage, and the CEO limitations.[32]

The Carver model clearly had some advantages. It forced the MMA board to return to first principles and to define the mission of the organization in very explicit language. In so doing, the MMA board reaffirmed that the churches it represented were the owners of the organization and structured its meetings to include regular input from denominational staff members, pastors, and thought-leaders.[33] Clarifying the "ends" also sharpened the board's understanding of each aspect of MMA's complex organization and prompted it to create clear criteria for assessing the performance of its products and services. How, for example, was mutual aid or stewardship to be defined? If these principles had ongoing value, how should they be monitored or assessed? Did the fraternal benefit program qualify as mutual aid or was it really charity? Addressing these, and many other similar questions, was a salutary exercise for board members.

Reading through the MMA board minutes from 2000 to 2010 one cannot help but be impressed by the earnestness with which the board set about to implement policy governance. Although the model came under critique for its mechanistic rigor, the initiative did force the MMA board to define its role in much more explicit language and to be more transparent about the overarching goals they wanted the organization to pursue.[34]

MMA: THE STEWARDSHIP AGENCY OF MENNONITE CHURCH USA

The process of denominational integration might have been the occasion for MMA to spin off from the church as an independent organization. Instead, MMA publicly embraced its new identity as the stewardship agency of MC USA in the opening decade of the new century, claiming stewardship education as a central focus of its mission. Stewardship, of course, was not a new theological concept. Anabaptist-Mennonites had been using the term since at least the 1930s.[35] But Brenneman elevated stewardship to a central theme in MMA's strategic plan.

In contrast to mutual aid, stewardship was an expansive concept. It pointed first to a theological awareness that humans were not owners but merely stewards of the resources entrusted to them by God. And it implied a clear responsibility for Christians to tend those resources carefully, without prescribing exactly how that would look in practice. Stewardship could mean radical and sacrificial generosity; but it could also evoke the parable of the talents, which suggested that gifts should be multiplied rather than hoarded. Stewardship encompassed resources beyond money or traditional financial assets, like time, talents, or health. Stewardship could mean thoughtful planning for retirement that ensured you would not become a financial burden on your children or congregation; or an insurance plan against catastrophic healthcare costs that could lead a family to bankruptcy; or a commitment to investing only in companies whose practices conformed to a set of ethical criteria.

One expression of stewardship in the 1990s focused on health. To be sure, MMA leaders had long recognized the importance of preventative medicine. Already in the 1950s, H. Clair Amstutz, a local Goshen physician who sat on various MMA boards, was writing a regular column in Mennonite periodicals that underscored the importance of diet and exercise as an expression of a healthy Christian life. In the 1970s and 1980s the editors of *Sharing* magazine featured numerous articles on preventative health, particularly in response to rising healthcare costs and the industry-wide recognition that even small health-related changes in large pools of insured people could significantly reduce medical expenses. But in the 1990s, MMA's focus on the stewardship of health took on a new level of urgency. Virtually every issue of *Sharing* magazine, for example, included some reference to stress management, weight loss, or the benefits of regular exercise. When studies by the Mennonite Automobile Aid revealed that Mennonite drivers were just as likely to cause accidents as other groups, MMA incorporated safe driving under its stewardship rubric.

A series of brochures and seminars encouraged patients in the healthcare system to question their family doctor about the utility of various tests, or to demand greater clarity regarding billing, including a careful review of itemized expenses. On the surface, these admonitions reflected basic consumer common sense—the sort of thing that most people would do before contracting services with a plumber or a car mechanic. But the culture of the doctor-patient relationship in the United States suggested that it was unseemly for patients to ever question the doctor's "orders." And frank conversations with physicians about pricing structures or comparative costs seemed to turn a relationship built on trust into a commodity. But as the challenge of controlling healthcare costs escalated, such conversations became imperative—an extension of what it meant to be a good steward of one's health and money.

In the spring of 1997, MMA undertook a comprehensive revision of its Wellness Program and launched a new series of booklets, edited by Kelli Burkholder King, called the Healthy Living Series. Each of the booklets in the series explored some aspect of stewardship around the general theme of "Keeping Mind, Body, and Spirit Well." In 1999 the series, now renamed "Stewardship for Life," expanded to include additional material on mental illness and physical disabilities.

Another educational initiative that had significant implications for controlling medical costs focused on the realities of death and dying. With the introduction of specialized treatments for end-stage heart disease or various forms of cancer, hospitals could keep people alive long after there was any reasonable hope for recovery. These developments in medical technology raised new awareness about quality of life, and the amount of resources that were being spent in the final stages of life to postpone the inevitability of death. These were all complex questions, of course, touching on finances, ethics, emotions, and religious convictions. MMA educators, collaborating extensively with medical experts, theologians, and pastors, framed the dialogue in the context of stewardship, reminding Christians that death is not the final word and encouraging families and individuals to make deliberate choices about end-of-life care rather than leaving those decisions in the hands of hospitals or insurance companies. MMA actively encouraged all of its members to prepare advance directives, to formalize a will, and to bring their financial affairs into order. [36] A book sponsored by MMA on these themes, *Medical Ethics: Human Choices*, sold nearly twelve thousand copies in five years.[37]

One of the most visible MMA initiatives to promote stewardship in the 1990s was Brenneman's decision to employ Lynn Miller as a full-time stewardship minister. A gifted pastor, teacher, and storyteller with a colorful life history, Miller brought a passionate commitment to simple living. In 1997, after serving for a time as the denomination's "Firstfruits Teacher," Miller joined the MMA staff. Miller's infectious enthusiasm and vivid imagination for practical application made his presentations memorable. Although his critique of capitalism and consumerism irritated some listeners, his teachings were deeply theological and firmly grounded in Scripture. For nearly a decade, Miller pursued an itinerant ministry, popularizing the Stewardship Wheel, a visual representation of holistic stewardship. He also worked closely with the SRI component of the Praxis Mutual Fund, and he wrote several books on themes

Stewardship Minister Lynn Miller traveled across the country, delivering his memorable teachings, including "Stewardship is the act of organizing your life so that God can spend you."

of generosity and simple living.[38] "Stewardship," Miller was fond of saying, "is the act of organizing your life so that God can spend you."[39]

In an effort to bring the theme of stewardship even more centrally into the forefront of its public identity, MMA introduced a new educational initiative in the fall of 2000 called Stewardship University. The concept behind Stewardship University was that of extension education—MMA would design a full curriculum of classes around the theme of stewardship, provide teachers, and host a weekend of seminars in Mennonite communities throughout North America, enabling ordinary church members to work their way through the curriculum.[40] Mark Vincent, who had assumed the role as Director of Stewardship Ministries for MMA in August, 1999, took initiative in designing the curriculum. In addition, MMA stewardship staff promoted *Good $ense Ministry*, a nondenominational curriculum rooted in biblical principles that offered free counsel on budgeting and financial management for MMA members who needed assistance with their personal finances.[41]

FRATERNAL BENEFIT FUNDS

By the late 1990s, the amount of money available for redistribution in MMA's fraternal benefits fund had grown to more than $3 million per year. Approximately 60 percent of the money was set aside in the Sharing Fund for direct support of needy members at the congregational level. In 1992, Brenneman appointed Phyllis Mishler to manage the Sharing Fund program and encouraged her to make the fund more visible.[42] In 2004, $1.8 million in Sharing Fund (leveraged to $3.13 million with congregational matches) benefited 1,158 churches and 3,316 households.

The remainder of the fraternal funds supported a wide range of specific programs administered either by MMA, the denominations represented on MMA's board, or other church-related institutions.[43] In the Mennonite Church, for example, the fraternal funds regularly supported projects related to the Mennonite Minorities Council. The Community Service Grant helped congregations fund local projects such as preschool programs or food pantries; the Annuity Scholarship Program awarded modest student grants to families who held MMA annuities; the Urban Initiative Fund designated funds for inner-city projects; and the Pastoral Leadership Program supported seminary students as well as pastors who were pursuing continuing education. In 1994 MMA created the Community Development Investment program that offered low interest loans to housing projects, especially in urban centers. Ten years later, in 2004, MMA reported that it had invested $10 million in the program.

In 1998 MMA enacted a policy of adding an annual tithe of 10 to 30 percent of the net gain from each of its corporate entities to the fraternal fund; and MMA staff devoted enormous energy to ensure that the money they dispersed reflected the priorities of the church and members they served.[44] In so doing

Phyllis Mishler, as Sharing Fund Manager, had the pleasure of giving millions in grant dollars to people in need, matched by congregational gifts. STEVE ECHOLS

MMA modeled the same principles of stewardship it was promoting to the broader church.

It is difficult to assess the long-term impact of MMA's educational programs on the church. But the resolute focus on stewardship—and on holistic ways of thinking about money, time, talents, and health—was clearly the leading edge of the organization's public identity throughout the 1990s.

The Model Challenged: Healthcare Reform, Legislative Engagement, Dissenting Voices

Brenneman's motto of "the best of business and the best of church" succinctly captured the new confidence and energy that characterized MMA during his early years as CEO. Yet understandings of how to define "the best of business" or "the best of church" differed, sometimes widely. Nowhere were these tensions more apparent than in the public debate that unfolded in the late 1990s around MMA's position regarding national healthcare reform. The controversy over national healthcare reform raised significant questions about Christian faith and witness that pointed toward deeper tensions within the wider Anabaptist-Mennonite community.

In the presidential election of 1992, Bill Clinton was swept into office in part because he promised the American people fundamental reforms in the area of healthcare. The aims of his proposal seemed beyond reproach: promote better health, prevent health insurance companies from denying coverage to sick people, and solve the primary cause of bankruptcy in the United States by making health insurance available to everyone.

But, as with all complex social problems, the devil was in the details.

At the center of the Clinton healthcare proposal was a vision of replacing the employer-based model of health insurance with a series of regional health alliances, operated by states, that would control costs and oversee plans. Under the Health Security Act (HSA), employers would pay 80 percent of insurance premiums, with individuals funding the remainder. Private insurance companies that wanted to remain in business would need to accept all applicants without conditions and regardless of preexisting conditions.

Although MMA had quickly expressed support for the principle of universal healthcare, the Clinton plan posed a problem. As a fraternal benefit society, MMA was required to restrict its membership to a defined group of people—the Anabaptist-Mennonite community of churches. If the legislation went forward, MMA would have to give up its fraternal status, and with it the fraternal benefit dollars that many regarded as essential to the organization's identity.

Xuan-Huong Thi Pham (Lisa) became an advocate for her congregation, Vietnamese Christian Fellowship, Falls Church, Va. The church used Sharing Fund grants to help refugees who left Vietnam after the Vietnam War and who had experienced financial needs in resettlement.
MARK BEACH

Brenneman was optimistic that a legislative amendment could be found that would enable MMA to maintain its existing health plan, and he appointed Karl Sommers to serve as the organization's liaison in Washington, D.C., working alongside a lobbyist hired by the Fraternal Benefit Association.[45]

Throughout 1993, as Karl Sommers was meeting with lobbyists and lawmakers, MCC's Peace Section office in Washington, D.C., had been actively rallying support among allies and its own Mennonite constituents for alternative legislation that would fund a national healthcare plan with public money—the so-called single-payer model. When it became clear that MMA was seeking an exemption from the HSA model and, furthermore, that the majority of MMA members did not support a single-payer system, the stage was set for a public controversy that seemed to pit MCC against MMA.[46] Although both organizations endorsed the fundamental principle of universal coverage, critics of MMA quickly framed the differences in theological language. MMA, they argued, was only interested in institutional preservation and the self-interests of its Anabaptist-Mennonite members. By contrast, in its support for nationalized healthcare, MCC was taking the high road in advocating on behalf of all marginalized people.

By the summer of 1994, several meetings among MMA and MCC leaders had clarified their positions in an amicable way. But the controversy revealed a political and cultural divide in the Anabaptist-Mennonite world that would persist and deepen in the coming decades. In the end, the Clinton healthcare legislation ultimately failed in Congress. MMA lived on as a fraternal organization, and the national healthcare crisis would continue to simmer for another generation.

DISSENTING VOICES AND TENSIONS

In the midst of the debate over strategies for healthcare reform, Ted Koontz, a professor of ethics at Associated Mennonite Biblical Seminary and newly-appointed member of the MMA board, posed a series of even more substantive criticisms. In July of 1993, a year after his appointment, Koontz sent a lengthy letter to other members of the MMA Board outlining his disquietude with several aspects of MMA's corporate culture and strategic directions.[47] Koontz framed his concerns within the larger context of Christian ethics—specifically, his assumption that "if we believe that Christian ethics make a difference, then it seems reasonable to assume that a church organization should operate in some ways differently from those organizations which have no connection to the Christian faith."[48] Although MMA had been running ads in various church papers calling attention to its "margin of difference," Koontz was not convinced that MMA's products and policies were actually that different from its secular counterparts. His long list of pointed questions included the following:

1. MMA's emphasis on estate planning and deferred giving was in tension with the biblical call to give generously and spontaneously out of one's firstfruits. The church had immediate needs; yet MMA's charitable giving model promoted a "last fruits" mentality that encouraged hoarding, with charitable gifts deferred until late in life after assurances that one's own needs were met.

2. MMA's emphasis on retirement planning also encouraged asset accumulation, which increased the gap between the rich and the poor in Anabaptist-Mennonite communities and congregations. Instead, Koontz challenged MMA to promote programs of wealth redistribution that would reduce the number of fellow church members who were living below the poverty line.

3. Behind MMA's understanding of stewardship as "the wise management of financial resources" was an assumed goal of independence or self-sufficiency that seemed to "directly undermine the sense of mutual vulnerability, mutual care, and mutual reliance, which is at the base of community and of mutual aid." "If all we at MMA do in helping with estate planning is to 'crunch numbers,' using the standing forecasting models in the financial planning industry,"

Koontz asked his fellow MMA board members, "why should we bother to do this as a church institution?"[49]

Koontz followed up his written concerns with numerous personal meetings with board members and MMA leaders, offering a series of constructive suggestions along with his critique.[50]

Although Koontz eventually resigned from the MMA board in frustration, Brenneman did embrace his suggestion that MMA host a major study conference on mutual aid and stewardship.[51] Many of the presentations at the academic symposium that ensued in 1996 celebrated the continuity of MMA's work within the long Anabaptist-Mennonite tradition of mutual aid and stewardship. Yet several of the contributors picked up on Koontz's concerns. In an essay titled "Mutual Aid as 'Practice'", for example, Joseph Kotva, Jr., a Mennonite philosopher active in the field of healthcare ethics, argued that MMA had failed in its mandate at the point when the fraternal benefits programs began to overshadow voluntary contributions and the organization started to screen applicants with preexisting illnesses in its health insurance policies.[52] In another essay, Keith Graber Miller, a professor of ethics at Goshen College, made a similar argument, suggesting that at its core MMA was no different than secular insurance agencies.[53] Donald Kraybill, one of the volume's editors, responded to the critique with a thoughtful defense of MMA's "margin of difference;" but the sense that something fundamental had changed in the organization since its beginnings in 1945 could not be shaken.[54] "My fear," reflected Richard Reimer, MMA board chair at the time of the symposium, "is that as we become more and more acclimated to mainstream middle America, we will accept the values of a people who appear to be concerned mainly about their own financial well being, and that we may well lose sight of our heritage of mutual aid."[55] Steve Bowers, senior editor on the Marketing team, articulated a position that was somewhere in the middle. "One of the primary assets of MMA," he suggested,

> is that it is not strictly a business. It is an organization with a strong religious foundation. . . . We go the extra mile beyond the legal agreement. But helping meet the needs of the people in the church also requires that MMA act as a responsible business. . . . Bankruptcy is not good stewardship. The result is an MMA that often finds itself caught in the middle of the conflict between the church and the world. . . . Standing on that fault line. . . is often a very uncomfortable position for MMA and the Mennonite Foundation . . . [but this is] exactly where MMA and the Mennonite Foundation need to be.[56]

The Best of Business and Church: Healthcare Access and the Emergence of the Corinthian Plan

As the twentieth century drew to a close it became clear that the national healthcare crisis that generated so much public debate in the mid-1990s was not going to be quickly resolved. Few people defended a system that left so many Americans without health insurance or forced them into bankruptcy when overwhelmed with medical bills. But the political debate over the government's role in funding healthcare and in shaping decisions about end-of-life treatment had become toxic. Those deep disagreements were also reflected among MMA's own members. Indeed, part of what made the heated exchange between MCC and MMA over the Clinton plan so painful was the fact that both groups could claim to be representing the voice of their Anabaptist-Mennonite constituents.

Still, even as hopes for a national solution dimmed, MMA and others continued to seek common ground within the church. In 2001, a series of surveys and focus groups conducted by the Anabaptist Center for Healthcare Ethics (ACHE) concluded that healthcare costs and access were among the most important concerns of MC USA members. At the MC USA delegate assembly in 2003, the church called for a resolution clarifying the church's position on healthcare and a plan that would "demonstrate our commitment, as a community of faith, to universal access to health care."[57]

The form that this plan should take was left unclear. On the one hand, the resolution stipulated that it should incorporate the principle of "access to health care for all persons." Then it immediately qualified that ambitious goal by recognizing that "the starting point in this project will be Anabaptist congregations and the lives they touch." The model was to include an emphasis on health promotion, healing, and caring, along with a "recognition of our mortality and the limits required by stewardship of scarce resources."[58]

In the fall of 2003, ACHE recruited nineteen people from across the church—healthcare professionals, leaders of provider organizations, ethicists, theologians, and MMA representatives—to carry out the assignment. In February of 2005 the group presented a draft resolution to the MC USA Executive Committee. The language was bold, describing the national healthcare system as "sick." It "suffers from complexity, greed, racism, fear of death, and lack of concern for the common good."[59] The draft statement went on to commend the services of MMA, while also noting the "uncharitable character of commercial underwriting practices which it has had to adopt." It called on Mennonite employers to provide employees with fair wages and benefits, "including access to health insurance coverage for employees and their dependents." To the government, the statement insisted that "healthcare is a basic need for all people, . . . not a luxury reserved for the privileged." Although the draft stopped short of advocating for a universal healthcare plan, it did call for an extension of Medicare and the State Children's Health Insurance Program, and encouraged a careful study of alternative healthcare models in other countries.

By April, however, the language of the resolution had undergone significant revisions, particularly in regard to public policy. In a section headed "Our Witness," specific recommendations to the government were eliminated and replaced with the phrase: "We join other faith-based communities in urging our government to establish policy for a system of healthcare in which everyone, everywhere in the United States has access to basic, affordable healthcare, and where the risks and expenses are shared by all."[60]

At the church's national assembly in Charlotte in the summer of 2005, delegates overwhelmingly affirmed both the Healthcare Access Statement as well as a study document called *Healing Healthcare: A Study and Action Guide on Healthcare Access in the United States*, which they recommended to congregations for discussion and response.[61]

After 2005, responsibility for moving the conversation forward shifted to several smaller reference groups with staff support provided by MMA's Karl Sommer and Glen Miller, a retired medical doctor who served as a part-time program manager. One reference group, focused on public policy, sought to formulate a statement of "foundational beliefs" that Mennonites could affirm when evaluating legislative proposals or communicating with legislators.[62] A second group focused on the challenges faced by church-related institutions— retirement centers, nursing homes, hospitals—around the question of healthcare access. A third group convened conversations with Anabaptist-Mennonite business leaders and healthcare professionals.

As the conversation proceeded it became clear to all three reference groups that the most pressing unresolved issue regarding healthcare access in the church was the vulnerability of pastors. The majority of congregations in MC USA at the time had sixty or fewer members, making it difficult for them to provide their pastors with health insurance.[63] The most significant development, reported Miller, was a public commitment by MMA to develop a new health insurance plan for church workers and pastors.[64]

By the time of the MC USA assembly in the summer of 2007 the reports, recommendations, and resolutions of the reference groups took up thirteen pages of the delegate handbook.[65] Included in the presentation was a proposal from MMA to provide health insurance for pastors and church workers as an "application of denomination-wide mutual aid."[66] In his introduction of the proposal, MC USA executive director Jim Schrag framed the decision in stark terms: "Will we be a church that is marked by a loose association of congregations and agencies making decisions that are based primarily on their own separate self-interest, or will we be a church where the parts are committed to the good of the whole and to strong, interdependent relationships?" Keith Harder, MC USA's project manager for the proposal, concurred. "Ultimately, this project . . . is not primarily about insurance or about economics or about church structures. It is primarily about God's work in our midst and God's calling on our lives."[67]

Though some of the details remained to be worked out, the basic outline—now dubbed the Corinthian Plan—explicitly sought to recover the basic principles of churchwide mutual aid. It envisioned a funding model based on congregational assessments, with premium costs adjusted according to membership. Wealthy congregations were asked to make "mission" contributions to subsidize the premiums for pastors in low-income congregations. Congregations whose pastors had health insurance through their spouses were assessed at half the cost of the basic plan. At the same time, MMA administrators recognized that the Corinthian Plan would need to be affordable; it would need to incorporate sound actuarial, insurance, and business principles. Participants needed to be good stewards of their own health. And, not least, membership would need to "reflect a favorable risk profile." MC USA delegates gathered in San Jose, California, in the summer of 2007 passed the resolutions by a wide margin.

Conclusion

In 2005, as his tenure as CEO drew to a close, Howard Brenneman had good reason to be proud of the accomplishments of the past decade. MMA health insurance plans had stabilized, membership in the organization had grown, and MMA seemed to be infused with a new culture of confidence. Brenneman unabashedly borrowed from the business logic of the day. He drew on the counsel of outside consultants, introduced systematic strategic planning, diversified products and revenue streams, embraced marketing, and aggressively promoted a new model of distribution. Between 1992 and 2005, MMA introduced the Praxis Mutual Funds and a new Trust Company, and it implemented a model of policy governance for its board, while broadening the composition of board membership to better reflect the breadth of its Anabaptist-Mennonite constituency. But MMA also played a significant role in helping the church through the organizational complexities of denominational integration; it fully accepted its identity as "the Stewardship Agency" in the newly-created MC USA, and made good on that claim with a host of stewardship education initiatives. By the turn of the century, MMA was one of the most visible and recognized agencies of the church.

At his final MMA board meeting in June of 2005, Brenneman's parting counsel echoed his familiar refrain of "the best of business and the best of church." "Stay close to the church in a broad sense," he admonished the board,

> stay focused on the broader Anabaptist constituency; pay attention to the middle market; listen to the extremes for constructive criticism, but stay away from divisive issues; find a way to follow Anabaptists to the urban centers and market to them even though they may not be attending an Anabaptist church; and work with the church on leadership issues and balance.[68]

That counsel would prove prescient for the challenges MMA and the church would face in the coming years.

From MMA To Everence

*Succession Challenges, Restructuring,
and a New Name (2005–2014)*

$\mathcal{O}$n the morning of March 31, 2010, an MMA press release distributed to all the Mennonite media outlets as well as local newspapers and TV stations announced that MMA had reached a decision regarding its new name. In the fall of 2009, MMA leaders had reported their intention to rebrand the organization following a new partnership MMA had forged with Mennonite Financial Federal Credit Union. In the months prior to the announcement there was widespread speculation—and no shortage of suggestions, particularly among MMA staff members—about what the new name was going to be. But when, just ahead of the public announcement, president and CEO Larry Miller informed the MMA board, meeting in Sarasota, Florida, that the organization was adopting the name "Everence," his announcement was initially met with an awkward silence. The immediate response of the Anabaptist-Mennonite public was equally tepid. And some were negative. "I'm sorry," wrote one commentator in response to the online article in *The Mennonite Weekly Review*, "but this whole name change/press release is laughable."[1]

Yet by November, when Everence officially became the new identity of Mennonite Mutual Aid and Mennonite Financial Federal Credit Union, the name had already begun to feel familiar. Within a year, according to all accounts, the organization's board, members, and broader public had fully embraced Everence and the new logo. Although some veteran employees or older members would continue to refer to "MMA," most staff regarded the change as a symbol that the organization fully embraced all employees, regardless of their denominational background. In the end, Everence proved to be a well-chosen moniker—a name that rolled off the tongue naturally and seemed somehow appropriate for a church agency focused on stewardship and generosity that also provided health insurance, financial counseling, investment options, and banking services.

The new name was more than a marketing ploy. Since at least 1992, when Howard Brenneman assumed leadership of the organization, MMA had been in a process of a profound transformation, responding quickly to changes that were taking place in both the church and the broader society. To be sure, virtually all the subsidiaries established at the beginnings of MMA in the early years still existed in some form. But by 2010 MMA had moved from a relatively small church institution—uncertain about its future in the face of astronomical healthcare costs—to a diversified and thriving faith-based financial services organization whose reach extended far beyond the constituency of the Mennonite Church USA and whose programs included mutual funds, trust services, and a full-fledged credit union.

Surviving Succession

Late in 2003 Brenneman had signaled his intention to retire at the end of July of 2005, thereby giving the MMA board ample time to plan for an orderly transition in leadership. At the time of his departure MMA was clearly a healthy, vibrant organization. All of which makes the troubled story of the events surrounding the presidential transition deeply surprising.

In the spring of 2004 the board appointed a Succession Committee and created a budget for its work. Gene Yoder, president and CEO of Greencroft Retirement Communities, was the chair of the Succession Committee. Carol Suter, MMA board chair, was also a member of the committee and took a very active role in the process. Suter, a Mennonite lawyer, had joined the MMA board in the early 1990s, recruited by Howard Brenneman after she had done some legal work for the organization. Brenneman, she later reflected, "had been an excellent manager and leader for twentieth century corporate America." But in her eyes, the twenty-first century would require a new kind of leadership if MMA was going to make the move from "good to great." "We were looking for people who could imagine new product lines and new ways of delivering services, people who had another level of business experience."[2]

The work of the Succession Committee proceeded, like most executive searches, in secrecy. In contrast to earlier searches, the committee determined early in the process that it would employ the services of a corporate executive search firm, eventually settling on the Chandler Group, a small company operating out of Minneapolis. The search committee made it clear to the Chandler Group that this was to be a national search, extending beyond candidates in the Anabaptist-Mennonite world.[3] Most of the candidates in the church, they reasoned, were already known to the committee; the search firm would expose the committee to a broader range of leadership talent.

Previous MMA leaders, of course, had been drawn from inside the church—indeed, from inside the organization itself. Both Dwight Stoltzfus and James Kratz had been senior managers at MMA before being selected as CEOs. Howard Brenneman was a partial exception—prior to his service at MMA he had been a corporate executive. But Brenneman had also previously served on the MMA board, was well-known in Mennonite circles, and firmly anchored in the Mennonite church. To be sure, MMA had always been open to broadening its identity beyond narrow denominational borders. So in some ways, the door had been opened for a CEO who did not fit the traditional mold.

By late spring 2005, a candidate was chosen. The transition process then needed to move rather quickly because the appointment required approval from the MC USA Executive Board, whose next meeting was scheduled for July 4, 2005, immediately prior to the denomination's delegate assembly in Charlotte, North Carolina. At the assembly, the Succession Committee planned to announce the new president and introduce him to the larger church.[4]

A NEW KIND OF LEADER

In the end, it came as a surprise to MMA employees and the broader church when the search committee announced Terry (Skip) Nagelvoort as their candidate.[5] Nagelvoort, who was unknown in the wider Anabaptist-Mennonite community, had been an investment banker and financial analyst with several Wall Street firms in New York City in the late 1970s and 1980s, before establishing his own boutique investment firm, Nagelvoort & Co. His religious affiliations had been with Reformed and Presbyterian churches, but during his time in New York he identified strongly with nondenominational groups, including the New York Stock Exchange Bible Study, the National Prayer Breakfast, and other "marketplace ministries."[6] Over a twenty-year period, Nagelvoort's investment firm initially specialized in investment banking; later it bought, operated, and sold a series of small diverse companies. At his interview, search committee members were impressed by his charisma, his business experience, his Christian testimony, and his enthusiastic embrace of MMA's mission.[7]

On July 4, Suter, along with Jim Schrag, executive director of MC USA, introduced Nagelvoort to the MC USA Executive Board, who approved his appointment. At that time, Schrag said, "Skip is clearly comfortable with church service and theology in ways that make him well-suited for the leadership role at MMA." The following day, Schrag presented Nagelvoort to the MC USA delegate assembly saying "His faith perspective is very compatible with Mennonite Church USA and our missional focus."[8] For his part, Nagelvoort expressed his appreciation for the distinctive values of the Anabaptist-Mennonite tradition and his intention to join a Mennonite congregation. "I feel very comfortable with the Mennonite/Anabaptist community," he told the assembly in Charlotte, "because it has taken faith so seriously. Personal standards and commitments are high."[9]

Nagelvoort started at MMA on August 1. However, when the organization conducted a background check on Nagelvoort—a routine legal procedure required of all financial institutions when hiring a new executive leader—new information emerged about his former business experiences.[10] On September 21, only seven weeks after his appointment, the MMA board abruptly announced that they had accepted Nagelvoort's resignation. Although both Nagelvoort and the board members declined to comment on the reasons for the sudden turnabout, Robert Rhodes, a journalist for the *Mennonite Weekly Review*, reported that on June 29, 2005—less than a week before his formal appointment as MMA's CEO—Nagelvoort had filed for Chapter 7 liquidation and personal bankruptcy protection in U.S. Bankruptcy Court.[11] "MMA officials and a search committee that recruited Nagelvoort," Rhodes wrote, "were not aware of his pending bankruptcy until after he had started work at MMA."[12]

The events that led to Nagelvoort's resignation are not in the public record. In the immediate aftermath of the revelation, perspectives differed on what the news of his bankruptcy and his nondisclosure of the information meant for his future at MMA.[13] Technically, filing of personal bankruptcy did not legally disqualify a person from serving as president and CEO of a financial institution. In the end, however, Nagelvoort agreed to resign as MMA's president and chief executive officer.

Although the immediate issue was resolved, the episode marked a difficult moment in the history of the organization. As a financial services organization—but also as a program agency of the church—MMA relied heavily on the confidence of its members that it was a trustworthy organization. For many

A trusted long-term leader, Steve Garboden served as a transition president until Larry Miller was chosen.

employees and board members the incident raised questions about all the factors that led to the crisis.

So it came as a great relief when, shortly after Nagelvoort's resignation became public, the MMA board of directors announced that Steve Garboden, a twenty-nine-year veteran of MMA, had agreed to serve as MMA's interim CEO and president.[14] Garboden had joined the organization in the fall of 1976, where he quickly developed expertise in the growing field of Information Technology. From there he became Vice President for Information Services under James Kratz, before moving into health insurance during the tumultuous years of the late 1980s and 1990s. Along the way, Garboden earned a reputation as a gifted analyst, an idealist deeply committed to the principles of mutual aid, and a leader of unquestioned personal integrity. "You could just feel the relief when it was announced that Steve would step into the role," several long-time MMA employees later recalled.

Beyond the immediate priority of restoring confidence in the organization, the future challenges Garboden and the organization confronted in the fall of 2005 remained significant. Under Brenneman, MMA had stabilized its position in health insurance, diversified its offerings, broadened its base, and significantly increased its assets and reserves. Nevertheless, healthcare costs remained a national preoccupation, and the viability of the MMA Trust Company and MMA Praxis Mutual Funds was by no means assured.

There were other long-term issues to face as well. For years, MMA employees had struggled to accommodate themselves to a building with leaky roofs, erratic temperatures, and outdated offices. MMA's approach to sales and distribution needed to be upgraded. And despite various attempts, Brenneman had not fully resolved the longstanding challenge of integrating the various components of MMA's operation—especially Mennonite Foundation, the Trust Company, and Praxis Mutual Funds—into a coherent legal and operational whole.[15]

For eighteen months, however, Garboden's steady presence enabled MMA to move forward while giving the reconstituted search committee the time it needed to identify a new CEO and president.

A Stable Path Forward: Larry Miller

At an MC USA executive board meeting in early February of 2006, Garboden assured church leaders that MMA "wants to be accountable to the church, to build trust through predictability and accountability in the next search process, and to work at a deliberate pace that is done well."[16] A few weeks later, a new CEO transition team, now chaired by MMA board member Pat Swartzentruber, reconvened.[17] In June the committee reported to the board that a survey regarding key traits needed in the next CEO revealed that "the single biggest category of comments dealt with the person being part of the Anabaptist community." Every respondent had also ranked "trustworthiness" as "extremely important."[18]

When the committee announced in October 2006 that Larry Miller, president of Mennonite Financial Federal Credit Union in Lancaster, Pennsylvania, had accepted the position as president and CEO of MMA, the news was greeted across the church and within the organization with enthusiasm. Miller had grown up in the Mennonite farming community of Kalona, Iowa. At the age of twenty-four, after a short stint with the Federal Land Bank, he became the manager of a credit union in Hampton, Iowa, and then took a similar role at a savings and loan bank in Mount Pleasant, Iowa. In 1990, eager to return to the world of financial cooperatives, he accepted a new position as manager of the Pennsylvania Mennonite Federal Credit Union in Scottdale, Pennsylvania.[19]

Under his leadership the credit union expanded rapidly. In 1998 Miller moved the company's headquarters to Lancaster, Pennsylvania, closer to the heart of a large Mennonite community. Several years later, he negotiated a new charter that enabled the growing organization—now renamed the Mennonite Financial Federal Credit Union—to serve Anabaptist-Mennonites from across the nation. When Miller arrived, the Pennsylvania Mennonite Federal Credit Union had $6 million in assets; when he left in 2006 the organization claimed assets of $75 million and had expanded to include seven branches.

Coming into MMA as former president of the credit union, Larry Miller was soon able to start the process of affiliating the organizations.

In his role as CEO of the credit union Miller had enjoyed positive relations with MMA. He frequently met for breakfast with the local MMA representatives in Lancaster and he had a warm relationship with Howard Brenneman, who would occasionally speculate with him about the possibility of integrating banking services into the MMA organization. At the time, MMA's Trust Company held a bank charter, but used it mostly for investment transactions. In conversations with Brenneman, the question was whether future MMA banking services would be best expanded under the Trust Company or reconceived in the form of a credit union. When the new MMA search committee contacted him in August of 2006, Miller sensed a calling and accepted the invitation. On January 22, 2007 he assumed responsibilities as MMA's seventh president and CEO.

Miller soon became known for his ready laugh, his congenial personality, and his disarming modesty. He was also a churchman, deeply respectful of MMA's connection to the church and committed to nurturing the underlying values that had long been a part of MMA's corporate identity. Since virtually all of Miller's experience had been in banking, early in his tenure Miller often relied on members of the MMA staff to guide the organization through the maze of legal regulations, actuarial details, and market forecasts.[20] Yet behind his modest demeanor, Miller was fully prepared to make bold changes that would significantly reshape MMA as the organization moved confidently into the twenty-first century.

THE GREAT RECESSION OF 2007–2009

When Miller arrived at MMA, no one could have predicted that within a few short months the country would be plunged into the greatest economic crisis since the Depression. Economists do not all agree on the causes of the Great Recession of 2007–2009. Most, however, suggest that a major contributing factor were the subprime loans offered by many commercial banks that induced consumers to borrow heavily for home mortgages in a context of rapidly rising home prices.

MMA investment managers had been wary of subprime loans and were not heavily invested in these mortgages and home equity loans. But there was no escaping the impact of the crisis. Almost overnight the stock assets in the MMA Praxis Mutual Fund family dropped from $700 to $500 million. MMA members with investments in the Mennonite Retirement Trust, the MMA Trust Company, or the Mennonite Foundation looked on helplessly as their portfolios shrank dramatically. In February of 2009, MMA staff reported to the board that the organization had lost $3.3 million in 2008. Total assets under management had decreased in a single year by 22 percent.[21]

The recession also brought to the foreground an especially difficult set of questions that had been swirling for some years around the under-performance of the MMA Praxis Core Stock Mutual Fund. In February 2007, only weeks after Miller's arrival, John Liechty, president of the fund, noted that the "socially responsible investing screens have been a drag on [growth fund] performance for the past six years."[22] The observation touched off a significant debate, heightened by the pressure leadership had already been feeling from investors. It was true that the core stock fund's returns had lagged behind the S&P 500 index. But when performance was compared with other indexes using SRI screens, the Praxis fund was actually on target. The difference, Liechty suggested, "is really the responsibility of the board that has set policy for SRI practices, not the underperformance of the investment advisors."[23] So the question turned to whether the board should change the metrics of evaluation to SRI-screened benchmarks or, perhaps, to create a set of metrics for evaluating the "missional performance" of the funds.

Over time, the MMA Praxis Mutual Funds survived—indeed, surpassing the $1 billion mark within the coming decade. But the reckless actions of the large investment firms leading up to the recession prompted sweeping changes by both Congress and the Securities and Exchange Commission—including the Dodd-Frank Wall Street Reform and Consumer Protection Act in 2010—that nearly overwhelmed small investment firms like MMA with a host of new and complex regulations.

All this meant that Miller was moving into a new and complicated financial organization at precisely the moment when the national economy was in crisis, followed by a new wave of regulations for MMA programs that were already heavily regulated. At virtually the same time, the election of Barack Obama renewed the national debate over healthcare reform, which raised further questions about the sustainability of MMA's individual healthcare plans. That MMA was able to navigate these challenges in a way that enabled the organization to not only survive, but to actually grow, is a testimony to the creativity and hard work of Miller and his leadership team.

In the space of three short years Miller negotiated a formal affiliation between MMA and the Mennonite Financial Federal Credit Union, restructured the legal relationships of MMA and its subsidiaries, initiated dramatic changes within his management team, undertook a large-scale renovation project at the MMA headquarters, significantly transformed the distribution and sales model of the organization, closed out the individual healthcare line of insurance, and led MMA in a major rebranding initiative that included a name change. By 2010, Everence appeared to have weathered the worst of the Great Recession and emerged stronger than ever.

During the Great Recession, many people like Ruth Furr, Harrisonburg, Va., started to question the stability of their financial situation and sought help from MMA's partner, LSS Financial Counseling. HOWARD ZEHR

MMA Affiliates with Mennonite Financial Federal Credit Union (2007)

When Miller arrived early in 2007 he brought with him a lifetime of experience with credit unions. So it was not a surprise that one of his first major accomplishments was the successful integration of Mennonite Financial Federal Credit Union with MMA. The marriage of the two organizations was not a simple matter. It called on the creativity of lawyers, accountants, marketing experts, and board members to find their way through a labyrinth of paperwork. It also required key leaders to set aside familiar habits and personal egos as they worked to integrate two corporate cultures. But the formal affiliation between MMA and Mennonite Financial Federal Credit Union late in 2007 was a signature success of Miller's tenure as CEO.

In contrast to a bank, which is a for-profit business owned by shareholders or individuals, credit unions are not-for-profit organizations owned by their customers, who are called members. Like banks, credit unions accept deposits, make loans, and provide a wide array of other financial services. But they are democratic—each member has one vote in board elections, regardless of the amount of their investment. Moreover, credit unions are explicitly cooperative institutions, designed to "serve people, not profits." In an age before online credit ratings, when loans were often based on family connections and established credentials, credit unions enabled ordinary people to borrow small sums of money at reasonable rates of interest. In the classic phrase of the credit union movement, "I save so that you can borrow."

Throughout its history, the idea that MMA should add a credit union to its roster of subsidiaries had surfaced repeatedly, but never found the traction it needed to move forward. In the 1950s and 1960s, for example, Howard Raid frequently expressed his hope that the MMA board would take up the task.[24] In 1968, John Rudy proposed that MMA conduct a survey of local Mennonites in the Goshen area regarding their interest in a credit union.[25] In the early 1970s, MMA responded positively to a request from the Minority Ministries Council to explore the possibility of creating credit unions in urban areas that were underserved by commercial banks.[26] In 1973 John Rudy revived the idea once again, this time framed as part of a larger vision for a "Menno Investment Service."[27]

All of these efforts culminated in the fall of 1977, when Rudy cited information from various state credit union associations in support of his recommendation that the MMA board establish a "Mennonite Credit Union" in Elkhart County, Indiana.[28] The board initially agreed, but charged Rudy and Swartzendruber with the task of testing the concept first with an in-house credit union for MMA employees. In February 1978, however, the MMA leadership wavered, overwhelmed by more immediate challenges. At its spring meeting, the board finally rejected Rudy's proposal, concluding that "such a program should come into existence as a local grassroots activity rather than as a program of MMA. Credit unions are owned by members and not by organizations such as MMA."[29]

Still, the idea refused to die. In 1982, after various local business leaders and pastors continued to press MMA to consider the idea, Rudy tested the waters yet again, noting that "new regulations have allowed credit unions to greatly expand their services."[30] But once again, the idea failed to gather momentum.

A CREDIT UNION EMERGES IN PENNSYLVANIA

Meanwhile, elsewhere in the Anabaptist-Mennonite world several local credit union initiatives had taken hold, both in Canada and in the United States. The most successful of these ventures in the United States started in April of 1955 among the employees of the Mennonite Publishing House in Scottdale, Pennsylvania.[31] A combination of low salaries and the fact that most employees were new to the area made it very difficult for workers at the publishing house to obtain loans at the local savings bank. With the blessing of the organization's general manager, A. J. Metzler, the Mennonite Scottdale Credit Union opened with eight charter members.[32] Within a month membership had grown to 54 participants with $1,150 in savings and $265 in loans.

In the years that followed, the Mennonite Scottdale Credit Union (MSCU) slowly grew as the association opened its membership to employees from nearby Laurelville Mennonite Camp and Provident Bookstores, which the publishing house owned and operated. That growth became exponential in the early 1980s when J. Lorne Peachey, who had served on the credit union's board and for a time as its treasurer, was hired as the first full-time manager.[33] In 1983 the National Credit Union Administration rejected Peachey's application for a national charter; but they did allow the credit union in Scottdale to broaden its membership to include all Mennonites in the state of Pennsylvania. Two years later, now operating as the Pennsylvania Mennonite Credit Union, Peachey opened a branch office at the Provident Bookstore in Lancaster, Pennsylvania. Peachey also began to promote the credit union to church-related institutions in Pennsylvania, particularly in the Belleville and Lancaster communities, offering payroll deduction services, checking accounts, access to fair loans, and competitive interest rates on savings accounts.

As interest in the credit union concept spread to other Mennonite communities—with new organizations emerging in Ohio (1985) and Illinois (1988)—administrators and board members began to gather on a regular basis to encourage each other and to exchange information. A 1987 retreat at Laurelville Mennonite Church Center hosted by Pennsylvania Mennonite Federal Credit Union and the Mennonite Savings and Credit Union of Ontario was particularly significant in creating the Association of Mennonite Credit Unions, helping to forge a sense of collaboration among the smaller credit unions that eased the path for later mergers.

When Larry Miller arrived on the scene in 1990 as the Pennsylvania Mennonite Federal Credit Union's new president, growth only accelerated. By the mid-1990s, the credit union was offering its members home equity loans, VISA credit cards, debit cards, and ATM services. In 1998 Miller relocated the headquarters from Scottdale to Lancaster, where membership was growing most rapidly, and rehired J. Lorne Peachey to oversee marketing. Five years later, Miller successfully applied for a national charter with an expansive definition of membership that included all "active members or participants of a congregation recognized by Mennonite World Conference . . . and employees of institutions or businesses where two-thirds of the controlling interest is Mennonite."[34] Under the new charter the Pennsylvania Mennonite Federal

J. Lorne Peachey, left, was a leader during the early years of the credit union in Pennsylvania.

The credit union brought strong relationships with multiple Amish communities. At one point, it provided mortgages to Amish families establishing a farm community near Marathon, N.Y.

ELLEN ZASLAW

Credit Union became the Mennonite Financial Federal Credit Union. At the time of Miller's arrival the credit union had 3,200 members; in 2004, the organization had become a national body, with membership of 8,000, six branch offices, and assets of $60 million.[35]

By 2005, the parallel trajectories of MMA and the Mennonite Financial Federal Credit Union seemed destined to intersect. Not long before his departure, Brenneman charged Rod Diller, head of MMA's Trust Company, to lay the groundwork for MMA to (finally!) create a credit union.[36] From Brenneman's perspective, a credit union clearly fit with the larger goals of diversifying the range of financial services that MMA offered to its members. Another, equally significant, goal was to broaden MMA's market to include a younger demographic. For many years, MMA leaders had been aware that many of their strongest and most visible products—e.g., Medicare Supplement, Mennonite Foundation, and MMA Praxis Mutual Funds—were most relevant to members who were over fifty years old. By contrast, the services offered by a credit union—home mortgages, car loans, credit cards, check writing services, or certificates of deposit—were more likely to appeal to younger adults. In addition, MMA already had offices where the Mennonite Financial Federal Credit Union was looking to expand. And, as a membership-driven organization, many of the credit union's programs—including the Rebate for Mission credit card—aligned well with MMA's commitment to stewardship and mutual aid.

THE AFFILIATION TAKES HOLD

Soon after Larry Miller left Mennonite Financial Federal Credit Union to assume leadership of MMA, conversations regarding a possible merger moved forward. At its June 2007 meeting the MMA board acted "to provide consumer banking services to members and to pursue an affiliation with Mennonite Financial Federal Credit Union."[37] On December 13, 2007, MMA employees

celebrated the grand opening of a Goshen branch of Mennonite Financial
Federal Credit Union.

Not surprisingly, however, the details associated with merging the two operations were extremely complicated. As a member-owned organization with
its own board, the credit union was legally obliged to retain its own identity,
distinct from MMA. Technically, the new relationship was a "deep affiliation"
rather than a formal merger.[38]

Kent Hartzler, who was appointed president and CEO of Mennonite
Financial Federal Credit Union after Miller's departure, would play a key role
in working through the complicated alignment of strategic priorities and financial relationships that followed. Hartzler had stumbled into the world of credit
unions when, in 1998, Miller recruited him from the Mennonite Publishing
House to create a marketing department at the Pennsylvania Mennonite Credit
Union. Hartzler soon became a passionate supporter of the credit union philosophy. Within a few years, he moved into a new role as a lending officer,
and then as vice president of lending. The long-standing working relationship
between both Miller and Hartzler undoubtedly eased the complex negotiations that ensued as MMA and the Mennonite Financial Federal Credit Union
found their footing in the new affiliation.

From left, Kent Hartzler, Larry Miller, and James Horsch (board chair) celebrate the
new Mennonite Financial Federal Credit Union headquarters in Lancaster.

MMA, of course, was the larger partner in the arrangement, capable of underwriting some of the risk involved and providing a useful infrastructure for expanded operations. But whereas Mennonite Financial Federal Credit Union was accustomed to making quick adjustments in response to a changing market, MMA was somewhat encumbered by the complexity of its organizational structure and various regulatory constraints. This meant that the two organizations needed to find ways of integrating not only the logistical details of their separate operations but also the corporate cultures that each brought to the relationship. The rebranding initiative that followed in 2010 helped to ease these differences, but the process was not easy.

In February 2009, the two boards revised the "Terms of Affiliation" in order to provide for "more clarity in the [credit union] business plan."[39] In June, recognizing that more conversation was needed about the "appropriate and adequate 'glue' [needed] to hold the two organizations together,"[40] the two groups agreed to include Mennonite Financial Federal Credit Union's financial statements in MMA's quarterly and annual reports. In addition, Hartzler became "a full functioning member of the MMA Executive Team," and MMA became the "sponsoring organization" for the credit union, providing its office technology, capital management, accounting, marketing, and human resource services, while also purchasing or subsidizing the rent of several credit union offices.[41] MMA also provided significant infusions of capital on several occasions "without any expectation or obligation of repayment" to assist the credit union in meeting its capital obligations as part of a shared commitment to a strategy of steady growth.[42]

Despite the complexities, the advantages of the new arrangement soon became apparent.[43] The Mennonite Financial Federal Credit Union broadened the scope of MMA's membership, made the organization more visible and relevant to younger people, and ensured that ordinary members had a full array of banking services at their disposal.

Administrative Restructuring (2008)

CORPORATE ENTITIES ARE UPDATED

With the credit union's affiliation with MMA, an already complex organizational chart became even more bewildering. Like the Mennonite Mutual Aid Association, which comprised the products associated with the fraternal benefits association, the Mennonite Financial Federal Credit Union was an organization owned by its members who elected a board to represent their interests.

This legal and organizational complexity was replicated in a dozen different ways with other parts of the organization. Long-time MMA employees often describe the organization as analogous to the 1110 North Main Street building itself. Over time, the basic structure has undergone numerous renovations, additions, and reconfigurations—each carried out under different circumstances and with different goals. The end result was a functional, but extremely complex, structure whose interior hallways, plumbing, and ductwork did not always align. On various occasions, outside consultants or concerned regulators had identified the legal, fiscal, administrative, and regulatory complexity of MMA as a matter of significant concern. It was not always clear which of the various subsidiaries were operating within the letter or the spirit of the law. In October 2007, Mel Claassen, MMA's Chief Financial Officer, outlined a plan that would simplify the MMA corporate structure, making it easier to transfer capital and to manage risks and liabilities across the various subsidiaries.[44] Several months later, in early 2008, Karl Sommers presented the board with the new model as developed by the law firm of Ice Miller in Indianapolis.[45]

Under the new plan, some of the familiar MMA entities—among them Mennonite Foundation, the Mennonite Mutual Aid Association (the fraternal benefits association), Mennonite Financial Federal Credit Union, and Mennonite Retirement Trust remained virtually unchanged. The new arrangement, however, created a holding company system, under the ownership of the fraternal benefit association, that allowed MMA to take advantage of corporate organizational simplification and tax opportunities. While Mennonite Church Buildings as a tax-exempt entity owned most of the properties on behalf of MMA, a new entity was created known as MMA Real Estate Holdings to manage the property acquired through the church loan program. MMA Capital Management continued to serve as the investment advisor for Praxis Mutual Funds. MMA Securities was formed as a broker-dealer in order to receive commissions and other forms of compensation from ProEquities, a brokerage service, relating to the sale of Praxis Mutual Funds and other investments. MMA simplified the sale of insurance products through MMA Distribution, and repurposed the MMA Insurance Company as the home for the Third Party Administration services that MMA offered to self-funded insurance pools. The newly-formed MMA Holding Company brought all the taxable entities of MMA—including MMA Capital Management, MMA Distribution, the Trust Company, and MMA Insurance Company—under one roof. All benefits and wages for MMA staff were paid and provided by MMA InSource, LLC.

For most lay people, the legal reorganization did not seem to make great advances in simplifying a bewilderingly complex organizational structure. But the new alignments were a needed response to growing realities of regulatory oversight, management of risks and liabilities, and changing tax laws.

MANAGEMENT AND ORGANIZATIONAL SHAKEUP

At the same 2008 board meeting that approved the new organizational design, Miller also reported his intention to simplify and streamline the organizational structure and the executive leadership team.[46] Miller preferred an organizational structure with clearer lines of authority and a smaller group of senior leaders.[47] For the first year of his tenure, Miller had worked hard to understand MMA's inner workings. But by 2008 he was ready to restructure the management team in a way that better fit his style of leadership. In his report to the board, Miller expressed concern about "the siloing of departments" and his desire for the various components "to work as one team for the good of MMA." To achieve these ends, he gave notice that "in 2008 we will implement some bold changes, which will no doubt create anxiety."[48]

Drawing on the counsel of an outside consultant, Miller first reduced the number on the senior leadership team from eight to four. This meant, of course, consolidating key leadership positions. Miller encouraged long-time veterans in the company to apply for the newly-defined positions; but he also made it clear that no one was guaranteed a job in the new structure.[49] When the dust settled, two vice presidents—Mel Claassen and Rod Diller—remained in upper management positions, Claassen as senior vice president and chief financial officer, and Diller as senior vice president of sales and distribution. Two new faces were promoted from lower ranks within the company—David Gautsche as senior vice president of products and services and Jim Alvarez as senior vice president for corporate services. But the outcome of the process meant that at least four other senior management people—Karl Sommers, Steve Garboden, Steve Martin and John Leichty—who collectively represented more than a century of combined years of experience with MMA, would leave the organization.

Second, the restructuring meant that some departments now related to senior leaders in a new way and with a new alignment of functions. These changes were most evident in the dismantling of the Fraternal Benefits Department that oversaw MMA's work with the church and its Sharing Fund. That department's staff was reassigned to other areas, with the largest group—the church relations representatives— moving under field offices. It took several years for the reconfiguration of church relations and fraternal benefits to settle into a new mode of operating.

While some affirmed the decision as a necessary, albeit painful, move—one that reflected a management style that fit well with the direction the organization was moving—the shock to many staff members was nevertheless real.[50]

NEW MODEL OF SALES/DISTRIBUTION

And there were other changes in store as well. Even as he was moving to restructure the organization, Miller introduced a new sales distribution model that would "bring all field distribution under one leadership with a sustainable business model that would combine and streamline all MMA products and services." The larger goal, he told the board in the February 2008 meeting, was to create "a sales force driven by church and member relationships."[51]

Marketing, sales, distribution, and customer service had always been a challenge for MMA. Early in its history, the organization relied on reports in church papers, informative brochures, and occasional visits to pastors by its "field service men" to promote MMA products. Congregational representatives, serving as volunteers, handled most of the direct contact with MMA members. As the Hospital-Surgical Plan became more complex, MMA shifted to a sales model that relied on licensed insurance agents in Mennonite communities who agreed to represent MMA as part of their larger portfolio of products. Congregational advocates continued to promote stewardship education and handled the logistics of Sharing Fund grants, but sales commissions were directed to these independent agents who related to regional MMA representatives—known whimsically as the "twelve apostles." On the upside, the agency model forced MMA products to be competitive alongside commercial alternatives; and it incentivized agents with commissions on the sale of MMA products. But even though many of the independent agents were members of Anabaptist-Mennonite congregations, they had no real reason to educate clients on the larger faith component of MMA's identity and often found it easier to promote other competing products, whose companies launched national marketing campaigns and often rewarded sales staff with incentive trips or subsidies for conventions.

In the face of these challenges, Rod Diller took a bold step in moving the sales and distribution model in a different direction. In an effort to improve the alignment of MMA's health insurance and financial services, and to sharpen MMA's identity as the stewardship agency of the church, Diller proposed that MMA would actually purchase the agencies that represented MMA products

Financial representatives like Jay Kready, Mount Joy, Pa., became MMA employees when the organization reorganized its sales and distribution system.
MATTHEW LESTER

and services, thereby bringing the sales representatives into the organization as MMA employees. The negotiating process that ensued was slow and often complicated. The new model required MMA to invest heavily, not only in the real estate and portfolios of existing agencies, but also in the infrastructure required to support the new field offices.

In the fall of 2010 Diller offered a preliminary report to the board. Significant progress had been made in forming core markets, integrating teams, working out compensation models, enhancing sales support, and cultivating a culture of professionalism. Nevertheless, in the five-year planning projection, Diller anticipated that the new model would not reach a financial break-even point for at least three years, with the hope of becoming profitable by 2014.[52]

A MAJOR BUILDING PROJECT LAUNCHED (2008–2012)

In the midst of these major changes in management and sales, Miller also elected to move forward with a long-anticipated building project. The offices at the 1110 North Main Street location, acquired in 1971, had solved a pressing need for space. But from the start the property also had significant structural problems. At the time of the move, the board had hoped to use the original building for ten years, assuming it would then be torn down and replaced by a new structure. Instead, they settled on two major renovation projects—first in 1978 and then again in 1984—that expanded and reconfigured the original design.

By 2005 MMA had outgrown the facility once more, and problems with the existing structure could no longer be ignored. Despite the renovation efforts, the MMA offices located in the original part of the building were notoriously cold in winter and had no central air conditioning for the hot summer months. Cables from the rapidly expanding IT department were visible in public hallways, the customer reception area was small and unwelcoming, and there was simply no longer any space to squeeze in more cubicles for new employees, despite numerous creative efforts to realign the modular walls.[53]

For nearly a decade, the board had been setting aside money in anticipation of a major construction project that would replace the original building and include several new additions. When Miller arrived in early 2007, he and the board agreed that it was time to set a plan in motion. Jane Bowers, who had served as MMA's Facilities Manager since 2000, took the lead. From the outset the building committee was committed to model stewardship practices in the design and construction process by incorporating sustainable features such as passive solar heating and bioretention ponds. Their goal was to meet the Leadership in Energy and Environmental Design (LEED) Gold certification standard.

As it happened, the building project began in the midst of an extremely difficult economic environment. In the fall of 2007 the housing market collapsed,

In 2008, MMA tore down the original structure at the site of its headquarters, remodeled its current space, and added a major new wing.

the stock market plummeted, and the national economy contracted. Locally, unemployment in Elkhart County in 2008 reached 20 percent. Nevertheless, money for the project had already been set aside. At a time when local builders were laying off workers, the board reasoned, launching a major building project sent a strong signal to the community that MMA was confident about the future. At its June 2008 meeting the MMA board approved $8.3 million for the building project and signed a contract with D. J. Construction.[54] The blueprints called for the addition of nearly 45,000 square feet to the original footprint and a complete renovation of another 40,000 square feet of the original building.

The first phase of the project, completed in 2009, added nearly 25,000 square feet to the back of the building and included a rain garden, a bio-retention pond, and an expanded parking lot. A second phase in 2010 focused on new office and conference rooms and the creation of a customer reception area in the front of the building. The final, most complicated stage of the project—the complete renovation of the existing structure—took another two years to complete. Each stage required significant planning to ensure that the work of the 230 employees at the Goshen offices was not unduly disrupted. At times, some of the staff was forced to temporarily relocate to a small underground building on the property—affectionately known as the Bunker—until they could return to the newly-furnished workspace. Bowers, working closely with Eunice Culp, vice president for Human Resources, orchestrated the complicated dance of construction schedules, shifting office space, and design and decor decisions, while also keeping a close eye on the budget and on the sustainability goals needed for LEED Gold certification,[55] which the building was eventually awarded in 2013.

FROM MMA TO EVERENCE (2010)
Even while the building project was still underway, Miller initiated yet another change that would have far-reaching consequences for the sixty-five-year-old organization. When Orie O. Miller declared in the fall of 1943 that the new program he envisioned would be called Mennonite Mutual Aid, there was never an open debate about the name. Each word seemed an appropriate description of the mission and identity of the new initiative. A generation later, Mennonite Mutual Aid enjoyed high visibility and a positive reputation in most Anabaptist-Mennonite communities.

Yet there were some limits inherent in the name as well. Membership in MMAA, the fraternal benefit association that housed the health and life insurance products, had always included denominations beyond those in the Mennonite family—Mennonite Brethren and Brethren in Christ were strong supporters, as were several groups of Quakers and members of the Missionary Church.[56] By 2010 at least one-third of MMA's members came from denominations other than MC USA. Moreover, denominational affiliations and allegiances were waning at the turn of the twentieth century; and in some circles, the term *Mennonite*—like *Amish*—was strongly associated with a particular ethnic folk culture.

In addition to all of these considerations, the products and services that MMA was offering in 2010 had moved well beyond the Burial Aid and Hospital-Surgical mutual aid plans of the 1950s and 1960s. They now included a wide range of insurance options, retirement programs, financial planning and trust services, mutual funds, stewardship education resources, and a vehicle for promoting charitable giving in the Mennonite Foundation. For a time, the marketing wisdom under Howard Brenneman had been to address this reality by dropping the label Mennonite Mutual Aid and simply using the acronym MMA. But that strategy had its own challenges, among them the fact that MMA was mostly associated in popular culture with "Mixed Martial Arts"! When Mennonite Financial Federal Credit Union joined MMA in 2008, it seemed to Miller and others that the time had come for the organization to consider a new name.

In the spring of 2009 Steve Bowers, Director of Marketing, set the process in motion with an intensive search for a company that would assist MMA and Mennonite Financial Federal Credit Union in the rebranding effort. They eventually settling on FutureBrand, a marketing firm specializing in corporate name changes. In the first phase of the research, MMA employees were invited to submit suggestions, with proposals ranging from silly to serious. By the time the process came to an end, representatives of FutureBrand had identified four possibilities, which they presented to the executive team. One of the options, "Kefa"—which they associated with Simon Peter, or Cephas, and the suggestion of "built on the rock"[57]—was soon eliminated since a coffee company in California already had adopted the name and would not allow MMA to consider it. In the end, the leading recommendation was for "Everence," which connoted words like reverence, forever, and permanence. At an MMA board meeting in Sarasota, Florida, in February, 2010, FutureBrand proposed the new name along with a redesigned brandmark—a cross-shaped vine image, inspired by the New Testament metaphor for Jesus (John 15:5), that suggested the interconnected nature of a living community. Although board members were initially lukewarm in their response, following a PowerPoint presentation that offered a fuller rationale for the name and the brandmark they reportedly stood and applauded.[58]

On March 29, 2010, Miller sent a letter to all MMA and Mennonite Financial Federal Credit Union members explaining the rationale behind the name change. A news release posted a few days later announced the name change to the broader public, noting that the official transition to Everence would take place on November 1, 2010.[59] In a conference call with media outlets, Kent Hartzler, CEO of Mennonite Financial Federal Credit Union, noted that Everence "is a name that does not give the impression that we are exclusively for Mennonites. . . . This is important as we reach out to a broader audience of potential members who are not Mennonite but who are attracted by the faith aspect of our business."[60] All the press releases associated with the name change assured readers that Everence would continue to be an agency of Mennonite Church USA, committed to stewardship education and accountable to the church's Executive Board.

Public reaction to the name change was initially mixed.[61] Paul Schrag, editor of the *Mennonite Weekly Review* expressed concern that the impulse to drop the name "Mennonite" would inevitably lead to a growing sense of distance from the Anabaptist-Mennonite theological tradition that had given birth to the organization.[62] But the criticisms soon faded. In the months that followed, MMA management and marketing personnel reported that reactions to the name change in most settings mirrored that of the board in their Sarasota meeting—an initial response of surprise, followed by slow acceptance, and eventually, strong affirmation.[63]

By late 2010 most of the legal details related to the name change had been completed. Everence replaced MMA as the new name for the umbrella organization, and was also incorporated into most of the associated and affiliated entities. Thus, Mennonite Financial Federal Credit Union became Everence Federal Credit Union; the MMA Association became Everence Association; and MMA Praxis Mutual Funds became Praxis Mutual Funds: A Fund Family of Everence.

Relations to MC USA

Like the CEOs who had preceded him, Larry Miller was deeply committed to maintaining close ties to the church and nurturing the faith-based values that had long been part of the organization. As he assured MMA members in his announcement of the name change, "our Anabaptist faith foundation and our relationship to the church remains unchanged."[64] Yet clearly, as attitudes toward the denomination and its agencies changed—as Mennonites became more pragmatic in their investment decisions and as the national debate around healthcare reform became increasingly polarized—the nature of relationship with the church *did* change.

On the one hand, throughout the opening decade of the twentieth century, MMA actively supported many MC USA initiatives.[65] MMA, for example, funded two major churchwide research projects—"People in the Pew" (2004) and "First Fruits Giving" (2004–2005)—and continued to sponsor the work of Marty Lehman, MC USA's director of finance, as she helped the newly-integrated denomination to clarify its funding model. In 2006 and 2007, Lehman traveled extensively throughout the church explaining the concept of firstfruits giving and promoting the Generosity Project. In 2006, the organization agreed to house the Creation Care Network on behalf of the denomination, and provided significant subsidies for that work to move forward.[66] MMA staff continued to host Stewardship University weekend seminars, particularly in the region around Lancaster, Pennsylvania. And, thanks in part to the regular "linkage with owners" reviews mandated by the Carver model of board governance, the MMA board spent a portion of every meeting listening to the perceptions and expectations regarding MMA from a wide variety of church constituencies.[67]

At the same time, however, relationships with MC USA were clearly becoming more complex, particularly as various denominational agencies struggled to meet their budgets. One expression of these internal tensions was a decision by a subcommittee of the Mennonite Educational Agency (MEA) to reallocate endowment funds that had been entrusted to MMA on behalf of the denomination's colleges. In March 2006, MEA's pooled endowment fund had assets of $146 million. Traditionally, 70 percent of these funds had been lodged for investment with the Mennonite Foundation. In 2008, however, in the midst of the Great Recession, the MEA investment committee reduced that amount to 60 percent, choosing to increase investments with other mutual funds that seemed to promise better performance. Shortly thereafter, an investment consultant hired by MEA put Mennonite Foundation on notice that they were going to establish a direct relationship with outside investment managers, which implied a further decline in funds held by the foundation to around 40 percent of the overall endowments. The committee's explanation for shifting the funds was their concern regarding the management fees charged by the foundation. Representatives of the foundation responded by noting that the investment management fees helped to "fund the cost of stewardship education, charitable estate planning, and resource support to MEA institutional development offices." In the end, however, those arguments were not persuasive.[68] At the March 2008 MMA board meeting John Liechty, president of the Praxis Mutual Fund, reported that the Mennonite Education Agency, had "elected to move to an 'enhanced indexing' investment strategy for their endowment fund. As a result, they liquidated nearly all of their direct investments in Mennonite Foundation, leaving only $8 million invested in the MMA Praxis Intermediate Income Fund."[69]

At the same MMA board meeting, members heard that the MC USA Executive Board intended to restructure its governance in such a way that the boards of the various denominational program agencies would be consolidated under a single centralized MC USA board. The concerns motivating the proposal were understandable. When MMA had formed in 1945, the Executive Committee of the (Old) Mennonite Church General Conference had full control of the new organization. Virtually every significant decision made by the MMA board required approval from the central authorities of the church. Over time, however, the growing complexity of MMA—with its various subsidiary companies and the increasing role of government regulation—gradually diminished the nature of denominational oversight. To be sure, MMA leaders continued to meet regularly with the Mennonite Church executive committee, the church nominated a majority of MMA board members, MMA reported faithfully to district conferences and churchwide assemblies, it supported the work of the church with fraternal funds, and it remained highly visible in its educational role. But the actual authority of MMA's operations—fiduciary control of its assets, for example, or the decision to create the Trust Company, or to move into mutual funds—was held by the MMA board, and only reported to the MC USA executive board.

The initiative in the spring of 2008 to bring all the program agencies of the church under a single unified board marked a bold move on the part of church leaders to recover operational control over its various agencies—and, not least, over their assets as well.[70] As the newly-formed denomination struggled to find its identity and a stable source of funding, there was a certain logic in the Executive Board's effort to claim a more prominent role in shaping the church's vision and controlling its resources. But agency leaders and their board members saw the matter quite differently. For MMA—clearly the organization with the most resources—the proposal was unrealistic, not least because of the many regulatory agencies to whom MMA was accountable. Over the course of several meetings, MMA board chair LaVern Yutzy, speaking on behalf of the board, made a compelling case, citing the complexity of MMA's legal and fiduciary requirements along with the fact that MMA's membership and board included members of groups beyond MC USA.[71]

In the end, the proposal came to naught. But the failed initiative signaled clearly what had been the de facto reality for a long time: MMA was connected to MC USA by a dotted, not a solid line. The church's Executive Board retained the right to approve the MMA CEO and to nominate board members; but beyond that the relationship would continue to be defined by advice, counsel, good will, and the weight of tradition.[72]

Winding Down Individual Health Insurance — ACA Healthcare Reform (2010–2013)

On March 23, 2010, President Obama signed into law the Patient Protection and Affordable Care Act—commonly abbreviated as ACA and known informally as Obamacare. The legislation, which had been deeply embroiled in partisan political debate, marked the most significant regulatory overhaul of the nation's healthcare system since the passage of Medicare and Medicaid in 1965. The goal of the Affordable Care Act was to increase the number of Americans covered by health insurance and to reduce healthcare costs. Among the most significant aspects of the legislation was a provision that prohibited insurance companies from denying coverage to anyone on the basis of preexisting medical conditions, assuming they met certain requirements. In addition, employers with more than fifty employees were required to provide them with healthcare insurance. In many states, the ACA expanded eligibility for Medicaid coverage; and the legislation created a new system of healthcare exchanges that would sell insurance at a subsidized rate, depending on income. Anyone who did not get health insurance would be charged an annual penalty.

Ever since the healthcare crisis of the late 1980s, MMA—like virtually all health insurance companies—had struggled to create healthcare plans that would adequately cover medical expenses at a cost that policyholders could afford, and based on actuarial data that gave the plans a realistic chance of remaining solvent. By 2010, as the national debate over the ACA was reaching a bitter climax, Everence had managed to survive as a provider of health insurance. But the long-term outlook was not promising. Thus, when faced once again with the question of whether it would seek an amendment to the national legislation in order to continue serving only members in the Anabaptist-Mennonite tradition, Everence chose not to pursue that legislative battle. Instead, the ACA provided a framework for the organization to bring its individual health insurance program to an end.

How to do that gracefully, in a way that did not expose its most vulnerable members to needless anxiety about their transition into a new plan, required a great deal of planning and energy. The challenge of winding down the individual healthcare program fell largely to David Gautsche, vice president for Sales and Services. Two years ahead of the transition to the new system, which was scheduled to begin in 2014, Everence policyholders began to receive information about the ACA in the mail and on the Everence website. In 2013 Gautsche embarked on a nationwide tour of communities with heavy concentrations of Everence healthcare members. Along the way, he explained the details of the new program and outlined the steps by which individuals—even those who were quite ill—could transition into new healthcare plans. In principle, the promise of ACA to provide universal healthcare met the hopes expressed in the MC USA Health Care Access statement that church delegates had affirmed in 2007. The Affordable Care Act did indeed make it possible for people who would have previously been denied health insurance by commercial companies to receive coverage; and for many people—though not all—coverage became more affordable, especially for those who qualified under the new regulations for Medicaid.

THE CORINTHIAN PLAN: MUTUAL AID REVIVED

Even as Everence was in the process of closing out its individual health insurance policies, it was also giving major attention to a new plan for pastors that had emerged out of the lengthy churchwide conversations around healthcare access.[73] At the MC USA general assembly in 2009, Ervin Stutzman, the denomination's executive director, announced that the church was moving forward with the Corinthian Plan—an approach to health insurance for pastors and church workers based explicitly on the principles of mutual aid that had been so central to the formation of MMA some seventy years prior.[74] The name of the plan came from Paul's letter to the church at Corinth, where he encouraged them to emulate the generosity of the Macedonian churches who "gave as much as they were able, and even beyond their ability." (2 Corinthians 8:3).

The genius of the Corinthian Plan was the creation of a self-funded pool of insured pastors and church workers that was sufficiently large—and sufficiently funded—to guarantee coverage to all qualified applicants, regardless of their medical history. In order to make the plan work, large or wealthy churches needed to contribute more to the plan than smaller congregations.

If a pastor already had coverage through a spouse's plan, the congregation would still make a contribution to support premiums for pastors who otherwise could not afford to buy health insurance. The plan had high deductibles, integrated with a Health Savings Account, and included a requirement that all participants adhere to a wellness program focused on preventative practices. One clear benefit of the Corinthian Plan was its portability—pastors who moved from one congregation to another did not have to worry about reapplying for health insurance. MC USA owned and sponsored the plan; but since its inception in 2010 Everence has provided the infrastructure needed to manage enrollment, set the premiums, and oversee the finances.[75]

Thus far, the Corinthian Plan has been remarkably successful—a model of mutual aid that has enabled congregations throughout the country to support each other in a very concrete and practical way. In August 2018 some 321 congregations were part of the plan, enabling 215 churches to provide health coverage for 796 pastors or church workers.[76]

Conclusion

In October of 2013, Larry Miller announced that he intended to retire as Everence's CEO and president by the following fall, after eight years of service to the organization. Like all leaders, Miller built on the foundations of his predecessors. But he also left a profound mark on the organization. In less than a decade, Everence had weathered the Great Recession, renovated its corporate headquarters, redesigned its sales and distribution system, and closed out its individual health insurance program in a way that enabled its members, even those who were quite sick, to maintain coverage. At an even deeper level, MMA was transformed by its new alliance with Mennonite Financial Federal Credit Union—a partnership profound enough to merit an entirely new name. With close to eighty thousand members and managed assets of $2 billion, Everence had become a full-service financial organization.

EIGHT

Everence Today

(2014–2020)

*O*ne of the newest Everence offices, situated within the Esperanza Health Center in the Kensington neighborhood of Philadelphia, symbolizes a significant moment in the organization's 75-year history. Kensington is not a wealthy community. Indeed, it represents a part of Philadelphia that financial institutions generally avoid. Yet as Leonard Dow, the banker-turned-pastor who directs the project, frequently repeats, one goal of the new office is precisely to "engage folks with financial services who have traditionally been left out of that world."[1] The initiative is also unique in the history of Everence in that its membership will almost certainly include a higher percentage of African Americans, Hispanics, and Asians than any of its other locations. And the new office will draw heavily on the latest in communication technology, connecting local Kensington residents who are seeking basic banking services with Everence representatives in other locations via videoconferencing. The branch will be a test of a new generation of high tech "kiosk banking" that is likely to be the wave of the future for many financial institutions.

In all of these ways—serving members in a major urban context who are racially and ethnically diverse, drawing on cutting edge technology—Everence is breaking new ground, living into a bold future. But in another sense, there is nothing unusual about these innovations. As it has done throughout the past seventy-five years, Everence continues to go "where the people go"—in this case to a growing number of urban Anabaptist-Mennonites and other supporters of these faith-based values who are looking for financial services that will truly serve their needs.

It is fitting that the Everence branch of the future is being tested in Philadelphia. The City of Brotherly Love is home to Germantown Mennonite Church, the oldest Mennonite congregation in North America, whose roots go back to 1690. In the centuries that followed, Anabaptist-Mennonites largely avoided the bustling metropolis of Philadelphia, settling instead in agrarian communities north in nearby Franconia township and westward in Lancaster County. But in 1899 the General Conference Mennonite Church established the First Mennonite Church of Philadelphia, whose "Menno-Friendly Benefit Association," a burial aid society, survived through the 1950s. In the early

Staffers Bryant Keal, Leonard Dow, Natalie Martinez, Randy Nyce, and Kevin Gil (from left) by an old bank vault in the building where Everence opened an office in Philadelphia. MATTHEW LESTER

1930s, several African Americans began to attend services at the Lancaster Conference Mennonite mission church near Norris Square in the Kensington neighborhood.[2] By the 1960s there were more than a dozen Anabaptist-Mennonite churches in Philadelphia; and in more recent decades, the city has become home to numerous additional congregations founded by immigrants from India, Vietnam, China, Ethiopia, and elsewhere. By the time the Everence Financial office opened in Kensington, Anabaptist-Mennonites in Philadelphia were worshiping in more than a dozen different languages.[3]

Leonard Dow, the visionary pastor, banker, and community organizer who heads the office, embodies that story. Born and raised in Philadelphia, Dow first encountered the Mennonite tradition in 1978 as a high school student at Christopher Dock Mennonite High School in Lansdale, Pennsylvania, and then as a graduate of Eastern Mennonite University in Harrisonburg, Virginia. Soon after graduation, he began working at the Univest bank in Souderton, Pennsylvania, where he noticed that loans in that largely Mennonite community "recycled" money whereas wealth in the African American Philadelphia neighborhoods where he grew up seemed to only flow out. In 1999, Dow became pastor of the Oxford Circle Mennonite Church, located in one of Philadelphia's most ethnically diverse neighborhoods. Like the theologian-economists who founded MMA two generations earlier, Dow was committed to bringing faith and economic practice together. So he established the Oxford Circle Christian Community Development Association, a nonprofit organization whose vibrant community center helped to transform the neighborhood. Dow's theological grounding, his commitment to the principles of mutual aid, and his ability to build partnerships were fully aligned with the Everence spirit. Those same traits will be crucial to the success of the new Kensington office.

A New CEO

Philadelphia is also close to the heart of Ken Hochstetler, Everence president and CEO since 2014. Although Hochstetler grew up in Goshen, Indiana—with a paper route that included deliveries to both of the Eighth Street homes that once housed MMA's earliest offices—he spent most of his adult life living in the Mennonite community of Souderton, Pennsylvania, just thirty-five miles north of Philadelphia. Anabaptist-Mennonites in eastern Pennsylvania had a long tradition of integrating faith and business. Many of the leading businesses in the area were established by Anabaptist-Mennonite families, who had a reputation for channeling their wealth to worthy causes.[4] Indeed, a significant percentage of MMA's charitable assets during its rapid growth in the

Joining Everence in 2014, Ken Hochstetler, current president and CEO, is leading the organization into serving more diverse and urban areas, like Philadelphia.

second half of the twentieth century derived from Anabaptist-Mennonite family businesses and farms in the region.

Hochstetler, who came from a more traditional midwestern Mennonite background, flourished in this setting. While completing an MBA program at Lehigh University in Bethlehem, Pennsylvania, he began working as a commercial loan officer with Meridian Bank. In 1991, he joined Univest Corporation, in Souderton, Pennsylvania where he worked for over twenty years, becoming senior executive vice president, with various leadership roles in its transition from traditional banking to broad financial services provider. While at Univest, he gained extensive experience in banking, insurance, investments, charitable services, and financial planning. As a member of Blooming Glen Mennonite Church, Hochstetler was nurtured in church leadership and stewardship practices. He also became deeply involved with Mennonite Economic Development Associates (MEDA), serving as a long-time board member at both the local and the binational level.[5] For Hochstetler the idea of "the best of church and best of business" was deeply integrated into virtually every part of his life—so much so that when, in the spring of 2014, the Everence search committee invited him to serve as its president and CEO, it seemed like a job for which he had been preparing his entire life.[6]

When Hochstetler joined Everence in August of 2014, he quickly recognized that the organization had a strong foundation and was poised for growth. A year after his arrival, Hochstetler and his leadership team developed a five-year plan outlining the strategic priorities of Everence in the years leading up to the seventy-fifth anniversary celebration.[7] The foundation of the strategic plan was a mission statement that any of MMA's earlier leaders would likely have recognized and affirmed—to "help people and institutions integrate their faith and values into their financial decisions to accomplish their stewardship goals." Based on that mission statement Everence today operates by the same fundamental principles that guided the small staff in the late 1940s who over-saw CPS loans, launched the Burial Aid and Hospital-Surgical Aid plan, and envisioned the Survivor's Aid program—namely, its products and services must produce operating income so that its growing membership can, in turn, prac-tice faithful generosity. The form those principles have taken across the years have varied enormously, of course. The size, scope, and complexity of Everence today would, no doubt, stagger the early pioneers of the mutual aid movement. But they would recognize the essential components.

It is difficult to capture fully the breadth of the Everence identity—the rich diversity of its products and services, the multifaceted nature of its external relationships, the layers of operational interactions that move its work forward, or the nuanced considerations that go into the difficult decisions of its leader-ship. But one glimpse into the character of Everence today is suggested by five simple aspirational statements that comprise the Everence Strategic Plan 2020, formulated in 2016. Each of them emerges out of a historical context; and each illuminates a set of questions and challenges that will continue to shape the Everence identity in the future.

Everence Today

1. WE WILL BE AN EMPLOYER OF CHOICE WITH A WORKFORCE THAT REFLECTS GROWING DIVERSITY

For much of its history MMA's board, employees, and membership reflected the gender assumptions and racial profile of the Anabaptist-Mennonite churches it served—which is to say that the organization was overwhelm-ingly white and dominated by males. The first female MMA board member, Mary Swartley, was not elected until 1980. Shortly thereafter she was joined by Miriam Weaver, and then by Mary Conrad, bringing the total number of women on the board to three in 1984. That number increased to five in 1986, and since then has never been less than five, with at least three women—Mary Swartley, Beryl Brubaker, and Carol Suter—serving as board chairs.[8]

Integrating women into the upper management of the organization proved to be more difficult. In 1972, MMA had nine hiring classes for ranking its fifty-four employees in terms of their wages or salaries. All thirty-three of the employees in the bottom three wage groups were women; only Maggie Glick, listed in Class IV as a "field services promotion assistant" was salaried. Which meant, of course, that the twenty highest paid employees in 1972 were all men.[9]

In 1987, Steve Garboden, writing on behalf of MMA's executive leadership team, informed the board of an "affirmative action" plan to recruit and promote women within the organization. Although there were fifteen women in managerial positions, none had advanced into vice presidential roles. "There is no overt prejudice toward including women in Division Management," Garboden asserted, but if changes are going to happen "we need to take active steps to counter the momentum which is implicit in our society."[10]

But a year-and-a-half later, after a Women in Leadership seminar for division managers, Garboden lamented the lack of progress and called on the personnel department to create a mentoring system, a trainee program, and to identify "five outside persons for women manager candidates and to review career/education possibilities with them."[11] In 1991, Shirley Yoder, who had served on the MMA board from 1986 to 1990, was appointed vice president of Corporate Services. Shortly thereafter, Eunice Culp also moved into a vice president position with responsibilities for Human Resources.[12]

An even bigger challenge for the organization was addressing the deep institutional racism that permeates virtually every aspect of American society. For much of MMA's early history, references to race simply do not appear in the sources—a measure of the insularity of the organization and the churches that it served. In 1968, following news of the assassination of Martin Luther King Jr., Lowell Nissley wrote a long editorial in the MMA office newsletter, in which he agonized about the complacency of Mennonites in the face of racial injustice. "In the light of this man's life," Nissley asked,

> what do we here at Mennonite Mutual Aid feel? We who are so concerned for people with burdens. We who are dedicated to weeping with those who weep. . . . Is this maybe our trouble—we don't think of the negro, the Mexican, the poor, as our neighbor? . . . It seems to me the time has come and long overdue for us to build a fire under our feelings, or someone else will likely do it for us.[13]

In the spring of 1971, MMA made a first gesture to embrace the racial diversity of the Mennonite Church by creating the Congregational Health Improvement Program, an initiative directed primarily to low income congregations in south Texas—most of them Spanish-speaking—to help members purchase health insurance.[14] Yet progress was slow. In 1978, MMA employees

Working with many Spanish-speaking churches, Stewardship Consultant Martin Navarro was invited to Puerto Rico to lead a spiritual and financial wellness retreat for pastors after Hurricane Maria.

noted in their organizational review that none of the many MMA brochures were available in Spanish and that the organization had almost no Spanish-speaking employees. Two years later, the MMA board appointed Macler Shephard as its first African American member, though it appears as if he, along with Rafael Ramos, who was appointed in 1984, served only a single term. LeRoy Berry Jr., an African American Mennonite college professor and lawyer, also cut short his tenure with the MMA Board.

To be sure, MMA fraternal funds subsidized virtually all the work of Mennonite Minority Ministries in the 1970s and 1980s, along with numerous specific projects initiated by African American, Native American, and Hispanic church leaders. And MMA provided significant financial support to the Damascus Road antiracism training program in the 1990s. But bringing racial diversity into the Everence membership or into the organization itself was difficult. In the ambitious ten-year strategic plan introduced in 1995, MMA anticipated the significance of the Internet, the need to market to a younger generation, and the likely waning of denominational loyalties; but an outreach to the church's racial/ethnic groups does not appear anywhere in that expansive vision of the future.

With the formation of MC USA at the turn of the century, the new denomination made a formal commitment "to honor the dignity and value of all racial/ethnic people in Mennonite Church USA, ensuring just and equitable access to church resources, positions and information."[15] In 2007, church leaders conducted an internal review to assess the progress of each agency toward reaching that goal. In their report, MMA administrators noted that most of their management team had participated in Damascus Road antiracism training; but they also confessed that "MMA has not yet found the best model for building stronger relationships with our Racial/Ethnic constituency."[16] MMA could identify congregational advocates in one hundred of the 158 racial/ethnic churches in MC USA, but also recognized that only six of its three hundred employees were people of color.[17] Their report went on to note that Spanish-speaking communities were "the fastest growing segment within MMA's eligible church denominations," and concluded with a commitment to invest $500,000 to recruit employees of diverse backgrounds, provide bilingual services, subsidize financial counseling, and develop a Spanish version of the organization's website.

This context helps to clarify why an explicit commitment to diversity is a key component of the Everence strategic plan today. In 2015 Everence created a "specialist" position for a Stewardship Consultant who would expand relationships with Spanish-speaking individuals and congregations around the country. The first person to serve in that role, Martin Navarro, has helped Everence develop a more realistic understanding of what it means to expand its reach to include racial/ethnic groups. But it is not enough, as Navarro has noted, to simply translate a brochure into Spanish or to make the same product

Everence has begun recruiting more college interns to experience the organization during summer months, including this group in 2018.

available to Spanish-speakers. If Everence is truly going to serve the needs of the Hispanic community, it will require a deep understanding of the particular needs and context of the group it wishes to serve—which might include entirely new products.[18] Currently, numerous Spanish speakers serve as Everence financial consultants, stewardship consultants, or church relations representatives, with additional bilingual staff assisting customers at Everence Federal Credit Union. The Everence website now features an enlarged Spanish language section with materials specifically designed for a Hispanic market.

At an Everence board meeting in February 2016, Hochstetler, along with Eunice Culp, vice president of Human Resources, proposed the creation of a diversity and inclusion plan.[19] The plan—which brought Aphaphanh Nussbaum to Everence in 2018 as its Diversity and Recruitment Coordinator and created a Diversity and Inclusion advisory group—has slowly begun to see results. Whereas in 2014, only 3.1 percent of the Everence workforce were people of color, that number had grown to 10 percent by the end of 2019.[20] Changes are also evident at the top levels of leadership. Included among the nine members of the Everence senior leadership team today are three women (Eunice Culp, Madalyn Metzger, and Julie Hertzler) and two persons of color (Jim Alvarez and Madalyn Metzger); nearly twenty women represent Everence in its various offices as financial representatives, financial and stewardship consultants, or financial planners.[21] For all staff, Everence has also worked intentionally at cultivating a work environment that "fosters inclusion, sensitivity, understanding, and mutual respect."[22]

As part of its current strategic commitment to invest in its employees, the Human Resource department has regularly conducted surveys to assess engagement and address employee concerns. The evidence also suggests that employee turnover at Everence is much lower than comparable companies; and most open positions are quickly filled—suggesting that Everence enjoys a good reputation in the local community.[23] Finally, the organization has developed an extensive paid summer internship program, with a long-term view to cultivating future employees and leaders who reflect the diversity of the contemporary church.

2. WE WILL DEEPEN OUR CUSTOMER RELATIONSHIPS IN TERMS OF PRODUCTS AND EXPERIENCE

Everence today has seventy-eight thousand members and clients living in all fifty states, with offices in some twenty-six different locations. Like similar organizations, the challenge of connecting with individual members in a meaningful and personalized way is ongoing. During the first half of its existence,

MMA distributed its mutual aid plans, insurance products, and stewardship educational materials through volunteer representatives in local congregations who were supported by regional staff members. In the 1980s, as these products became increasingly complicated, MMA turned to independent licensed agents as its primary point of contact with members. Today, distribution of most Everence products occurs through Everence employees in its field offices.

But beyond the formal channels of sales and distribution, numerous other face-to-face interactions help to link Everence with its members. Every day, for example, Everence Federal Credit Union staff enable hundreds of banking transactions and confer with dozens of clients—including many churches and small businesses—regarding loans. Everence financial consultants meet regularly with individuals, families, and business owners to review their financial goals. Stewardship consultants offer counsel on charitable planning, donor advised funds, bequests, and gift annuities. Everence managers tend to relationships with churches and organizations regarding group health and retirement plans. And staff correspond every day with congregational advocates about stewardship education resources and the details of Sharing Fund grants. In April 2019 Everence established a Customer Engagement Center, with the goal of not only responding quickly to queries from its members, but also to contact members proactively—even if their investments with Everence are relatively small.[24] The Marketing department has also worked hard to differentiate its messages to appropriate segments of Everence members, while also ensuring

Everence has invested in offices in regions around the country, including this new space in North Newton, Kans.

that its brand promise ("guided by Christian values [we will] cultivate and grow the resources that enrich our communities and the lives we share") will be unmistakably clear in its sales and marketing campaigns.

In 2014, Everence launched a comprehensive and highly personalized approach to financial planning. Using the Everence Vine brandmark as a framework, conversations usually begin with four basic aspects of steward-ship—discover and plan for God's purpose; live responsibly; prepare for the future; give generously—before moving to specific "branches" connected to the vine such as cash flow, investment, taxes, and charity. Online access to Vine Vision 360 enables Everence members to organize and track their cash and monitor savings, charitable giving, and investments.

Everence continues to have a local presence in more than one thousand congregations through its congregational Stewardship Advocates—volunteers trained and encouraged by Everence staff members to promote steward-ship ministry and assist with applications for Sharing Fund grants. In 2018 Everence, in collaboration with *The Mennonite Inc.*, sponsored "Smart Living, Simple Money," a podcast produced by young adults about connecting their experiences with faith and values. In another outreach to youth intended to encourage savings, Everence Federal Credit Union has offered a special account for young people that earns a higher rate of interest.

It may be too early to assess the full impact of these recent efforts to deepen member relationships, but several surveys have reported very positive re-sponses, with overall customer satisfaction increasing from 84 percent in 2004 to 94 percent in 2018, far higher than the general market.[25]

3. WE WILL CREATE AN ENVIRONMENT THAT ENCOURAGES DIGITAL INNOVATION

In the fall of 1991, as James Kratz was preparing to vacate his office after seven-teen years of service to MMA, he paused to reflect on the growing significance of technology in the organization. Among church-related institutions, MMA had long been at the cutting edge of new technology, and Kratz took some pride in the growing sophistication of MMA's use of computers. "Between 1978 and 1984," he recalled, "we completely switched over to automation. It was a change that was inevitable, and we couldn't function without it." But then he also added a cautionary note. "I still have some reservations," he wor-ried, "about what computers do to personal relationships."[26]

What Kratz could not have foreseen in 1991 was the way in which rap-idly advancing technology would dominate virtually every aspect of MMA's work during the next two decades, first with the increasing capacity of its IBM mainframe, then with the introduction of desktop computers, and now with the digital revolution unleashed by the ever-expanding capacity of the Internet.

Today, Everence is living into the reality of the digital world. Like most modern banks, Everence Federal Credit Union enables its customers to carry out nearly all of their banking transactions using smartphones or a personal computer. Shareholders of Praxis Mutual Funds can conduct transactions in their accounts from the comfort of their homes. The Everence Marketing team manages various social media accounts that keep members informed about financial tips, new products, or perspectives on changing market trends. The Everence website offers a wide array of stewardship educational materials, along with full explanations of its many departments and services. Responding to stringent federal regulations, Everence has invested millions of dollars in digital security, assuring members that their money and personal information are secure. State-of-the-art teleconference rooms enable Everence employees to hold meetings across vast geographic distances; and increasingly, financial advising and other customer service functions are being handled via video-conference as a way of connecting members with just the right staff person, regardless of where they happen to live.

In these, and many other ways, Everence has already fully embraced digital innovation. Looking forward, perhaps the bigger challenges will be the unintended consequences of the digital revolution. Although each new technological advance presents itself with an aura of inevitability, Everence leaders of the future will need to make conscious choices about how technology will shape the identity of the organization. One essential aspect of the digital world, for example, is the principle of speed. We can now check our balances on the hour if we wish, invest in the stock market before breakfast, transfer money from one account to another with a few keystrokes, pay bills while we sleep, and deposit checks without leaving our homes. With these expectations now firmly in place, Everence will now need to continue upgrading those systems if members are going to remain loyal. Once you step on the escalator of accelerating expectations it is very difficult to step off.

An even more significant challenge posed by the digital revolution—not just for Everence, but for all humanity—is its impact on relationships. At the heart of the Christian narrative, as it unfolds in the story of creation, is a conviction that God created human beings to live in relationships of trust and transparency. To be sure, these relationships have been distorted by sin; but at their very core, humans yearn for intimate relationships. Modern people like the efficiency and convenience that digital technology offers; but it is also becoming increasingly evident that the nature of a relationship changes fundamentally when it is conducted through the abstract medium of the Internet rather than face-to-face. Electronic communication enables transactional connections, but ultimately, it is no substitute for embodied human relationships. Indeed, despite the fact that we are more electronically connected with each other than ever before, a recent major study reports that a staggering 47 percent of Americans of all ages often feel alone, left out, and lacking meaningful connection with others.[27]

It is unrealistic to expect Everence employees to have personal relationships with each of its seventy-eight thousand members. But a powerful theme in the Anabaptist-Mennonite tradition is its emphasis on communities shaped by love, compassion, and generosity. Moving into the future, how will Everence nurture relationships within the organization and with its members that honor and promote these essential qualities? Whether digital technology will be a helpful tool or an obstacle in reaching these goals will say much about the creativity of Everence leadership in the coming years.

From left, Angelo Perera, Sara Alvarez Waugh, Levi Wilson, and Steven Craft receive the organization's internal Commitment of Excellence Award from President Ken Hochstetler (center). The award recognized the team's efforts in digital innovation with the 2017 launch of the organization's new website.

4. WE WILL SATISFY CUSTOMER NEEDS WITH PRODUCTS THAT ARE UPDATED AND COMPETITIVE

Ever since the years of helter-skelter growth in the first decade of its existence, Everence has continuously adjusted its products and services to meet the changing needs of its members. Some products, like the Thrift Accumulation plan or Menno Insurance Service, quietly disappeared.[28] The decision in 1998 to close out the automobile insurance program, which had been an active part of the organization for forty years, was more controversial.[29] Some initiatives that Everence once administered—life insurance, for example, or the Community Development Investment program—are now brokered through other companies.[30] In describing the many products and services that comprise Everence today, employees frequently turn to the building at 1100 North Main Street as a metaphor. Entering from the front, the building looks deceptively simple. An aerial photo, however, reveals a large sprawling complex of buildings behind the facade, all clearly connected to each other and part of the same structure, but nearly invisible to the person walking in the front door.

In general, Everence offers five categories of products:

- *Banking* through Everence Federal Credit Union
- *Insurance*—including Medicare Supplement, GroupCare health plans, and other insurance plans
- *Investments*—particularly Praxis Mutual Funds, with its strong legacy of "stewardship investing," and asset management services provided by Everence Trust Company
- *Charitable giving*—including Everence Foundation, donor advised funds, and charitable gift annuities
- *Financial planning*

In the world of financial institutions, Everence is a fairly small company offering its members a large range of options. "We already have a broad range of products," Hochstetler reflected. "Our opportunity is to serve more members with our current offerings. Our challenge is to keep them updated and competitive, and to develop additional solutions for emerging needs." At the same time, in a world where Everence must compete with its counterparts for quality and price, it faces the additional challenge of demonstrating that these products and services reflect the distinctive values that Everence has claimed for itself as a church-related organization. Sometimes—as with the case of socially responsible investments, the fraternal funds, or the Corinthian Plan—the "margin of difference" is obvious. In other instances, however, such as financial planning, the qualities that distinguish the Everence approach rely heavily on

With friend Talisa Lopez-Garcia, Brenda Brown (right) is an Everence member who was drawn to its Medicare Supplement plan because of the organization's faith mission. ELAINE KESSLER

the individual advisor's expertise in charitable services and the nature of the personal interaction.

One product did get a visible overhaul in 2017 when Everence Federal Credit Union revised the charitable feature of its credit card. Today, the MyNeighbor card enables members to direct 1.5 percent of the money they spend to a charitable organization of their choice; in one year alone a nonprofit organization designated by sixty-eight MyNeighbor cardholders received close to $18,000. Within two and a half years, Everence has donated nearly $1 million to a host of local and global nonprofits through the MyNeighbor program.[31] Whereas the Everence Foundation supports the generosity of wealthier people, the MyNeighbor card enables the average person to express their generosity.

Going forward, Everence will need to continually emphasize the "value proposition" of products and services like the MyNeighbor card if it is going to distinguish itself in the marketplace of financial institutions. In the early 1970s, arguments in favor of socially responsible investing seemed to be at the fringe of the investment world. Today, these basic concepts have become mainstream, with virtually every major investment firm offering an SRI (or ESG—environment, social, and governance) screened fund.

Looking to the future, what are the cutting-edge ethical questions that Everence might take the lead in addressing? Could the creativity that made Everence a pioneer in the world of SRI investing inspire it to respond in new creative ways to the growing wealth inequality in our country? To do more about the massive burden of student debt borne by many young people? Or, even more audaciously, to address the climate crisis that the coming generation is now facing?[32]

5. WE WILL STRENGTHEN OUR CHURCH, COMMUNITY, AND FRATERNAL CONNECTIONS

According to the bylaws of Mennonite Church USA, Everence is the denomination's Stewardship Agency, one of five churchwide programs linked to the church through regular reports, reviews, and by the denomination's hand in approving the appointment of its CEO. But Everence also nurtures relationships with many other denominations and church networks whose values align with the Anabaptist-Mennonite tradition, and it identifies itself even more

The MyNeighbor credit card allows its users to donate 1.5 percent of the money they spend on the card. Kari Cullen (left), a credit branch manager in Belleville, Pa., gave $500 to Jane Neff, Director of Shelter Service, from members who chose it as their charity of choice in 2017.

Vanessa Caruso, with her son, chose to work with Everence on financial planning to help her and her husband Steven manage their money. JENNA STAMM

broadly as a "financial organization dedicated to the principles of Christian stewardship." At the same time, Everence is also a part of many local communities. And it cultivates a host of other relationships with partners in the world of SRI investing, various trade associations, Mennonite Health Services, and parachurch organizations like MEDA and Mennonite World Conference.

At various times in its history, Everence leaders have cultivated some relationships more than others. Howard Brenneman, for example, made a concerted effort to connect more intentionally with local civic leaders and organizations, a posture that Ken Hochstetler has strongly affirmed through such things as employee service days, support of the United Way Campaign, and corporate sponsorship of regional cultural programs and events. Hochstetler has also nurtured strong connections with the American Fraternal Alliance, the Church Benefit Association, rkGoBig (the Credit Union's shared services organization), and the Christian Investment Forum, which all help to ensure that the organization does not become unduly preoccupied with its own internal realities.

Yet within the long arc of Everence history, its relationship with the church and its identity as a Christian organization will likely require significant ongoing attention. Clearly, many of the traditional ways that Everence has demonstrated its commitment to the church in the past remain vibrant and strong. Since 2013, Everence has helped to channel nearly $400 million to worthy causes, a remarkable redistribution of wealth that has enabled scores of schools, hospitals, mission and service organizations, retirement homes, and church-related projects to thrive. Everence makes very little profit on the Mennonite Retirement Trust, Corinthian Plan, or the health insurance pools it administers, seeing them as a service to the church. And the long legacy of stewardship education continues to be at the forefront of the organization's identity.

But in other ways, the challenge of holding together "the best of church and best of business" has been made much more complicated by the widespread collapse of public confidence in church-related institutions and by the associated rise in the number of people—especially young adults—who check "none" when asked about their church affiliation. For many young people today, Christianity has come to connote a rigid and narrow-minded worldview, closely associated with racism, misogyny, and homophobia. Although the rising generation may affirm values like "peacemaking," "environmentally

Everence works with many organizations, such as Garden Spot Village, where CEO Steve Lindsey shows its innovative greenhouse to Everence staffer Nikki Shingle. Everence has an office at Garden Spot to help its retired residents with financial matters. KATE LOPEZ

sensitive," or "socially responsible," any explicit links between these values and the teachings of Jesus in the New Testament can be met with skepticism. For Everence, this means that an organization whose distinctive identity has been inseparable from the teachings of Jesus will need to find new ways to claim its deeply religious roots while also attracting a younger market.

Equally challenging will be the task of defining the Everence Christian identity within its own membership. In recent years, Hochstetler has worked very intentionally to broaden the family of denominations that Everence serves. Today that list includes a wide spectrum of groups, more than thirty altogether, ranging from conservative Amish-Mennonite churches to very progressive Quakers—a remarkable assembly in light of the polarized character of contemporary American culture. Although few of the Everence products and services invite theological controversy, litmus tests of one sort or another inevitably arise. In the area of socially responsible investments, for example, determining what qualifies as "socially responsible" inevitably has a theological component. In recent years, several investment firms, appealing to more conservative and evangelical investors, have developed their own mutual funds using screens that represent their convictions on various conservative social issues, such as same-sex marriage or abortion. By contrast, Everence current shareholder advocacy focuses on the themes of environmental sustainability, ending modern slavery, and addressing inequality, topics that may not attract all Christian investors.[33]

Closer to home, Everence continues to negotiate its public identity as an agency of Mennonite Church USA at a time when the denomination itself is undergoing deep divisions over issues related to gender, sexuality, and church polity.[34] Thus far, however, most members and congregations who related closely to Everence in the past have retained their ties to the organization even after leaving MC USA. And indeed, Everence continues to be a welcome framework for ongoing conversations and relationships among various Anabaptist-Mennonite groups in an era otherwise marked by fragmentation and division.

One concrete example of this bridge-building role emerged in 2016 when Everence received a $1 million grant from the Lilly Endowment to develop a Pastoral Financial Wellness Program. Piloted first within MC USA and the Conservative Mennonite Conference, the program provided direct financial support to pastors—with matching funds from their congregations or conferences—for debt relief, financial education, and personal financial planning. In 2019, following the pilot program's resounding success, Lilly provided an additional $1 million grant, which Everence used to expand its Pastoral Financial Wellness Program to active and credentialed pastors from all of Everence's partner denominations.[35]

On the eve of its seventy-fifth anniversary, Everence appears to be a strong and vibrant organization, clearly on a trajectory of growth. Yet even as Everence celebrates that milestone from a position of financial health, the perennial questions of mission and identity refuse to go away. During the first half of its history, MMA defined itself primarily in the language of mutual aid. Beginning in the 1990s, the organization embraced the themes of stewardship and generosity. Now as it looks to the future, Everence will once again need to identify and embrace its defining motif. As Everence moves into the next chapter of its history as "a Christian-based, member-owned financial services organization,"[36] how will those Christian commitments find expression? Will the carriers of a Christian identity be found primarily in the distinctive nature of its products and services? In the character and quality of Everence employees? In the commitments of Everence board members? In the tone and example of the CEO? Or in something else altogether?

None of these questions, of course, are new. From its beginnings in 1945, Everence—like all church-related institutions—has always faced the challenge of maintaining some kind of healthy equilibrium between the competing claims of it faith commitments and the daily pressures of the marketplace. What is new today is not these deeply embedded tensions, but rather the changing contexts within which those tensions will find expression and the new faith-based solutions that will emerge in the coming decades.

Looking to the Future

In 1945 MMA consisted of a two-room loan office in Goshen with $8,750 in start-up capital. Today, Everence—the successor to that tiny initiative—is a modern organization with some 380 employees working in nearly thirty locations and managing assets of more than $4 billion. In the seventy-five years between 1945 and 2020—the span of a single lifetime—the nature of mutual aid, stewardship and generosity among Anabaptist-Mennonites in the United States has been fundamentally transformed.

At each step of the way, of course, there have been critics, worried that the history of Everence is a parable of a larger narrative of Anabaptist-Mennonite complicity with modern capitalism or a story of the commodification of human relationships.[37] Behind most of the criticism lies a concern that the teachings of Jesus about love, trust, vulnerability, and generosity are fatally compromised whenever money emerges as a medium of exchange or whenever Christians organize institutions as a means of expressing these virtues. Yet unless one is going to withdraw from modern society altogether and commit to a communal life of free exchange or bartering, *some* form of financial transactions will be inevitable. And if Christians are going to enter into a common enterprise of any sort, *some* form of organization is going to emerge in which policies and procedures will be essential to the organization's success.

Of course, no institution—least of all one with roots in the church—is above critique. But there is no starting point of purity; no historical "golden age" when Anabaptist-Mennonites somehow practiced mutual aid perfectly; no realized ideal that can stand in absolute judgment of every other effort to live out one's faith in the context of a changing culture. The history of the early church and the history of the Anabaptist movement both bear witness to a wide variety of earnest efforts to give expression to Christ's teachings on wealth, community, and generosity.

Currently, the fastest growing groups in the Anabaptist-Mennonite movement are found in settings outside of Europe and North America. Indeed, since 2001, 93 percent of the growth of the Anabaptist-Mennonite family has taken place in Africa, Asia, and Latin America.[38] Not surprisingly, each of these groups that have claimed a voice within the Anabaptist-Mennonite movement express their understandings of Christian faith and life in ways that are relevant to their particular culture. This, most Christians would agree, is exactly as it should be: faith must be "inculturated."

So it is with Everence. Everence has always existed at the intersection of the biblical understanding of *incarnation* and the secular concept of *incorporation*. Both of these parallel terms—incarnation and incorporation—derive from Latin roots; and both attempt to describe a reality that strains human comprehension. The incarnation (from *carne*, or flesh) points to the mystery that God—creator of the universe—entered into the world of time and space in the person of Jesus. In Jesus the "Word became flesh." Followers of Jesus do not claim perfection; nor are their practices all the same. But through the Holy Spirit, the body of Christ is still present in the world—the Word is still made flesh—wherever believers bear witness to the way of Christ in their daily lives. When Anabaptists spoke of economic sharing or community of goods, they did not mean something abstract—it was a concrete, tangible expression of their new life in Christ. And when that sharing happens today with an attitude of joy and gratitude to God, Christians participate in the incarnation, making the Spirit of God visible in the world.

At the same time, church-related institutions like Everence also exist in the secular world as a corporation. In the Western world, corporations enabled new forms of organization and commerce to emerge, which have proven to be remarkably useful. Yet like incarnation, the word incorporation (from *corpus*, or body) is an effort to describe a body that is invisible. Some scholars call corporations "legal fictions"—even though they do not take up space in the world, corporations can nevertheless own property, pay taxes, obey laws, hire employees, build factories, borrow money, and contribute to political campaigns.[39] In the modern world, the high priests of corporations are not clergy but judges, presiding over sacred rituals that enable modern people to believe that corporations are real.

On July 19, 1945, the first official act of the Mennonite Mutual Aid committee was to become incorporated as a not-for-profit company. In the years that followed, virtually every entity that MMA created took on a legal identity as a corporation. By the "useful fiction" of incorporation, Everence has been able to act collectively on behalf of thousands of individuals, receiving their money, writing checks, enacting policies, and bearing a legal responsibility to treat them and the resources entrusted to the corporation in a responsible and transparent way.

In itself, incorporation is not an inherent threat to the church's understanding of the incarnation. Corporations, subject to regulatory laws, have enabled church-related institutions to do things that they would not have been able to do on their own. But one should never lose sight of the quasi-religious—and hence, the idolatrous—quality that is also part of the world that corporations inhabit.

Everence, like all church-related institutions, is not a congregation—we should not expect to find in it the fullest expression of the incarnation. But neither is Everence merely a corporation. The future of Everence will depend on the capacity of its leaders, its employees, its members, and the churches that it serves to consciously live between the radical freedom of the incarnation and the regulatory world of the incorporation—deeply attentive to the call of Jesus to "give to all who ask," while also creatively engaging the laws, economic currents, and cultural context of the world in which it lives.

In the summer of 1995, at the celebration of its fiftieth anniversary, the MMA planning committee organized a futuristic exhibit at the joint Mennonite Church and General Conference Mennonite Church delegate convention meeting in Wichita, Kansas. The display featured a guided tour in a "time-travel machine" that first transported the viewers back to the inspiring story of

Anabaptist beginnings in 1525 and the importance of economic sharing in the churches they formed. A series of video clips featuring the founders of MMA then reviewed that vision as it had developed over the past fifty years. But the central focus was on the future—the year 2025 when Anabaptists around the world would commemorate the five hundredth anniversary of the first baptisms in Zurich, Switzerland. In this vision of the future, the church was racially and ethnically diverse; Anabaptist-Mennonites in 2025 were recognized around the world as peacemakers; and newfound wealth was freely shared with those in need. The video accompanying the exhibit concluded with a scene of baptism, as those attracted to the movement voluntarily committed themselves to Christ and following in the way of Jesus.

Clearly, the reality of Everence today does not have the same sci-fi edge as the scene imagined in the 1995 exhibit. But in some ways the stories unfolding at the new Everence office in the Kensington neighborhood of Philadelphia; or an Everence financial consultant in Kidron, Ohio, offering comfort and counsel to a widow; or a congregation in Virginia whose support of the Corinthian Plan enables a pastor in rural Nebraska to afford health insurance; or a Quaker meeting in Kansas transformed by the practices of stewardship—these stories, multiplied a hundred times over, are no less farsighted or bold.

How Everence will write the next chapter of its future remains to be seen. But the trajectory is clear. Everence was built on a long and rich tradition. Everence remains attuned to the leading of the Spirit. And Everence is attentive to the future, eager to play its part to ensure that the five-hundred-year legacy of Anabaptist-Mennonite mutual aid, stewardship, and generosity will endure for future generations—going, in good conscience, "where the people go."

Notes

Epigraph
"Report of the Insurance and Investment Study Committee," *Twenty-Eighth Mennonite General Conference, Kitchener, Ontario, Canada, August 26–30, 1953* [Proceedings] (Scottdale, PA: Mennonite Publishing House, 1953), 71–80, 74.

Introduction
1 "What We Do Together: The State of Associational Life in America," https://www.lee.senate.gov/public/_cache/files/b5f224ce-98f7-40f6-a814-8602696714d8/what-we-do-together.pdf.
2 "Report of the Committee on Industrial Relations," *Twenty-Third Mennonite General Conference: Organization, Minutes, Reports, Ministerial List, Officers and Committees Elected, Ministers and Delegates in Attendance, Goshen, Ind. August 18–24, 1943*, 28.
3 *Building Communities of Compassion: Mennonite Mutual Aid in Theory and Practice*, ed. Willard Swartley and Donald B. Kraybill (Scottdale, PA: Herald Press, 1998), 13.

Chapter 1
1 The literature on the Anabaptist movement is vast. For a basic introduction see C. Arnold Synder, *Following in the Footsteps of Christ: The Anabaptist Tradition* (Maryknoll, NY: Orbis Books, 2004).
2 For more on Anabaptist beliefs and practices concerning wealth, see Peter James Klassen, *The Economics of Anabaptism, 1525-1560* (The Hague: Mouton, 1964) and James M. Stayer, *The German Peasant War and Anabaptist Community of Goods* (Montreal: McGill-Queens University Press, 1991).
3 *The Chronicle of the Hutterian Brethren*, 2 vol. (Rifton, NY: Plough, 1987), 1:81. The text cites the following Bible verses: Isaiah 23:18; Acts 2:44-45; Acts 4:34-35; and Acts 5:1-11.
4 The best account of the early Hutterite movement can be found in Werner O. Packull, *Hutterite Beginnings: Communitarian Experiments during the Reformation* (Baltimore: Johns Hopkins University Press, 1995).

258 / WHERE THE PEOPLE GO

5 As historian Werner Packull has demonstrated, the same basic commitment to the practice of mutual aid expressed in this Swiss Congregational Order of 1527 was also echoed in an influential *Discipline of the Believers* (ca. 1529) and expressed in even greater detail around 1540 in *A Church Order for Members of Christ's Body* by the Anabaptist Leopold Scharnschlager (Packull, *Hutterite Beginnings*, 33–53).

6 *Anabaptism in Outline: Selected Primary Sources*, ed. Walter Klaassen (Scottdale, PA: Herald Press, 1981), 236.

7 Willard Swartley, "Mutual Aid Based in Jesus and Early Christianity," in *Building Communities of Compassion*, ed. Willard Swartley and Donald B. Kraybill (Scottdale, PA: Herald Press, 1998), 34.

8 Cf. Stayer, *The German Peasants' War and Anabaptist Community of Goods*, 139–159; and Robert Friedmann, "Economic Aspects of Early Hutterite Life," *Mennonite Quarterly Review* 59 (July 1956), 259–266.

9 *Chronicle of the Hutterian Brethren*, 1:84.

10 Indeed, many of their earliest statements of faith, including the Congregational Order of 1527, seemed to suggest that a common purse was biblically mandated.

11 Stayer, *The German Peasants' War and Anabaptist Community of Goods*, 104.

12 Hans Pauli Kuchenbecker, "Das Bekenntnis der Schweizer Brüder in Hessen," *TA, Hesse* (Marburg: G. Braun, 1951), 434–436. Emphasis added.

13 Harold S. Bender, "The Discipline Adopted by the Strasbourg Conference of 1568," *Mennonite Quarterly Review* 1 (January 1927), 57–66.

14 Leonard Gross and Jan Gleysteen (trans.), "The Concept of Cologne," *Mennonite Yearbook* (Scottdale, Pa.: Mennonite Publishing House, 1991), 8–10.

15 *Montbeliard Mennonite Church Register, 1750–1958*, trans. and ed. Joe A. Springer, 2 vol. (Goshen, IN: Mennonite Historical Society, 2015), 1:303.

16 "Foundation of Christian Doctrine," in *The Complete Writings of Menno Simons*, ed. and trans. John C. Wenger (Scottdale, PA: Herald Press, 1956), 110–111.

17 "Why I Do Not Cease Teaching and Writing," in ibid., 307.

18 E.g., "They are so bent on accursed profit that they exclude God wholly from their hearts." ("True Christian Faith," in ibid., 369). See also Menno's denunciation of the gap between the wealthy and the poor in his "Reply to False Accusations," ibid., 558–559.

19 Historian Mary Sprunger has provided a detailed description of these activities. Cf. Mary Sprunger, "Mutual Aid Among Dutch Waterlander Mennonites," in Swartley and Kraybill, *Building Communities of Compassion*, 144–167.

20 Ibid., 148–154.

21 Theron Schlabach summarizes the Oberholtzer story and the emergence of the General Conference Mennonite Church in helpful detail. See *Peace, Faith, Nation: Mennonites and Amish in Nineteenth-Century America* (Scottdale, PA: Herald Press, 1988), 118–140.

22 "John H. Oberholtzer," *Mennonite Encyclopedia*, 4:13.

23 Cf. Helen Kolb Gates, *Bless the Lord, O My Soul* (Scottdale, PA: Herald Press, 1964); Joseph Liechty, "From Yankee to Nonresistant: John F. Funk's Chicago Years," *Mennonite Quarterly Review* 60 (July 1985), 203–247.

24 *Herald of Truth* 10 (October, 1873), 167. The primary sources related to this story are helpfully gathered in *Brothers in Deed to Brothers in Need: A Scrapbook about Mennonite Immigrants from Russia, 1870–1885*, ed. Clarence Hiebert (Newton, KS: Faith and Life Press, 1974).

25 Theron F. Schlabach, *Peace, Faith, Nation*, 278. For a detailed account of the migration and the role of the Mennonite Board of Guardians, see pp. 254–294.

26 At the turn of the nineteenth century, for example, Catholic, Jewish, and Lutheran immigrant aid societies raised millions of dollars to assist newcomers from various parts of Europe in the transition to their new culture. Cf. John Bodnar, "Ethnic Fraternal Benefit Associations: Their Historical Development, Character, and Significance," in *Records Of Ethnic Fraternal Benefit Associations In The United States: Essays And Inventories*,

ed. Susan H. Shreve and Rudolph J. Vecoli (St. Paul: Immigration History Research Center, University of Minnesota, 1981), 5–14. Bodnar argues that cultural preservation was more important than economic benefits in early years.

27 Benedict R. Anderson, *Imagined Communities: Reflections on the Origin and Spread of Nationalism* (London: Verso, 1983).

28 Cf. Theron F. Schlabach, "Reveille for *Die Stillen im Lande*: A Stir Among Mennonites in the Late Nineteenth Century," *Mennonite Quarterly Review* 51 (July 1977), 213–226. In his recent history of Eastern Mennonite University, Donald Kraybill offers another useful overview of this dynamic era. *Eastern Mennonite University: A Century of Countercultural Education* (University Park, PA: Pennsylvania State University Press, 2017), 18–22.

29 James Juhnke, *Vision, Doctrine, War: Mennonite Identity and Organization in America, 1890–1930* (Scottdale, PA: Herald Press, 1989), 87–88.

30 In time these "conferences" of ministers became a shorthand for groups of churches themselves, ordinarily organized in geographic regions. For the sake of clarity, these groups of churches are referred to in the text as "regional," "district" or even "area" conferences, as the terminology itself evolved in an irregular fashion over time.

31 Ibid., 124–130, quote from 124.

32 To add even more confusion, when they met in an assembly they referred to themselves as the Mennonite Church General Conference.

33 "Daniel Kauffman," *Mennonite Encyclopedia*, 3:156–157. The *Gospel Herald* was formed in 1908 as the result of a merger of Funk's *Herald of Truth* and another paper published in Elkhart called *The Gospel Banner* (a waning interest in German had led to the demise of the *Herold der Wahrheit* in 1901).

34 John Ruth, *Maintaining the Right Fellowship: A Narrative Account of the Oldest Mennonite Community in North America* (Scottdale, PA: Herald Press, 1984), 293.

35 Cf. Horst Penner, *Ansiedlung mennonitischer Niederländer im Weichselmündungsgebiet von der Mitte des 16. Jahrhunderts bis zum Beginn der preussischen Zeit* (Weierhof: Mennonitischen Geschichtsverein, 1963), 19, 21. Remarkably, the association was still in operation until 1945, when most Mennonites were forced to flee the region as refugees during World War II.

36 Cf. J. Winfield Fretz, "Mutual Aid among Mennonites, I," *Mennonite Quarterly Review* 13 (January 1939), 36–46.

37 Ibid., 42.

38 A list of these organizations, along with the date of their founding and memberships (in 1956), can be found in "Mutual Aid," *Mennonite Encyclopedia*, 3: 799–800. By the 1950s, an additional seven automobile aid insurance companies had formed, along with at least fourteen burial aid societies, six hospital and surgical plans, and six loan aid organizations.

39 For a history of several specific plans, see Hubert R. Pellman, *Seventy-Five Years of Mutual Aid: Virginia Mennonite Property Aid Plan* (Harrisonburg, VA: Virginia Mennonite Property Aid Plan, 1989); Paul M. Lederach, *The Road to Goodville, 1926-2016: The Story of Goodville Mutual Casualty Company Through Seventy-Five Years* (New Holland, PA: Goodville Mutual Casualty Company, 2018); and *Fiftieth Anniversary: The Mennonite Mutual Fire Insurance Co., 1880-1930* (Newton, KS: Mennonite Mutual Fire Insurance Company, 1930).

40 Juhnke, *Vision, Doctrine, War*, 249–257.

41 See, for example, Jonas S. Hartzler and Daniel Kauffman, *Mennonite Church History* (Scottdale, PA: Mennonite Book and Tract Society, 1905), 244; and John F. Funk, *Sermon Preached by John F. Funk: At the Mennonite Church, Elkhart, Ind., Sunday, April 5, 1925*, 2nd ed. (Elkhart, IN: James A. Bell, 1928).

42 Quoted in Schlabach, "Reveille for *Die Stillen im Lande*," 213–214.

43 Marshall McLuhan, *Understanding Media: The Extensions of Man* (New York: McGraw-Hill Education, 1964).

44 Schlabach, "Reveille for *Die Stille im Lande*," 213–226.

45 Ibid., 216.

46 These concepts were first elaborated by Max Weber in *Economy and Society*, ed. Guenter Roth and Claus Wittich (Berkeley, CA: University of California Press, [1921], 1978).

47 Cf. Paul J. DiMaggio and Walter W. Powell, "The Iron Cage Revisited: Institutional Isomorphism and Collective Rationality," in *The New Institutionalism in Organizational Analysis* (Chicago: University of Chicago Press, 1991), 63–82; and Thomas H. Jeavons, *When the Bottom Line is Faithfulness: Management of Christian Service Organizations* (Bloomington, IN: Indiana University Press, 1994). Keith Graber Miller applies this critique to MMA in an essay titled "Mennonite Mutual Aid: A Margin of Difference?" in Swartley and Kraybill, *Building Communities of Compassion*, 264–292.

Chapter 2

1 *Mennonite General Conference Held at Kitchener, Ontario, August 27–29, 1935* [Proceedings], 8. The Executive Committee of the General Conference tended to the work of the group between its biennial meetings.

2 Ibid.

3 Ibid.

4 Cf. MacMaster, *Land, Piety, Peoplehood: The Establishment of Mennonite Communities in America, 1683–1790.* (Scottdale, PA: Herald Press, 1985), 48, 54, 162–166, 179, 188.

5 The group that did not continue the practice of community of goods became known as the "Prairieleut" and most of them later identified with Mennonites.

6 The 1936 census actually identified seventeen Anabaptist-Mennonite subgroups: most of them, like the Stauffer group who reported 161 members, were very small. See Paul Toews, *Mennonites in American Society, 1930–1970: Modernity and the Persistence of Religious Community* (Scottdale, PA: Herald Press, 1996), 29.

7 Gerlof Homan, *American Mennonites and the Great War, 1914–1918* (Scottdale, PA: Herald Press, 1994).

8 Duane C. S. Stoltzfus, *Pacifists in Chains: The Persecution of Hutterites during the Great War* (Baltimore: Johns Hopkins University Press, 2013).

9 Cf. Albert N. Keim, *The CPS Story: An Illustrated History of Civilian Public Service* (Intercourse, PA: Good Books, 1990).

10 The two largest regional conferences—Lancaster and Franconia—were not formally part of the General Conference, determined to guard their local autonomy, though they often participated in the general work of the larger church. Lancaster, for example, cooperated with the (Old) Mennonite Church on many initiatives, including Mennonite Central Committee, but created its own mission agency.

11 For a critical assessment of Kauffman and the larger consolidation of central authority see Leonard Gross, "The Doctrinal Era of the Mennonite Church," *Mennonite Quarterly Review* 60 (January 1986), 83–103.

12 The best example of this is the story of Goshen College, which Kauffman helped to close during the 1923–1924 academic year because of fears that its Bible and theology departments had become infected with the virus of Modernism. Kauffman himself served as president when the college was reopened in the fall of 1924 after overseeing wholesale replacements to the faculty. Cf. Susan Fisher Miller, *Culture for Service: A History of Goshen College, 1894–1994* (Goshen, IN: Goshen College, 1994), 87–122.

13 *Mennonite General Conference Held at Kitchener, Ontario, August 27–29, 1935* [Proceedings], 8.

14 Ibid.

15 Chris L. Graber, *Looking Backward: An Autobiography* (Goshen, IN: author, 1982), 48–50, 51–53.

16 "Report of the Christian Stewardship Study Committee," *Mennonite General*

Conference Held at Turner, Oregon, Ontario, August 25–27, 1937 [Proceedings], 36–38.
17 Ibid., 36, 38. Cf. Theron F. Schlabach, *War, Peace and Social Conscience: Guy F. Hershberger and Mennonite Ethics* (Scottdale, PA: Herald Press, 2009), 196.
18 J. Winfield Fretz, "Mutual Aid among Mennonites, I," *Mennonite Quarterly Review* 13 (January 1939), 28–58, and "Mutual Aid Among Mennonites, II: Mutual Aid Activities in a Single Mennonite Community," *Mennonite Quarterly Review* 13 (July 1939), 187–209.
19 Albert N. Keim, "My Brother's Keeper: Origins of Mennonite Mutual Aid," in *Building Communities of Compassion*, ed. Willard Swartley and Donald Kraybill (Scottdale, PA: Herald Press, 1998), 200.
20 "Report of the Christian Stewardship Study Committee," *Mennonite General Conference Held at Allensville, Pa., August 23–25, 1939* [Proceedings], 33–35, 34.
21 Hershberger attributed the problem to a lack of leadership: "I think it helps to explain why the Stewardship Committee didn't get much done: They didn't have any real leadership. . . . This was the Stewardship Committee's third report and it was the same story." Cf. Interview of Guy F. Hershberger by James Kratz and Dwight Stoltzfus [1986], transcript in folder labeled "Early MMA History," Everence Archives.
22 "Report of the Christian Stewardship Study Committee," *Twenty-Second Mennonite General Conference: Minutes, Reports, Ministerial List, Officers and Committees. Wellman, Iowa, August 26–29, 1941* [Proceedings], 9–11, 9.
23 Ibid., 11
24 Ibid. The report concluded with a call for a series of articles promoted in the *Gospel Herald* that would "bring this issue clearly before our brethren and sisters."
25 The General Problems Committee was a kind of clearinghouse that oversaw the work of various study commissions appointed to provide recommendations to the church on difficult questions of doctrine and practice.
26 "Report of the Christian Stewardship Study Committee," *Twenty-Third Mennonite General Conference: Organization, Minutes, Reports, Ministerial List, Officers and Committees Elected, Ministers and Delegates in Attendance, Goshen, Ind. August 18–24, 1943* [Proceedings], 29–31.
27 In contemporary usage the term *rehabilitation* referred to an effort to help young CPSers reintegrate into their communities and vocations.
28 Ibid., 31. For a fuller account of research carried out by J. Winfield Fretz among CPS men regarding the need for assistance with "rehabilitation" following the way, see Guy F. Hershberger, "Credits and Loans to Individuals: An Area of Christian Mutual Aid Activity," in *A Conference on Mennonite Mutual Aid, Atlantic Hotel, Chicago, Illinois, July 14–15, 1955* [proceedings], D1–D2.
29 "Report of the Christian Stewardship Study Committee," *Twenty-Third Mennonite General Conference, 1943* [Proceedings], 30.
30 Interview with Guy F. Hershberger by Leonard Gross, December 3, 1986. Transcript available in folder marked "Early MMA History," Everence Archives; see also the transcription of another interview with Guy F. Hershberger by James Kratz and Dwight Stoltzfus, which covers much of the same ground.
31 Miller first enunciated these three points in the "Report of the Committee on Industrial Relations," *Twenty-Third Mennonite General Conference, 1943* [Proceedings], 28. "In adopting the report [of the Industrial Relations Committee]," Hershberger recalled, "the General Conference gave us the green light to work on these basic problems."
32 Committee on Industrial Minutes, October 16, 1943. MC USA Archives, Committee on Industrial Relations, I-3-7.
33 Hershberger's weekly column addressed some aspect of the mutual aid initiative in the March 16, March 23, March 30, April 14, and April 21, 1944, issues of the *Gospel Herald*. Between March and August he published twenty columns on stewardship, community, or mutual aid.
34 [Guy F. Hershberger], "Mennonite Mutual Aid: A plan for the organization of a new

board to carry on an effective program of mutual aid within the Mennonite Church." Folder labeled "Early MMA History," Everence Archives.

35 Schlabach, *War, Peace, and Social Conscience*, 278–284 provides a detailed account of these efforts.

36 Orie Miller to Allen Erb, C. L. Graber, and Guy F. Hershberger, June 24, 1944. MC USA Archives, XII-8-1.

37 The specific confusion had to do with the fact that the brochure described the program as being for "the Mennonite Church and affiliated bodies." Hershberger and the others had intended this to mean all the conferences who were formally members of the General Conference, as well as the Lancaster and Franconia Conferences, which were only affiliated with it. The Virginia Conference opposed the inclusion of the Lancaster and Franconia groups.

38 Quoted in Schlabach, *War, Peace, and Social Conscience*, 280.

39 *Report of the Special Session of the Mennonite General Conference Held at Goshen College, Goshen, Indiana, August 15–18, 1944* [Proceedings], 5.

40 Orie Miller to C. L. Graber, August 19, 1944. MC USA Archives, XII-8-1.

41 C. L. Graber to Guy F. Hershberger, August 21, 1944. MC USA Archives, XII-8-1.

42 Hershberger was privately quite dismissive of Graber in his assignment to enlist support from conferences. "He was on the Stewardship Committee, and they never came through with a concept. He was mostly concerned about it having a charter and he didn't know how to get it done." Interview of Guy F. Hershberger by James Kratz and Dwight Gingerich [1986], transcript in folder labeled "Early MMA History," Everence Archives.

43 Guy F. Hershberger to C. L. Graber, July 7, 1944. MC USA Archives, XII-8-1.

44 John M. Snyder, "Is Mutual Aid Scriptural?" *Gospel Herald*, September 15, 1944, 474, 477. When Hershberger and others defended the proposal, Snyder responded with a sharp rebuttal of his own. John M. Snyder, "Some Thoughts on New Testament Mutual Aid," *Gospel Herald*, Dec. 22, 1944, 764–765, 772.

45 Guy F. Hershberger to Orie Miller, Aug. 26, 1944. MC USA Archives, XII-8-1.

46 Minutes of the Mutual Aid Committee, Adelphian Hall, Goshen College, May 31, 1945. MC USA Archives, XII-8-1.

47 The decision reached at the May meeting was affirmed by the end of the summer when an additional three conferences formally granted their approval.

48 Schlabach, *War, Peace, and Social Conscience*, 209, 204.

49 The house was located at the corner of Lafayette and 8th Street. The current numbering of houses on 8th Street has changed as neighborhood grew and new houses were built.

50 Harold Leon Swartzendruber, *Where the Corn Grew—Water Flowed Over the Dam: An Autobiography* (Goshen, IN: published by the author, 2003), 115.

51 For a fuller description of Miller's life and expansive role in the Mennonite Church see Paul Erb, *Orie O. Miller: The Story of a Man and an Era* (Scottdale, PA: Herald Press, 1969) and, more recently, John E. Sharp, *My Calling to Fulfill: The Orie O. Miller Story* (Scottdale, PA: Herald Press, 2015).

52 Swartzendruber, *Where the Corn Grew*, 49.

53 The authoritative biography of Hershberger is Theron F. Schlabach, *War, Peace and Social Conscience: Guy F. Hershberger and Mennonite Ethics* (Scottdale, PA: Herald Press, 2009).

54 At the meeting in Goshen on March 16, 1945, the group recognized that the mandate approved by the 1944 General Conference had replaced the reference to investments with "assist young married couples who need help in establishing a home and means of livelihood." This was the language of the mandate that was then approved at the May 31, 1945, meeting. Yet by the 1947 General Conference session, the mandate had reverted to the original with investments now appearing again.

55 Most of the loans were for agricultural-related pursuits: cows, tractors, farm

implements, broiler houses, etc. A few were business loans, but that was the exception. There was a short-lived program to fund Mennonite medical students, but that was really separate from the CPS loans.

56 C. L. Graber, "Finances for Mennonite Mutual Aid," *Gospel Herald*, January 11, 1946, 780.

57 "Categories of Capital for Mennonite Mutual Aid," Sept. 25, 1945. MC USA Archives, XII-8-1, Box 1/3. See also C. L. Graber and John M. Snyder, "Making Investment Funds a Means of Direct Christian Service, *Gospel Herald* (March 18, 1947), 1096. The interest charged to the loans was to be "as conservative . . . as possible" but "the same or less than comparable current rates of Government agencies."

58 MMA Board Minutes and Reports, Dec. 31, 1946. MC USA Archives, XII-9, Box 1.

59 MMA Board Minutes and Reports, April 12–13, 1957. MC USA Archives, XII-9, Box 1. The MMA reports in the biennial proceedings of the Mennonite Church General Conference sessions between 1945 and 1957 also give summaries of loan activity.

60 MMA Board Minutes and Reports, Aug. 26–29, 1947. MC USA Archives, XII-9, Box 1.

61 Swartzendruber, *Where the Corn Grew*, 116.

62 The Everence Archives contains two bound volumes of correspondence related to the collection of these loans, much of it highly detailed and deeply personal. A summary report in 1957 noted that delinquency of the CPS loans was about 4 percent of the total dollars loaned, though it jumped to 15 percent delinquency for loans outside the CPS program. Cf. MMA Board Minutes and Reports, April 12–13, 1957. MC USA Archives, XII-09, Box 1. A summary report in 1959 put the delinquent CPS loans at approximately $20,000 from twenty-three individuals. Cf. MMA Board Minutes and Reports, May 11, 1959. MC USA Archives, XII-9, Box 1.

63 MMA Board Minutes and Reports, Oct 16, 1956. MC USA Archives XII-9, Box 1.

64 Mennonite Church Executive Committee [Allen Erb] to Orie Miller, April 15, 1946. Miller responded somewhat testily five days later, writing "I believe you can appreciate that we should have some expression from the General Conference Executive Committee itself for our clearer guidance." MC USA Archives, XII-8-1.

65 The program, later assumed by Mennonite Medical Association, granted twelve loans totaling $20,000.

66 See references scattered throughout the Orie Miller correspondence files. MC USA Archives, XII-8-1, folders 10 and 11.

67 Between 1950 and 1959, when the loan program came to a definitive end, MMA had made around 100 of these loans, most of them between $500 and $2,000.

68 This arrangement with MCC, and the first of loans, were approved by the MMA board at its meetings on August 26–29, 1947. MC USA Archives, XII-9, Box 1. By August of 1947, $40,225 had been raised for Paraguayan refugees in the form of interest-free ten-year notes, with MCC overseeing the distribution of the funds and guaranteeing repayment.

Chapter 3

1 Action 22 at the MMA Board meeting on October, 28, 1960, MMA Board minutes and reports. MC USA Archives, XII-9, Box 1/19.

2 The meeting, and its larger context, are summarized in a letter from Swartzendruber to the MMA Board, May 12, 1961, Guy F. Hershberger MMA files, MMA Board minutes and reports, April 27–28, 1961. MC USA Archives, XII-8-2, Box 1/17.

3 "Report of the Christian Stewardship Study Committee," *Mennonite General Conference Held at Turner, Oregon, Ontario, August 25–27, 1937* [Proceedings], 37–38.

4 "Some Thoughts on Mutual Aid," *Gospel Herald* (Dec. 22, 1944), 765.

5 See, for example, John M. Snyder to MMA Directors, Oct. 5, 1946 and April 12, 1947. MC USA Archives, XII-8-1, Box 1/5.

6 Guy F. Hershberger, "Mutual Aid for Sharing of Losses in Case of Calamity, Sickness

or Death." MC USA Archives, XII-8-1, Box 1/5. Schlabach covers this debate in greater detail in *War, Peace, and Social Conscience*, 295–298.

7 Ibid.

8 See John M. Snyder to MMA Directors, April 12, 1947. Folder labeled "Insurance Debate," Everence Archives.

9 The results of the survey were reported in various contexts, but the most accessible can be found in MMA's 1947 report to the General Conference. *Twenty-Sixth [sic] Mennonite General Conference Held at Wooster, Ohio, August 26–29, 1947* (Scottdale, PA: Mennonite Publishing House, 1948), 55–56.

10 Ibid., 56.

11 The prolonged exchange leading to Snyder's resignation can be followed in Orie Miller's correspondence files from 1947. MC USA Archives, XII-8-1, Box 1/5. The story was complicated by the fact that the MMA board, following its own procedures, had been hesitant to grant Snyder a personal loan of $2,000 he had requested to help cover the losses of a failing tire repair business he had been running on the side.

12 MMA Board Minutes and Reports, May 19, 1949. MC USA Archives, XII-9, Box 1/5.

13 Report of Mennonite Mutual Aid, Inc., *Twenty-Sixth Mennonite General Conference, Eastern Mennonite College, Harrisonburg, Virginia, August 23–26, 1949* [proceedings], (Scottdale, PA: Mennonite Publishing House, 1949), 50.

14 MMA Board Minutes and Reports, Aug. 23, 1949. MC USA Archives, XII-9, Box 1/5.

15 MMA Board Minutes and Reports, Sept. 29, 1949. MC USA Archives, XII-9, Box 1/5.

16 MMA Board Minutes and Reports, March 24, 1950. MC USA Archives, XII-9, Box 1/6.

17 MMA Board Minutes and Reports, June 28, 1952. MC USA Archives, XII-9, Box 2/3.

18 MMA Board Minutes and Reports, Nov. 29, 1949. MC USA Archives, XII-9, Box 1/5. The board also proposed a six-month delay for surgical benefits for any applicant with preexisting conditions and warned that if "the number of poor risks is larger than what is generally good for the entire program it should be reported to the board."

19 Assessments were calculated on a sliding scale, depending on age. The payout for children under the age of eighteen was $100.

20 Cf. "Brotherhood Through Mennonite Aid, Inc." [brochure, probably from 1951]. "Mennonite Mutual Aid / Mennonite Aid, Inc.," Vertical File, Mennonite Historical Library. Later this was changed to two-thirds of the members, and later still to 40 percent of the congregation's members.

21 At its March, 13, 1950, meeting MAI staff reported 346 adults and 240 dependents in the new Hospital-Surgical plan and ninety-nine participants in the Burial Aid plan. Between 1950 and 1960 adult membership had grown to 23,500 participants. During that same decade, assessments increased from $40,000 to $910,000, claims jumped from $33,000 to $800,000, and internal operating expenses increased from $3,735 to 57,300. Cf. graphs prepared for "MMA Retreat, Nov. 19–20, 1976." MC USA Archives, XII-28, Box 1/12.

22 MAI Board minutes, Jan. 5, 1952. MC USA Archives, XII-8-1, Box 1/2.

23 MMA Board minutes and reports, Jan. 5, 1952. MC USA Archives, XII-9, Box 1/8.

24 MAI assessment letter, July 10, 1952. Folder labeled "Mennonite Aid, Inc.," Vertical Files, Mennonite Historical Library.

25 Mennonite Aid, Inc., minutes, Jan. 8, 1954. Survivor's Aid / Mennonite Aid Insurance, Inc. [expansion file], Everence Archives.

26 Ibid. Cf. "Catastrophe Aid: Supplement Aid to Needy M.A.I. Members Having Extensive Hospitalization or Surgical Expenses," [brochure], vertical files, Mennonite Historical Library.

27 Mennonite Aid, Inc., Minutes, Feb. 9, 1952. Survivor's Aid / Mennonite Aid Insurance, Inc. [expansion file], Everence Archives.

28 Mennonite Aid, Inc., Minutes, Jan. 8, 1955. Survivor's Aid / Mennonite Aid Insurance, Inc. [expansion file], Everence Archives.

29 Ibid. Previously, the one dollar annual contribution to the Catastrophe Aid fund had been voluntary.

30 Mennonite Aid, Inc., minutes, Jan. 8, 1955. MC USA Archives, XII-8-1, Box 1/15.

31 For a profile on Herr and his family see "Meet Aaron Herr: MMAA Claims Examiner," *Sharing* 1 (July, 1967), 4.

32 Swartzendruber, *Where the Corn Grew*, 136.

33 Harold Swartzendruber recounts this story in his autobiography. Swartzendruber, *Where the Corn Grew*, 38–39.

34 MMA Board minutes and reports, Oct. 8, 1952. MC USA Archives, XII-09, Box 1/8. For the Executive Committee's decision on Nov. 14, 1952, see "Report of Mennonite Mutual Aid, Inc.," *Twenty-Eighth Mennonite General Conference, 1953* [Proceedings], 51.

35 "Articles of Incorporation" (Dec. 30, 1952). MC USA Archives, Mennonite Foundation, XII-34, Box 1/2.

36 In a letter of Nov. 17, 1952, to the MMA Board reporting on the creation of a new board for the Foundation, Graber wrote "I think all of you understand why my name appears in this list since likely someone from Goshen and from the MMA office should be included. Harold Swartzendruber, of course, will do the work [!]." MC USA Archives, Mennonite Foundation, XII-34, Box 1/2.

37 Cf. Royden Loewen and Steven M. Nolt, *Seeking Places of Peace. Global Mennonite History Series: North America* (Intercourse, PA: Good Books, 2012), 222–228.

38 Cf. letter from Swartzendruber to Miller, Sept. 16, 1953, in which Swartzendruber reports on a trip to Indianapolis as part of his effort "to formulate the Automobile Aid Plan." A year later, in a letter of Nov. 17, 1954, to the MMA board, Swartzendruber reported that the Automobile Aid program was scheduled to start operations in January, 1955. MC USA Archives, XII-8-1, Box 1/15.

39 MMA Board Minutes and Reports, Oct. 5, 1954. MC USA Archives, XII-9, Box 1/10.

40 Swartzendruber, *Where the Corn Grew*, 129.

41 MMA Board Minutes and Reports, April 12–13, 1957. MC USA Archives, XII-9, Box 1/13.

42 MMA Board Minutes and Reports, Oct. 31, 1956. MC USA Archives, XII-9, Box 1/12.

43 For example, on Feb. 13, 1956, Swartzendruber recommended that MMA advance a loan of $15,000 at 6 percent for six months to Goodville to support their effort to establish offices in other states with heavy concentrations of Mennonites. MC USA Archives, XII-8-1, Box 1/16. On June 1, 1957, he reported to the board that "MMA has continued to use the services of Goodville Mutual Casualty Company . . . to provide liability insurance to members of our church. Their witness and testimony in matters of litigation are outstanding and are in keeping with the beliefs and practices of the Mennonite Church." Ibid. At the MMA Board meetings on April 25–26, 1963, Swartzendruber reaffirmed the relationship with Goodville Mutual Casualty Company, stating "we know of no facility to handle the 1953 request of the Mennonite General Conference for liability insurance provision that is better fitted to do it." Our aims "are very nearly the same," and "our 'hearts' are closer together than they have been for a long time!" MC USA Archives, XII-9, Box 1/27.

44 For a general history of Goodville, see Paul M. Lederach, *The Road to Goodville, 1926–2001: The Story of Goodville Mutual Casualty Company through Seventy-Five Years* (New Holland, PA: Goodville Mutual Casualty Company, 2002).

45 Orie Miller began urging Swartzendruber to establish a Goshen office in the fall of 1951. MC USA Archives, XII-8-1, Box 1/10.

46 In 1950, the assets of the nearly dormant corporation were transferred to the newly-created "Mennonite Educational Buildings, Inc.," chaired by C. L. Graber, whose major focus at the time was handling a loan to Goshen College for the construction of a new dormitory. For much of the organization's early history, including a helpful "Record of Minute Actions Leading Toward Formation of Mennonite Church Buildings, Inc.," see MC USA Archives, XII-4, Box 2 (minutes and reports, 1950–1968).

47 Most banks at the time had policies against lending money to church-related projects on a long-term basis.

48 Cf. "Introducing Mennonite Church Buildings, Inc. of the Mennonite General Conference." MC USA Archives, XII-4, Box 2/1. In a letter from Swartzendruber on September 29, 1956, Miller noted that in obtaining the General Council's approval for MCB, "MMA added a larger scope of service for it to render in the Constituency." MC USA Archives, XII-8-1, Box 1/17.

49 *Introducing Mennonite Church Buildings* [brochure], (1956). Mennonite Mutual Aid/Mennonite Church Buildings, Mennonite Historical Library vertical files.

50 MMA Board Minutes and Reports, April 3–4, 1956. MC USA Archives, XII-8-1, Box 1/16.

51 Swartzendruber, *Where the Corn Grew*, 133. In 1973 Swartzendruber noted that "MIS also stands as a possibility in providing insurance services to a larger Mennonite constituency should this become feasible and could broker or be agents for insurance services not feasible through our structure."

52 "Mennonite Retirement Plan," July 9, 1963 [news release]. MC USA Archives, XII-8-1, Box 1/28.

53 This became an issue in a 2001 review of MMA's legal structure when it became apparent that MRT had become informally incorporated into the MMA Board, thereby creating a potential conflict of interest. The review resulted in the creation of a separate MRT board of trustees. MMA Board Minutes and Reports, May 3–4, 2001, MC USA Archives, XII-9, Box 8.

54 Cf. *A Conference on Mennonite Mutual Aid, Atlantic Hotel, Chicago, Illinois, July 14–15, 1955* [proceedings]. Mennonite Historical Library, Goshen, Ind.

55 Ibid., C4–C6.

56 Cf. Howard Raid, *Twenty-Five Years—A Brief History of MMI* (Akron, PA: Mennonite Indemnity, 1983); also Edgar Stoesz, *Finding My Way: A Harvest of Memories* (Morgantown, PA: Masthof Press, 2018), 71–72.

57 In 1970, H. Ralph Hernley compiled the devotions from each of the AMAS meetings into a volume called *The Compassionate Community*, which MMA mailed to every Mennonite Church and General Conference Mennonite Church congregation. *The Compassionate Community*, comp. H. Ralph Hernley (Scottdale, Pa.: Association of Mennonite Aid Societies, 1970).

58 See, for examples, Ivan Lind's exasperated response to Herbert Troyer—both members of the Insurance Study Committee—when Troyer insisted that the local congregation was best suited to address the needs of widows and orphans. "I have not seen the church step out to help our widows," he charged. "Commonly, we see them let alone and hope that they make it, and sometimes accused them [of laziness] if they don't." Ivan R. Lind, "Statement on Life Insurance," Feb. 14, 1952. MC USA Archives, XII-8-2, Box 1/3.

59 By the 1940s the Brotherhood Mutual Life Insurance Company of Fort Wayne, Ind., was openly promoting life insurance products and making clear inroads into the local Mennonite community. Cf. William C. Ringenberg, *The Business of Mutual Aid: 75 Years of the Brotherhood Mutual Insurance Company* (Fort Wayne: Brotherhood Mutual Insurance Co., 1992); Schlabach, *War, Peace, and Social Conscience*, 315.

60 The plan did gain legal status in Kansas.

61 I. J. Rosenberger, *Life Insurance* (Scottdale, Pa.: Mennonite Publishing House, 1910), 5.

62 There "is no insurance that a company can give," argued Rosenberger, by which a person's "life can be restored." Rosenberger, *Life Insurance*, 10-11.) Cf. Daniel D. Miller, "Life Insurance," in *Bible Doctrine*, ed. Daniel Kauffman (Scottdale, PA: Mennonite Publishing House, 1914), 575–587; Daniel Bender, "Life Insurance," *Gospel Herald*, Sept. 28, 1919, 474–475; Harry A. Diener, "Life Insurance," *Gospel Herald* (Nov. 8, 1928), 674–675; John Snyder, "Mutual Aid Insurance," *Gospel Herald* (Dec. 22, 1944),

764–765; 772–773; Simon Gingerich, "The Insurance Phase of Mutual Aid," *Gospel Herald* (Dec. 22, 1944), 780.
63 Report of the Life Insurance Study Committee, *Twenty-Sixth Mennonite General Conference, 1949* [proceedings], 44.
64 The authors of the report noted that they focused almost exclusively on the question of insurance, leaving discussion of investments to the Committee on Economic and Social Relations and to the MMA board. Report of the Insurance and Investment Study Committee, *Twenty-Eighth Mennonite General Conference, 1953* [proceedings], 71–81. One reason the report took as long as it did was the clear opposition of Herbert N. Troyer, an early member of the committee, who had recently published a small book against life insurance. Herbert Troyer, *Life Insurance* (Scottdale, PA: Mennonite Publishing House, 1932). Troyer, a minister from Hartville, Ohio, and Carl Kreider, a professor of economics at Goshen College, clearly clashed on the committee. Ivan Lind, dean of Hesston College, where he also taught business, consistently supported Kreider in the exchange.—Schlabach, *War, Peace, and Social Conscience*, 309–313.
65 Report of the Insurance and Investment Study Committee, *Twenty-Eighth Mennonite General Conference, 1953* [proceedings], 71–81.
66 Ibid., 72–74.
67 Ibid., 75 [my emphasis].
68 Ibid., 77. The report described the Social Security system as a "noncommercial . . . retirement savings plan . . . and a means by which the state seeks to promote the welfare of the larger community. Social Security may rightfully be thought of as a means whereby the Christian can help to bear the burden of his neighbors who may or may not be members of the Christian brotherhood; and the Christian does have an obligation to his neighbor."
69 *Statement of Position on Insurance Adopted by Mennonite General Conference, Aug. 25, 1955* (Scottdale, PA: Mennonite Publishing House, 1955).
70 Ibid. In 1960 the Virginia Conference revised its statement on insurance, noting that MMA's "Survivors' Aid is the only plan that we know of that is truly based on the biblical basis of sharing one with another." Justus Driver to Friends, June 16, 1961. MC USA Archives, XII-8-1, Box 1/25.)
71 "Report of the Widows and Survivors Rehabilitation Sub-Committee to Mennonite Mutual Aid Board," August 23, 1957. MC USA Archives, XII-8-2, Box 1/24.
72 Ibid.
73 "Survivors' Aid: Systematic Planning to Provide Assistance in Case of Early Death or for Future Needs," [Brochure], Mennonite Historical Library, Goshen, Ind. In March of 1960, Swartzendruber attended a "Seminar School for Underwriters" hosted by the American United Life Insurance Company in Indianapolis, his first rudimentary encounter with the complex world of actuarial statistics.
74 Schlabach, *War Peace, and Social Conscience*, 315.
75 For a list of specifications supplied to the architect, see "New Office Building," Nov. 1, 1957, MMA Board Minutes and Reports. MC USA Archives, XII-8-2, Box 1/24.
76 For a useful listing of the employees and their tasks, see "Managers Report," Nov. 2, 1957, MMA Board Minutes and Reports.—MC USA Archives, XII-8-2, Box 1/24.
77 Ray Sala to H. Ralph Hernley, April 22, 1960. MC USA Archives, XII-8-2, Box 2/42.
78 Hershberger continued that Abe Hallman, Ralph Hernley, and Robert Krieder all shared the same opinion. Guy F. Hershberger to Orie Miller, April 25, 1960. MC USA Archives, XII-8-2, Box 2/22.
79 Aaron Herr to MMA Board, Oct. 25, 1961. MC USA Archives, XII-8-2, Box 2/43. Miller penciled in the margin of the letter: "read to 10/27 meeting; discussed with Aaron 11/1/61; no other ans."
80 Cresap, McCormick and Paget, Management Consultants, "MMA, Inc.: A Study of the Organization and Operation of MMA and its Affiliated Units" (the final report was issued on Sept. 11, 1961). MC USA Archives, XII-28, Box 1/14.

81 See, for example, the admonition by Lowell Nissley in the *MMA Office Mem-Oh!* (April 25, 1968), 2.
82 Ibid.
83 Noting that MMA staff had no routine system for reporting on work accomplished, no systematic system for collecting accounts receivable, and no cross-reference file, the CMP report placed a significant amount of the blame at the feet of Harold Swartzendruber: "The present manager has worked with such matters for a number of years, and has an unusual memory. Because of his knowledge of membership, he is opposed to creating a separate cross reference file." As a result, the general manager "ends up doing clerical tasks." Ibid.
84 Ibid., III-2.
85 Ibid.
86 Ralph Hernley, Luke Birkey, and Harry Wenger served on the committee, with H. Clair Amstutz and Albert Meyer as consultants.

Chapter 4
1 By the 1970s the denomination called the Mennonite Church General Conference, and also known as the (Old) Mennonite Church, increasingly was referred to simply as the Mennonite Church (MC).
2 Menno Schrag, "First Delegate Session," *Sharing* 1 (Jan. 1967), 4–5.
3 At a conjoint meeting on August 18, 1961, the MMA board and subsidiary boards received and accepted the CMP report in its entirety. MC USA Archives, XII-9, Box 1/21.
4 Letter from Aaron Herr to Orie Miller, April 4, 1961. MC USA Archives, XII-8-1, Box 1/25.
5 Ibid.
6 Letter from Arthur A. Smucker to Board of Directors, Mennonite Aid, Inc., June 26, 1962. MC USA Archives, XII-8-1, Box 1/26. Smucker also expressed astonishment that the Burial Aid program offered benefits of $750, an amount that "made a mockery of the Christian conviction that upon death the body 'returns to the dust'."
7 Letter from Neal O. Dubson to Harold Swartzendruber, July 26, 1961 (in response to Swartzendruber's letter of July 17, 1961, urging Dubson to register Mennonite Aid Insurance, Inc. with the state of Pennsylvania. Everence Archives, expansion file labeled "Survivor's Aid / Mennonite Aid Insurance, Inc."
8 Letter from Ralph Hernley to Abe Hallman, Aug. 28, 1962. Ibid.
9 Berman and Woodruff to Harold Swartzendruber, Jan. 17, 1963, ibid; Swartzendruber report on Jan. 18, 1963, meeting with National Congress of Fraternals representatives, ibid.
10 MAI Board minutes, April 25–26, 1963. Ibid.
11 Letter from Harold Swartzendruber to Edward J. Mullen, June 6, 1963. Ibid.
12 Letter from Charles Ainlay to Harold Swartzendruber, June 21, 1963. Ibid. Most of the issues, Ainlay reported, were policy questions, not matters of law.
13 Letter from Harold Swartzendruber to Edward J. Mullen, June 6, 1963. Ibid.
14 Swartzendruber, *Where the Corn Grew*, 142–143.
15 MMA Board Minutes and Reports, Nov. 8–9, 1963. MC USA Archives, XII-9-1, Box 1/29.
16 See letter of Edward Peters to Swartzendruber of May 22, 1964, where he summarizes his ongoing conversations with state officials and outlines in detail the next steps that MMA will need to take to become a fraternal benefits association. MC USA Archives, XII-3, Box 1/2. See also letter from Swartzendruber to Mennonite General Conference Executive Committee, Oct. 2, 1964. Ibid.
17 Initially, 395 (9 percent) of the 3,504 eligible members expressed objections to Medicare. MMA Executive Committee minutes, Jan. 13, 1966. MC USA Archives, XII-3, Box 1/4.
18 Memo from Swartzendruber to "members of the General Council" regarding

"Fraternal Status," Feb. 26–27, 1965. MC USA Archives, XII-3-1, Box 1/3.

19 "It would be expected," wrote Swartzendruber, "that Mennonite General Conference through this pattern would virtually be exercising control in the selection of the Board of Directors. However, it must be recognized that theoretically delegates could suggest other names that might be elected by the attending delegates (who in turn are the representatives of the membership of the association)." Ibid.

20 MMA Board Minutes and Reports, Nov. 12, 1966. MC USA Archives, XII-9, Box 1/29.

21 *What is Christian Mutual Aid?*, [brochure], (1966). Mennonite Mutual Aid/ Mennonite Church Buildings, Mennonite Historical Library vertical files.

22 *MMA Office Mem-Oh!*, Dec. 19, 1968.

23 "Mennonite Mutual Aid Report to the Facilities Study Committee," Jan. 11, 1966. MC USA Archives, XII-3, Box 1/4; MMA Board Minutes and Reports, April 15–16, 1966. MC USA Archives, XII-9, Box 1/38.

24 Report from Cresap, McCormick and Paget (Management consultants in Chicago, Ill.) to Harold Swartzendruber (April 7, 1967) on "Mechanization of Business Systems," fulfilling contract of Nov. 1, 1966. MC USA Archives, XII-28, Box 2/6.

25 Follow-up to CMP report, May 31, 1967. MC USA Archives, AMC XII-28, Box 1/7.

26 *MMA Office Mem-Oh!*, Sept. 28, 1967. The NCR 32 was one of the first true computers in the sense that it could modify its actions according to the results of a calculation.

27 "Report on Programs of MMA and its various Subsidiary Activities," Executive Committee minutes, June, 1963. MC USA Archives, XII-3, Box 2/7.

28 *MMA Office Mem-Oh!*, Oct. 24, 1968.

29 *MMA Office Mem-Oh!*, April 25, 1969.

30 "Wage Schedule," MMA Board Minutes and Reports, Nov. 1–2, 1957. MC USA Archives, XII- 8-2, Box 1/24.

31 Appended to Executive Committee minutes, July 9, 1964. MC USA Archives, XII-3, Box 1/2. Included in the plan was a provision for release time for service projects. Employees with three or four years of experience could take up to one week of unpaid leave; five-year veterans could have a week of paid leave for service; those with ten or more years could apply for "extended terms of service."

32 Ibid. The manual also implored employees to remember that they were "working for the Mennonite Church with its strengths and weaknesses, whose members are conservative and liberal, committed and nominal. . . . The challenge is to relate to our times."

33 Still, Swartzendruber noted that using anything higher than a 10 percent differential in classes VII, VIII, and IX would put those classes "out of reach" in terms of the compensation standard established by the denomination for leaders of other church institutions. Swartzendruber to MMA Executive Committee, Nov. 2, 1966. MC USA Archives, XII-3, Box 1/4. See also, "Report on Programs of MMA and its various Subsidiary Activities," June, 1963. MC USA Archives, XII-3, Box 1/1.

34 MMA Board Minutes and Reports, April 30–May 1, 1971. MC USA Archives, XII-9, Box 2/15.

35 "A Report of Mennonite Mutual Aid Association's 1973 Income and Expenses: MMAA Membership," *Sharing* 8 (July 1974), 9.

36 In 1969, for example, MMA received 710 requests for assistance from the Catastrophe Aid fund. 252 of the requests were granted, averaging $201 each, with a total disbursement of $50,844. *Sharing* 4 (July 1970), 7.

37 The CHIP program was launched in the spring of 1971; by 1976 at least fourteen congregations were participating in the plan. This is not to be confused with the later (1997) federal government program, jointly administered and funded by individual states, known as the Children's Health Insurance Program, commonly called CHIP.

38 By 1969, a Fraternal Activities Fund Committee, with members from each major Mennonite denomination, had developed guidelines for the fund. If, for example, a congregation had more than 50 percent of members enrolled in an MMA health plan,

they were eligible to apply for matching funds in support of needy members. Another aspect of the program focused on projects for the four denominations represented on the committee and on "Inter-Mennonite" projects. *Sharing* 4 (July 1970), 8.

39 MMA Board minutes and reports, May 14, 1982. MC USA Archives, XII-9, Box 3/14. Despite this slow start, annuities grew into a stable product. By 1991, 5,123 participants had invested nearly $8 million in the New Advantage Annuities. "MMA Reports Good Financial Results," *Gospel Herald* (April 30, 1991), 11.

40 Cf. MMA Executive Committee minutes, Aug. 4, 1970. MC USA Archives, XII-3, Box 1/8.

41 "Mennonite Mutual Aid Association Serving the Mennonite Conferences," report by Harold Swartzendruber to the Mennonite Church General Board, 1973. Cf. folder labeled "Historical Files." Everence Archives.

42 "Director Financial Services," *Sharing* 3 (Aug., 1969), 6.

43 Cf. Conrad Kanagy, *Roadsigns for the Journey: A Profile of Mennonite Church USA* (Scottdale, PA: Herald Press, 2007), 115–117.

44 "The Mennonite Foundation, Inc.," *Sharing* 1 (Jan. 1967), 9.

45 Lamar Nissley, "Brotherhood—the Victim of an Affluent Hangup," *Sharing* (July 1970), 1–2.

46 "Let's Talk About Money," *Sharing* 9 (July 1975), 12–13, 15.

47 Ibid.

48 *Sharing* 12 (Winter, 1978): John Rudy, "I Like Money!,"6–7. He went on to say, "but I don't *love* money."

49 Ibid., 7.

50 *Mennonite Foundation Annual Report, 1972*. Brochure in folder labeled "Historical Files." Everence Archives.

51 The Goshen College UnCommon Cause Endowment drive in the early 1980s eventually brought millions of additional dollars into the foundation.

52 The MMA Investment Policy Committee minutes of Sept 15, 1982 contain a useful historical review of earlier investment criteria. Folder labeled "Ethical Investment," Everence Archives.

53 Peter Landau, "Do Institutional Investors Have a Social Responsibility?," *Institutional Investors*, July, 1970, 25–36, 81–88. Del King, who served as MMA's investment manager in the early years of the Mennonite Foundation, also identified John G. Simon, Charles W. Powers, and Jon P. Gunnemann's *The Ethical Investor: Universities and Corporate Responsibility* (New Haven, CT: Yale University Press, 1972) as an influential text early in his career.

54 Milton Friedman, *Capitalism and Freedom* (Chicago: University of Chicago Press, 1962), 133.

55 Ibid.

56 Howard Raid to C. Norman Kraus, May 24, 1971. Everence Archives, file labeled "Praxis Mutual Funds."

57 MMA Board minutes and reports, April 7, 1972. MC USA Archives, XII-9, Box 2/17.

58 Interview with Delmar King, Aug. 13, 2018.

59 Initially, investments in U.S. Treasury securities were another gray area. MMA avoided them at first because they were used to finance military spending; but other people in the church pointed out that a major part of the federal debt also included social entitlement programs.

60 Earl Sears was appointed as "educational director" in 1972. *Sharing* 6 (Jan. 1972), 14.

61 *MMA Office Mem-Oh!*, June 8, 1967.

62 *MMA Office Mem-Oh!*, Dec. 19, 1968. In January of 1972, Maggie Glick beame editor of *Sharing*.

63 MMA Reports and Minutes, July 18, 1971. MC USA Archives, XII-9, Box 2/14. For the filmstrips themselves, see MMA Office of Communications files. MC USA Archives, XII-36.

64 Royden Loewen and Steve M. Nolt, *Seeking Places of Peace: Global Mennonite History Series: North America* (Intercourse, PA: Good Books, 2012), 240–241.

65 Ibid.

66 Guy F. Hershberger, "The Congregation and its Need for a Diaconate in a Changing Era," in "Report of the Mennonite Mutual Aid Association," Chicago, Ill., November 11, 1966.

67 However, many of the stewardship education initiatives that Rudy administered were covered by fraternal funds.

68 Letter of Ray Musser [a Brethren in Christ denominational leader from Upland, Calif.) to John Rudy, Nov. 27, 1976. In the letter Musser asked several questions about Mennonite Foundation and then requested a change in policy to allow for greater Brethren in Christ representation on the MMA board. La Mar Richert responded to the technical questions, but not to the more pointed question about board representation. On Dec. 3, 1977, however, Swartzendruber responded with detailed explanation regarding the formula for identifying the nine Mennonite Church, General Conference Mennonite, and Mennonite Brethren representatives on the board, who then elected eight additional people, selected with a view to experience and training rather than church affiliation, to serve for two-year terms. Swartzendruber always had several Brethren in Christ names on the list of potential nominees but "unfortunately, none of these were selected." Cf. MMA Board minutes and reports, Dec. 3, 1977. MC USA Archives, XII-9, Box 3/3.

69 Swartzendruber, *Where the Corn Grew*, 120.

70 "MMA Retreat, Nov. 19–20, 1976," [folder of presentations, agenda, and summary of findings]. Everence Archives.

71 Ibid.

72 Ibid.

73 CMP's report can be found in MMA Board Minutes and Reports, May 20–21, 1977. MC USA Archives, XII-9, Box 3/2. See also, "Why MMA is Reorganizing" *Sharing* 12 (Winter, 1978), 3–5.

74 "Swartzendruber Quits MMA Post," *Goshen News* [undated}. Newsclipping in folder labeled "Early MMA History." Everence Archives.

75 Swartzendruber, *Where the Corn Grew*, 148–149.

76 Ibid., 128.

77 Ibid.

78 J. Lawrence Burkholder, *Love and Justice in Mennonite Mutual Aid* (Akron, PA: Association of Mennonite Aid Societies, 1960).

79 Ibid., 5.

80 Ibid., 15.

81 Ibid.

Chapter 5

1 Video interview with James Kratz, [date unclear, but likely 1995], Everence Archives.

2 The story of this shift toward great political engagement has been recounted in various books, among them Donald Kraybill and Leo Driedger, *Mennonite Peacemaking: From Quietism to Activism* (Scottdale, PA: Herald Press; 1994); Keith Graber Miller, *Wise As Serpents, Innocent As Doves: American Mennonites Engage Washington* (Knoxville: University of Tennessee Press, 1996); and Perry Bush, *Two Kingdoms, Two Loyalties: Mennonite Pacifism in Modern America* (Baltimore, MD: Johns Hopkins University Press, 1998).

3 Royden Loewen and Steve M. Nolt, *Seeking Places of Peace: Global Mennonite History Series: North America* (Intercourse, PA: Good Books, 2012), 243–248.

4 In the words of historians Steve Nolt and Royden Loewen, "instead of reciprocal relationships of shared time and labor, church members increasingly calculated obligations in monetary terms and formalized relationships in premiums, insurance contracts, risk assessment, and hospital aid plans." Ibid., 238.

5 MMA's first female board member was appointed in 1980.

6 Ron J. Sider, *Rich Christians in an Age of Hunger: A Biblical Study* (Downers Grove, IL: Inter-Varsity Press, 1975): Doris Janzen Longacre, *More-with-Less Cookbook* (Scottdale, PA: Herald Press, 1976); Donald Kraybill, *The Upside-Down Kingdom* (Scottdale, PA: Herald Press, 1978). Each of the books sold more than one hundred thousand copies, with sales of the *More-With-Less Cookbook* approaching one million. Kraybill, along with Phyllis Pellman Good, also edited a provocative collection of essays several years later called *Perils of Professionalism,* which warned against the seductive nature of professional disciplines, whose values were often at odds with those of the New Testament. *Perils of Professionalism: Essays on Christian Faith and Professionalism* (Scottdale, PA: Herald Press, 1982).

7 Milo Kauffman, *The Challenge of Christian Stewardship* (Scottdale, PA: Herald Press, 1955). A second book by Kauffman, *Stewards of God* (Scottdale, PA: Herald Press, 1975), distilled his lifetime of teaching on the theme.

8 Cf. Daniel D. Kauffman, *New Frontiers: Stewardship and Mutual Aid* (Scottdale, PA: Association of Mennonite Aid Societies, 1966). Unsung heroes in the stewardship movement were Ray and Lillian Bair, whose *God's Managers: A Budget Guide and Daily Financial Record Book for Christians* (Scottdale, PA: Herald Press, 1985), offered a practical guide to budgeting and placed church at the center of household economics.

9 Stoltzfus was initially introduced as the interim president. In February of 1979, the position became permanent.

10 With a view toward a more formal review process of executives, the board stipulated that he would serve for a renewable three-year term. Cf. MMA Board minutes and reports, Feb. 24, 1979. MC USA Archives, XII-9, Box 3/8. The agreement called for his initial term to end on June 1, 1981, with a review process to start no later than January 1, 1981.

11 Interview with Sid Richard, Sept. 7, 2018. Richard credits Ron Litwiller for his role in defending both the principle of reserves and the actuarial department.

12 Andrea Zuercher, "His Aim: Extraordinary Smiles," *Sharing* (Summer, 1986), 6–7.

13 Ibid.

14 Ibid.

15 Ibid.

16 In 1977 some 360 congregations were participating in this program.

17 Andrea Zuercher, "His Aim: Extraordinary Smiles," *Sharing* (Summer, 1986), 7.

18 For the complete summary of suggestions coming out of the retreat, see the handwritten "Ideas List" dated Nov. 19, 1976. Special MMA Board Meeting, Nov. 19–20, 1976. Everence Archives.

19 For a summary of the May 12, 1977, CMP report and the formal effort of the MMA executive committee to respond to it, see "MMA Goals and Objectives Adopted by the Executive Committee, Feb. 26, 1977" and Dwight Stoltzfus's report to the MMA Board of May, 12, 1980. MC USA Archives, MMA Board minutes and reports, May 30, 1980, XII-9, Box 3/10.

20 In one of his first president's reports to the board, Stoltzfus affirmed that "the past six months have seen rapid movement toward the CMP management model." MMA Board minutes and reports, Nov. 17–18, 1978, MC USA Archives, XII-9, Box 3/7.

21 "Why MMA is Reorganizing," *Sharing* 12 (Winter, 1978), 15–16. Although the CMP report recommended that these positions be identified as "general managers," Stoltzfus preferred the traditional title of "director." In the coming years these titles would change with some frequency, with new positions created—director of fraternal activities (1978); director of church relations and services (1979); director of communications (1980); director of field services (1981).

22 Ibid.

23 Dwight Stoltzfus, "A Mutual Aid Vision," *Sharing* 19 (Spring, 1985), 19. The statement was reviewed and revised in 1989.

24 Jim Kratz to Dwight Stoltzfus, "Facility Needs and Planning," Feb. 8, 1983, which was included in the MMA Board minutes and reports, May 13, 1983. MC USA Archives, XII-9, Box 3/16.

25 The contract for the design and preliminary work was with Mennonite architect LeRoy Troyer, MMA Board minutes and reports, May 13, 1983. Ibid.

26 In November of 1970, MMA purchased a small IBM System 3/Model 10 computer, designed to process accident and health billing. The computer served MMA well until it was upgraded in March 1976, moving from punch cards to a disk memory system and doubling its core memory to 16,000 bytes. A year later, technicians installed an IBM System 3/Model 12 computer, that had 32,000 bytes of core memory. MMA Board minutes and reports, May 12, 1978. MC USA Archives, XII-9, Box 3/5.

27 "How MMA's Computer Helps 'John Miller,'" *Sharing* 20 (Winter 1986), 19

28 "MMA Marketing Task Force Progress Report, Nov. 4, 1980," MMA Board minutes and reports, Nov. 21, 1980. MC USA Archives, XII-9, Box 3/11.

29 Ibid.

30 Ibid. The report did encourage MMA to invest more resources in surveys, allowing members to express more clearly their concerns or wishes regarding MMA's services.

31 MMA Board minutes and reports, Nov. 12, 1982, Appendix B. MC USA Archives, XII-9, Box 3/15.

32 E.g., J. Marvin Nafziger, "Life's More Fun When You're Healthy," *Sharing* 10 (July 1976), 8–11; J. Marin Nafziger, "Positive Health and Lifestyle Pledge," *Sharing* 12 (Summer, 1978), 13–14; Ray and Lillian Bair, "Are You Fiscally Healthy? 6 Steps Toward Fiscal Wellness," *Sharing* 21 (July 1987), 14–15.

33 Cf. MMA Communication Services Department, MC USA Archives, XII-36, Box 1/2.

34 John H. Rudy, "Stewardship Challenges for Living and Giving," April 1983, included in MMA Board minutes and reports, May 13, 1983. MC USA Archives, XII-9, Box 3/16.

35 Steve Bowers, "John Rudy: The Life of a Steward," *Sharing* 24 (Winter, 1990), 10–13.

36 Cf. "Annual Report of the Administrative Services Division for 1981," Everence Archives.

37 "Position Paper on the Management and Use of Assets," May 29, 1980. MC USA Archives, XII-34. The very first set of ethical criteria for MMA investments, approved by the MMA Board in 1964, simply called for the avoidance of investments in "objectionable industries."

38 Cf. docket of materials labeled "Mennonite Mutual Aid, Investment Guidelines Review Committee, Sept. 15, 1982." Everence Archives.

39 "Investment Guidelines," *Sharing* 18 (Winter, 1984), 7.

40 This correspondence and the research related to it can be found in a folder marked "Ethical Investing," Everence Archives.

41 "Statement by Richard Reimer, Dec. 3, 1988, MMA Board Meeting," MMA Board minutes and reports, May 5, 1989. MC USA Archives, XII-9, Box 4/14.

42 Cf. folder marked "Ethical Investing," Everence Archives.

43 "PAX World Fund," *Sharing* 22 (Fall, 1988), 19. From 1982–1987 average returns on PAX funds amounted to 13.32 percent.

44 David Hostetler, "MMA Looking Toward 1993." Included in MMA Board minutes and reports, Nov. 18, 1983. MC USA Archives, XII-9, Box 3/17.

45 It did not take long for MMA to recognize the seriousness of the health care expense challenge. In a summary of "Healthcare Trends" presented to the MMA board in the spring of 1985, Ron Litwiller, vice president for Mutual Aid Services, warned that in the future MMA should expect "increasing pressure to deal with the needs of all Mennonites regardless of ability to pay." He also, however, anticipated that "basic care will be a right for all," assuming that the government would assume a much larger role in health care, and that MMA would need to have "established arrangements with physicians and

hospitals whereby services can be provided in the most cost effective way." MMA Board minutes and reports, March 28, 1985. MC USA Archives, XII-9, Box 3/21.

46 www.healthsystemtracker.org/chart-collection/u-s-spending-healthcare-changed-time/ (accessed Sept. 5, 2019). These figures are in constant 2017 dollars. By 2000, health expenditures had reached about $1.4 trillion, and in 2017 the amount spent on health had more than doubled to $3.5 trillion.

47 By 2017, the amount had risen to $10,739.

48 See also similar figures in Scot D. Yoder, "What is the Church Doing About the U.S. Health Care Crisis?" *Gospel Herald* (Oct. 20, 1992), 8.

49 There are numerous excellent histories of health care in the United States. Among the most accessible are Paul Starr, *The Social Transformation of American Medicine: The Rise of a Sovereign Profession and the Making of a Vast Industry*, 2nd ed. (New York: Basic Books, 2017); John C. Burnham, *Health Care in America: A History* (Baltimore: Johns Hopkins University Press, 2015); and Thomas W. Loker, *The History and Evolution of Healthcare in America: The Untold Backstory of Where We've Been, Where We Are, and Why Healthcare Needs Reform* (Bloomington, IN: iUniverse; 2012).

50 This is a point made by Jerry Troyer in "The Business of Caring: Why Do I Have This Pain in My Greenback?" *Sharing* 16 (Winter 1982), 15.

51 Laban Peachey, "Health Care Costs: What Can We Do about Them?" *Sharing* 21 (Summer, 1987), 18–19; Mary E. Klassen, "Tough Decisions," *Sharing* 21 (Winter, 1987), 19.

52 A survey of MMA members in 1989 made it clear that "the most important criteria for selecting health insurance are cost and benefits." Cf. "MMA's Health Members Say What They Think," *Sharing* 23 (Fall 1989), 8–9.

53 Between 1987 and 1992, MMA lost 20,000 health plan members. "Conference Address Health Care Concerns," *Gospel Herald* (Nov. 3, 1992), 11.

54 Interview with Peg Leatherman, Jan. 31, 2008; Steve Garboden, May 4, 2018; Eunice Culp, Aug. 21, 2018.

55 Kent Stucky, vice president for Stewardship Services, said of Kratz at the time of his hire that "He will continue to remind us that the congregation is the focus of both the spiritual and the economic parts of mutual aid; he knows how to differentiate mutual aid from commercial insurance." Helen Alderfer, "A New President for MMA," *Sharing* 20 (Fall 1986), 6–7.

56 James Kratz, "Report of the Executive Vice-President to the Board of Directors," MMA Board minutes and reports, May 9, 1986. MC USA Archives, XII-9, Box 4/3.

57 Jerry Troyer to Health Strategy Task Force, Sept. 19, 1988. Cf. MMA Board minutes and reports, Dec. 2, 1988. MC USA Archives, XII-9, Box 4/12.

58 Steve Garboden particularly emphasized this point as a rationale for finding a way forward even though the business logic would have been to close down the programs. Interview with Steve Garboden, May 4 and May 8, 2018.

59 "What Keeps Jack Going?" *Sharing* 17 (Summer, 1983), 10–11.

60 The response rate was 2,923 individuals (26 percent) and 131 employers (33 percent). Mary E. Klassen, "Tough Decisions," *Sharing* 21 (Winter, 1987), 18–19.

61 Folder labeled "Health Care Response," Everence Archives.

62 Ibid.

63 "More than Mutual Aid," *Sharing* 19 (Winter 1985), 19.

64 Folder labeled "Health Care Response," Everence Archives.

65 Karl Sommers, Jerry Troyer, and Laban Peachey to Division Management, "Price Competitiveness / Underwriting Recommendation," April 15, 1987, MMA Board minutes and reports, Nov. 7, 1987. MC USA Archives, XII-9, Box 4/8.

66 "Summary: Consultation with George Berry," July 9, 1985, MMA Board minutes and reports, Nov. 22, 1985. MC USA Archives, XII-9, Box 4/1. Among other things, Berry recommended that MMA focus on group plans and that MMA focus on selling "an idea rather than a product."

67 James D. Kratz, "Health Care: How Much Are We Willing to Pay?" *Gospel Herald* (Aug. 30, 1988), 590–591.

68 "What Would You Do?" *Sharing* 20 (Summer 1986), 11. It is striking that this is one of the first task forces with significant gender balance—five of the nine members were women.

69 "Does Love Let God?" *Sharing* 21 (Spring, 1987), 10–11. The book of essays arising out of Health Care Ethics Review was titled *Medical Ethics, Human Choices: A Christian Perspective* (Scottdale, PA: Herald Press, 1988).

70 *Sharing* 18 (Winter 1984), 4–7.

71 R. Clair Weaver, "Five Ways to Control Medical Care Costs," *Sharing* 18 (Summer 1984), 14, 15.

72 Vyron Schmidt to Jim Kratz, "New Educational Resource Benefit: Nurse in the Congregation," May 24, 1990, MMA Board minutes and reports, Aug. 9, 1990. MC USA Archives, XII-9, Box 4/20.

73 Steve Bowers, "Hey, MMA! What Are You Doing About Medical Costs?" *Sharing* 24 (Winter 1990), 7–9.

74 "Cost Containment Projects," April 3, 1986, MMA Board minutes and reports, May 9, 1986. MC USA Archives, XII-9, Box 4/3.

75 The traditional individual policy—Comprehensive Health Plan—had a maximum benefit per illness of $25,000.

76 Helen Alderfer, Michael Boge, Willard Krabill, Sid Richard, Carol Suter, Jerry Troyer, Beth Weaver, John Yoder-Schrock, and Scot Yoder, "MMA Organ Transplant Task Force Summary Report and Recommendations," July 17, 1990, MMA Board minutes and reports, Aug. 9, 1990. MC USA Archives, XII-9, Box 4/20.

77 "Wellness: A Personal Journey," *Sharing* 18 (Winter 1984), 16–17.

78 "How's My Mental Health Quiz," *Sharing* 19 (Winter 1985), 8–9.

79 "Stress at Every Age," *Sharing* 20 (Winter 1985–86), 12–13; Chester A. Raber, "Getting a Balance on Work," *Sharing* 16 (Winter 1982), 6.

80 Ann Raber, "Learn to Take Care of Yourself," *Sharing* 23 (Summer 1989), 10–13; Ethel Yake Metzler, "Take Care With Yourself," *Sharing* 19 (Fall 1985), 14–15.

81 Edwin F. Rempel, *Congregational Health Ministries Handbook: A Resource for Providing Health Ministries In and Through Congregations* (Elkhart, IN: Mennonite Health Association, 1987).

82 By 1982, the Fraternal Activities Department oversaw a budget of more than $900,000. Other sources of income for fraternal funds also came from investment income on surplus funds and voluntary contributions.

83 John L. Liechty, "Frequently Asked Questions Regarding Mennonite Mutual Aid Association's Fraternal Funds," July 21, 1982, MMA Board minutes and reports, Nov. 12, 1982. MC USA Archives, XII-9, Box 3/15.

84 "Budget Highlights," MMA Board minutes and reports, Nov. 20, 1981. MC USA Archives, XII-9, Box 3/13.

85 Every three years grants were also awarded to the Brethren in Christ Church, the Evangelical Mennonite Church, and the Evangelical Mennonite Brethren Church. In 1981 fraternal fund grants supported such projects as the Philadelphia Diamond Street Holistic Health Center, the printing of Spanish educational materials, Black/Hispanic Leadership Education Program, a Cheyenne Indian hymnbook, educational resources for people with disabilities, the Chicago Mennonite Learning Center, and a "More-with-Less" TV special.

86 In 1990 MMA appointed Phyllis Mishler to address individual instances where people were denied coverage and to seek support for them through the Alternative Resources initiative. Phyllis M. Mishler to Vyron Schmidt, "Alternative Resources Survey," July 25, 1990, MMA Board minutes and reports, Aug. 9, 1990. MC USA Archives, XII-9 Box 4/20.

87 "Mennonite Mutual Aid Corporate Marketing Plan, 1986–1988" [July 31, 1985]. MC USA Archives, XII-9, Box 3/2.

88 James Kratz, "Keeping the Links Strong," *Sharing* 20 (Winter 1985–86), 20.
89 James Kratz, "Whose Responsibility?" *Sharing* 21 (Winter, 1987), 20.
90 Paul W. Brunk, "Mutual Aid Counselors: An Emerging Dream," *Sharing* 21 (Fall 1987), 17–19.
91 James D. Kratz, "Health Care: How Much are We Willing to Pay?" *Gospel Herald* (Aug. 30, 1988), 590–591.
92 Ibid., 591.
93 Cf. folder labeled "Health Care Response," Everence Archives.
94 Ibid.
95 Ibid.
96 Vyron Schmidt, "Communication Task Force Report," Nov. 17, 1988, MMA Board minutes and reports, Dec. 2, 1988. MC USA Archives, XII-9, Box 4/11. In the MMA board meeting on May 3, 1991, Kratz reported a cumulative loss of 30 percent of membership in individual health care plans—a decline of nearly twelve thousand members. Cf. Steve Shenk, "MMA board okays new ways to deal with crisis in health insurance," *Gospel Herald* (May 21, 1991), 9.
97 Ivan Kauffman [Mennonite Church executive secretary] to George Dyck [MMA board chair], Jan., 1983, MMA Board minutes and reports, May 13, 1983. MC USA Archives, XII-9, Box 3/16.
98 Ibid.
99 99. James M. Lapp, "The Challenge of Mutual Aid in the 1990s," *Sharing* 24 (Spring 1990), 16.
100 Ibid., 17. In the same issue Steve Bowers, the editor of *Sharing*, reflected on Lapp's essay, noting that MMA has had to deal with "indefensible actions" by some members, where "in a number of cases, groups have attempted to transfer their healthy members to cheaper plans with other companies but leave their unhealthy members with MMA. Individual members have tried to do the same thing. How can this kind of thinking be justified in light of mutual aid?" "A Moment of Truth," *Sharing* 24 (Spring 1990), 18.
101 Interview with Karl Sommers, May 24, 2018; J. B. Miller, Nov. 6, 2019.
102 Steve Bowers, "Jim Kratz Looks Back on 17 Years at MMA," *Sharing* 25 (Winter, 1991), 12.

Chapter 6

1 J. Lorne Peachey, "White to MMA and MCC: 'Get Your Acts Together,'" *Gospel Herald* (April 26, 1994), 10.
2 For a helpful summary of this complex story see Jonny Gerig Meyer, "Sending Mixed Messages to Congress: Mennonite Involvement in Proposed National Health Care Reform, 1992–1994," *Mennonite Quarterly Review* 83 (April 2009), 181–220.
3 Hesston Manufacturing Company was first known for an auger Yost had invented for unloading grain from farm combines. In 1955, it introduced the first commercially available self-propelled windrower; then in 1967 it developed the first hydrostatic drive windrower. The company was also a pioneer in producing large bales, both square and round.
4 Steve Bowers, "A New President Looks Ahead," *Sharing* 25 (Winter 1991), 3–7; Interview with Howard Brenneman, Dec, 19, 2018.
5 Beryl Brubaker, then a member of the MMA board, recalls that in April of 1990, Brenneman gave a seminar to the MMA board. Drawing on his experience at Hesston Corp., he focused on the need for companies to diversify their markets. Interview with Beryl Brubaker, Dec. 17, 2018.
6 Interview with Howard Brenneman, Dec, 19, 2018.
7 Bowers, "A New President Looks Ahead," 5.
8 Brenneman also expected his management team to share in the difficult issues. In 2002, the midst of an economic slowdown, he ordered all of his managers to cut 10 percent from their budgets, which entailed laying off staff. All of those employees

received a phase-out package, which included financial assistance to retool and work with an outside firm that helped them with their job search, but managers recalled the decision with great pain.

9 "From Success to Significance," [three-ring binder]. Everence Archives.

10 These programs showed gains of $5.8 million in 1989 and $3.6 million in 1990.

11 Dwight Stoltzfus, "MMA Marketing," Oct. 19, 1977 [prepared for MMAA delegate meeting]. Folder labeled "MMA Marketing," Everence Archives.

12 "Mennonite Mutual Aid 1983 Marketing Plan," [final draft: January 6, 1983]. Folder labeled "MMA Marketing," Everence Archives.

13 Bowers, "A New President Looks Ahead," 5.

14 See, for example, Barth A. Hague, "Wherever You Need to Go: A Report on MMA's Latest Member Opinion Survey," *Sharing* 31 (Winter, 1997), 10–14.

15 Interview with Steve Bowers, March 8, 2018.

16 Steve Bowers, "A Symbol of Change, an Image of Stability," *Sharing* 27 (Fall 1993), 18.

17 Cf. "Mennonite Mutual Aid Video Clips for Stewardship Exhibit, April 26, 1995, First Draft" [transcript], folder labeled "MMA 50th Anniversary," Everence Archives.

18 The book, edited by New Testament scholar Willard Swartley and sociologist Donald Kraybill, was titled *Building Communities of Compassion: Mennonite Mutual Aid in Theory and Practice* (Scottdale, PA: Herald Press, 1998), playing on the title of an earlier collection of devotionals from the AMAS meetings that MMA published in 1970 called *The Compassionate Community*.

19 "President's Report," MMA Board minutes and reports, March 15–16, 2002. MC USA Archives, XII-9, Box 8.

20 Cf. Rick Stiffney, "The Self-Perception of Executives Concerning Their Role and Work in Shaping the Faith Identity of Nonprofit Mennonite/Anabaptist Organizations: A Collaborative Case Study and Narrative Approach" (PhD diss., Berrien Springs University, 2010).

21 Brenneman claimed that managed care had saved MMA $1.5 million through the first 8 months of 1993. Steve Bowers, "Health Care Reform: What Will It Mean for You and MMA?" *Sharing* 27 (Winter 1993), 5.

22 Karl Sommers also devoted a great deal of time exploring the feasibility of Long Term Care Insurance, anticipating greater demand from older adults who were looking for a hedge against rising costs of nursing care. In the end, however, MMA eventually opted to offer its members a brokered plan, administered by another company. Interview with Karl Sommers, May 24, 2018.

23 "Why Life Insurance?" *Sharing* 26 (Spring 1996), 7.

24 Delmar King, who had been recruited by John Rudy in 1971 to oversee investments for the Mennonite Foundation, noted especially the influence of a book by John G. Simon, Charles W. Powers, and Jon P. Gunnemann called *The Ethical Investor* (New Haven: Yale University Press, 1972). Interview with Delmar King, Aug. 13, 2018.

25 Praxis Mutual Funds added an international fund in 1997 in order to further diversify their investments.

26 Interview with Chad Horning, Aug. 31, 2018.

27 For example, Praxis commits approximately 1 percent of each fund to a Community Development Investment program.

28 In 1994 the foundation distributed $22 million to charities (more than triple the previous year), and 80 percent of those donations were directed to Mennonite-related organizations. [News report], *Sharing* 29 (Summer 1995), 2.

29 The prehistory of the merger goes back at least as far as 1977 when both groups began planning for a joint MC-GC binational assembly, which took place in Bethlehem, Pennsylvania, in 1983. There the two denominations adopted a resolution to continue on a path of intentional cooperation. Two years later, leaders formed a Cooperation Committee, and in 1989 at a binational joint assembly in Normal, Illinois, MC/GC delegates strongly affirmed the ongoing exploration of a possible integration of the two denominations.

30 In 2003 and 2004 MMA committed to "base and start up funds of $267,000 for each of the two years." Cf. "Funding Roundtable, Mennonite Church, USA," May 5–6, 2003, MMA Board minutes and reports, Aug. 1–2, 2003. MC USA Archives, XII-9, Box 8. In addition to funding Karl Sommers's role as a half-time consultant to the integration process, MMA also seconded Barth Hague, vice president for marketing, to lead a communications audit on behalf of the new denomination.

31 In 1998 the Canadian Mennonites opted out of the process to form their own integrated national church body.

32 For the fullest description of the substance of the MMA Boards definitions of these four categories, see "Policy Governance," MMA Board minutes and reports, Dec. 3–4, 2004. MC USA Archives, XII-9, Box 9.

33 A board review of the Ends Statements in the fall of 2007 changed the wording to define the purpose of MMA from empowering the "*Anabaptist faith community* to practice biblical stewardship" to empowering "*persons with Anabaptist faith* beliefs to practice biblical stewardship." "Notes from the Ends Development Session, Oct. 19, 2007." MMA Board minutes and reports, Feb. 22–23, 2008. MC USA Archives, XII-9, Box 9.

34 The Carver model of policy governance was eventually adopted by most agencies and institutions associated with MC USA.

35 See, for example, A. D. Wenger, "The Stewardship of Money," and M. C. Vogt, "The Stewardship of Talent," *Mennonite General Conference Held at Kitchener, Ontario, August 27–29, 1935* [Proceedings], 74–84, 84–88.

36 Sheldon Burkhalter, "When I Can No Longer Speak," *Sharing* 27 (Spring 1993), 11–13. The same issue of *Sharing* introduced a new resource titled *Life Choices: Guidelines for Creating Your Advance Medical Directives.*

37 *Medical Ethics: Human Choices*, ed. John Rogers (Scottdale, PA: Herald Press, 1988).

38 Cf. Lynn Miller, *Just in Time: Stories of God's Extravagance* (Scottdale, PA: Herald Press, 1997) and Lynn Miller, *The Power of Enough: Finding Contentment by Putting Stuff In Its Place* (Scottdale, PA: Herald Press, 2003).

39 For an example of Miller's activities during this period, including a list of his numerous congregational visits, see MMA Board minutes and reports, Aug. 12–14, 1999. MC USA Archives, XII-9, Box 8.

40 Randall Jacobs, Vyron Schmidt, Barth Hague, "Concept Platform: Stewardship University, rev. March 31, 1999." MMA Board minutes and reports, Aug. 12–14, 1999. MC USA Archives, XII-9, Box 8.

41 For a summary of these activities as reported by MMA field representatives, see "February 2003 Summary Activity Report from Church Relations Manager," in MMA Board minutes and reports, May 30–31 2003. MC USA Archives, XII-9, Box 8.

42 Steve Bowers, "She Loves Her Job," *Sharing* 27 (Summer 1993), 8–10.

43 For example, in the fall of 2001 Steve Garboden reported that MMA would be contributing $200,000 to MC USA in the coming year, $50,000 in the form of stewardship education and $150,000 as a direct subsidy. MMA Board minutes and reports, Aug. 3–4, 2001. MC USA Archives, XII-9, Box 8.

44 Reflections on the criteria governing disbursements of the fraternal funds and detailed reports of the actual distributions were part of virtually every board docket in the 1990s and early 2000s.

45 "MMA's Strategy for Responding to the Health Care Crisis, April, 1992," MMA Board minutes and reports, May 7–8, 1992. MC USA Archives, XII-9, Box 5.

46 The most comprehensive summary of this story is Jonny Gerig Meyer, "Sending Mixed Messages to Congress: Mennonite Involvement in Proposed National Health Care Reform, 1992–1994," *Mennonite Quarterly Review* 83 (April 2009), 181–220.

47 Cf. Ted Koontz to the MMA board members and Howard Brenneman, July 9, 1993 [thirteen-page, single-spaced letter], folder labeled "Health Policy and Correspondence," Everence Archives.

48 Ibid.

49 Ibid. See also Koontz's critique of MCC in Ted Koontz, "Commitments and Complications in Doing Good," *The Mennonite Quarterly Review* 70 (January 1996), 59–80.

50 On January 17, 1992, Koontz sent a list of detailed "brainstorms" to MMA board members that he hoped would "extend MMA's services to more of the church, especially to those who do not have the large financial resources which some of our programs require before they can be utilized." Other ideas included a Mennonite debt collection agency; stronger credit and debt counseling services; active tithing on MMA investment gains; and graduated premiums for health insurance. Folder labeled "Health Policy and Correspondence," Everence Archives.

51 For the correspondence around the planning of the study conference, see the folder labeled "Health Policy and Correspondence," Everence Archives.

52 Joseph Kotva Jr., "Mutual Aid as 'Practice,'" in Kraybill, *Building Communities of Compassion*, 71–74. "The current insurance products," Kotva argued, "are not mutual aid" (73).

53 Keith Graber Miller, "Mennonite Mutual Aid: A Margin of Difference?" in ibid., 264–292.

54 Donald Kraybill, "The Changing Face of Corporate Care," in ibid., 293–305.

55 Richard Reimer, "The Future of Mutual Aid and Stewardship," *Sharing* 29 (Summer 1995), 11.

56 Steve Bowers, "John Rudy: The Life of a Steward," *Sharing* 24 (Winter, 1990), 10–13.

57 The language of this resolution is contained in Karl Sommers, "Mennonite Church USA Health Care Access Commission: Report to the Executive Board of MC USA, Dec. 15, 2004), MMA Board minutes and reports, Feb. 11–12, 2005. MC USA Archives, XII-9, Box 9.

58 Ibid.

59 Karl Sommers, "Mennonite Church USA Health Care Access Commission: Report to the Executive Board of MC USA, Dec. 15, 2004" [in preparation for meeting with MC USA Executive Board on Jan. 13–15, 2005], MMA Board minutes and reports, Feb. 11–12, 2005. MC USA Archives, XII-9, Box 9.

60 Healthcare Access Commission, "Health Care Access Materials for Delegates, MC USA Charlotte 2005 Delegate Assembly, April 19, 2005," MMA Board minutes and reports, June 3–4, 2005. MC USA Archives, XII-9, Box 9.

61 Everett J. Thomas, "Mennonite Church USA Delegate Assembly," *The Mennonite* (July 26, 2005), 11.

62 The final recommendations listed five points: 1) Support a healthcare system in which risks, costs, and responsibilities are shared by all; 2) Eliminate financial and health status as barriers to healthcare access, giving special care to the weakest and most vulnerable members of our society; 3) Strengthen public health systems in order to create healthy communities; 4) Support and strengthen public insurance programs for vulnerable populations while comprehensive reform is being enacted; and 5) Openly address issues of quality, efficiency, and limits.

63 MMA's Covenant Mutual Benefits (COMB) health insurance was available in only ten of the twenty-one area conferences of MC USA. Although COMB guaranteed insurability and provided portable coverage among congregations, lower participation in the pool made it tempting for many congregations to choose cheaper coverage in the commercial market. At the 2005 MC USA delegate assembly, Steve Garboden expressed concern about the viability of the plan. "MMA Addresses Questions About COMB," *The Mennonite* (July 26, 2005), 5.

64 Cf. Glen E. Miller, "MC USA Healthcare Access Project Update, May 18, 2006," MMA Board minutes and reports, Oct. 21, 2006. MC USA Archives, XII-9, Box 9. At the time, employees in various church agencies were covered in one of five different insurance pools.

65 The delegate handbook can be found in MC USA Archives, Mennonite Church USA Convention Records, 2003–2009, EXL/003, Box 2. The committee's report to the 2007 delegate assembly in San Jose also summarized resources promoting stewardship of health.

66 Ibid. At the time, less than 40 percent of MC USA pastors were enrolled in the COMB plan.

67 Ibid.

68 "President's Report," MMA Board minutes and reports, June 3, 2005. MC USA Archives, XII-9, Box 9.

Chapter 7

1 Steve (April 14 at 5:32 p.m.) [comment section]. Cf. Paul Schrag, "MMA Renamed Everence," *Mennonite Weekly Review*, April 5, 2010. http://www.mennoworld.org/ archived/2010/4/5/mma-renamed-everence/?page=2 (accessed Sept. 8, 2019). See also, "MMA Adopts Its New Name—Everence," Mennonite Weekly Review, Oct. 25, 2010. http://www.mennoworld.org/archived/2010/10/25/mma-adopts-its-new-name-everence/.

2 Ibid.

3 Interview with Carol Suter, Dec. 8, 2018.

4 The search committee for MMA's new president included representation from the broader church—Jim Harder, president of Bluffton College, served as a representative of the MC USA Executive Board, and MC USA executive director Jim Schrag was present for all the interviews.

5 "Nagelvoort Introduced as MMA Chief," *The Mennonite* (July 26, 2005), 27.

6 Cf. http://boldministrynyc.blogspot.com/2009/02/bold-ministry-prayer-conference -call.html [accessed March 2019].

7 Interview with Bruce Harder, Sept. 22, 2018.

8 Robert Rhodes, "MMA introduces new CEO," *Mennonite Weekly Review*, July 18, 2005.

9 "Nagelvoort Introduced as MMA Chief," *The Mennonite* (July 26, 2005), 27.

10 After he started, at least two anonymous emails circulated reporting that Nagelvoort had serious issues regarding his finances.

11 Robert Rhodes, "MMA President Resigns; Had Filed for Bankruptcy on June 29," *Mennonite Weekly Review,* Oct. 3, 2005. http://www.mennoworld.org/ archived/2005/10/3/mma-president-resigns-had-filed-bankruptcy-june-29/?print=1.

12 According to court records, Nagelvoort had $9.1 million in liabilities and less than $50,000 in assets. Ibid.

13 Although some argued that bankruptcy should not automatically disqualify a person for senior management leadership, others noted that ProEquities had a policy that any-one with a bankruptcy in the past seven years could not represent them. MMA would likely have lost ProEquities as their primary brokerage firm if Nagelvoort had stayed on.

14 "Steve is a trusted and experienced leader, who is serving the organization well during this transition and has our full support," said Vice Chair LaVern Yutzy. MMA presidential transition press release, Nov. 4, 2005, Everence files.

15 For some sense of the complexity of the organization, when Garboden assumed the interim role, the MMA Board needed to take action to identify him as CEO of: MMA Stewardship Agency; MMA Association; Mennonite Foundation, Inc.; Menno Insurance Service, Inc.; MMA Church Buildings, Inc.; and Mennonite Mutual Aid, Inc. as well as the chair of MMA Community Development Investments, Inc.; MMA Trust Company; and Mennonite Retirement Trust.

16 Summary of MC USA Executive Board meeting Feb. 2–4, 2006, meeting included in MMA Board minutes and reports, June 2–3, 2006. MC USA Archives, XII-9, Box 9.

17 MMA Board minutes and reports, Feb. 25, 2006. MC USA Archives, XII-9, Box 9.

18 MMA Board minutes and reports, June 2–3, 2006. MC USA Archives, XII-9, Box 9. A typical comment read "I believe that serious consideration should be given only to

persons who are active members in a Mennonite Church (USA) congregation. While MMA serves many constituencies, this person must live the values of the sponsoring denomination."

19 Everett Thomas, "Larry Miller Named New MMA President," *The Mennonite* (Nov. 7, 2006), 27; interview with Larry Miller, Dec. 18, 2018.

20 Delmar King recalls working once with a seasoned consultant who told them that MMA was the most complicated business he had ever encountered, with the possible exception of American Express. Interview August 21, 2018.

21 MMA Board minutes and reports, Feb. 27, 2009. MC USA Archives, XII-9, Box 9 [CD-ROM].

22 MMA Board minutes and reports, Feb. 23–24, 2007. MC USA Archives, XII-9, Box 9.

23 Ibid.

24 The CMP report of 1961 refers to a conversation within MMA in 1954 about establishing a nationwide Mennonite credit union. Cf. "A Study of the Organization and Operation of MMA and its Affiliated Units (Aug. 18, 1961—preliminary report; Sept. 11, 1961 final report). AMC XII-28, Box 1/14. And the question reemerged in 1963. Cf. MMA Board minutes and reports, Nov. 8–9, 1963. MC USA Archives, XII-9, Box 1/29.

25 Cf. documentation in the folder labeled "Credit Union History," Everence Credit Union, Lancaster archives.

26 In May of 1972, Lupe de Leon Jr., who was carrying forward the initiative, reported that initial interest among Mennonites in South Texas, New York City, St. Louis, and Goshen had been high, but the local leadership was not equipped to carry through with the concept. De Leon also noted regretfully that he was "not available on the local level to see these projects through." MMA executive committee minutes, Nov. 4, 1971. MC USA Archives, XII-3, Box 1/9.

27 John Rudy, "Menno Investment Service," Oct. 1, 1973. Folder labeled "Credit Union History," Everence Credit Union, Lancaster archives. In April 1974, Rudy sent a letter to MMA congregational representatives to test the idea, asking for their opinion on a return postcard. In September, Swartzendruber reported that more than half of the respondents had voted against the idea.

28 Interest in credit unions was growing in Wayne County, Ohio, as well, with various pastors and local leaders asking MMA for counsel. MMA Board minutes and reports, May 20–21, 1977. MC USA Archives, XII-9, Box 3/2; and John Rudy, "Reflections on Credit Unions," MMA Board minutes and reports, Nov. 18, 1977. MC USA Archives, XII-9, Box 3/4.

29 Financial Services Committee report, Feb. 24, 1978; MMA Board minutes and reports, May 12–13, 1978. MC USA Archives, XII-9, Box 3/5. The report concluded, "at the present time priority should be given to MMA services other than credit unions."

30 John Rudy, File Memo, "Credit Unions, Jan. 20, 1982." At the margin of a 1992 copy of the memo Rudy scrawled, "Dwight, I'm scared to even mention credit unions again." The file memo was triggered by a January 18, 1992, article in the U.S. News & World Report titled "Credit Unions Take On Banking Goliaths," which emphasized the rapid growth of credit unions, due in part to their move into home mortgages and changes in regulations that allowed them to offer IRAs and "share draft" accounts that functioned like checking accounts.

31 The earliest Mennonite credit union in North America seems to have been Cross-town Credit Union, organized in 1944 to serve the Mennonites of Winnipeg, Man., soon followed by the Mennonite Scottdale Federal Credit Union, founded in 1955. In the meantime, credit unions emerged in a variety of other Mennonite communities: Hesston, Kans. (Central Kansas Federal Credit Union, 1960); Waterloo, Ont. (Mennonite Savings and Credit Union-Ontario, 1964); La Junta, Colo. (Mennonite Federal Credit Union, 1965); and Harrisonburg, Va. (Park View Federal Credit Union, 1969).

32 Unsecured loans were limited to one hundred dollars; but with collateral members could borrow as much as the fund could afford. Interest rates were 12 percent. Folder

labeled "Credit Union History," Everence Credit Union, Lancaster archives.

33 Interviews with J. Lorne Peachey (Oct. 30, 2019), Jack Scott (Oct. 30, 2019), and Kent Hartzler (Nov. 1, 2019).

34 This definition essentially aligned the membership of the Mennonite Financial Federal Credit Union with that of MMA.

35 In 2004 the MFFCU merged with two smaller credit unions in Ohio and Illinois.

36 MMA Board minutes and reports, Feb. 11–12, 2005. MC USA Archives, XII-9, Box 9.

37 MMA Board minutes and reports, July, 2007. MC USA Archives, XII-9, Box 9.

38 Interview with Kent Hartzler, Nov. 1, 2019.

39 MMA Board minutes and reports, Feb. 27, 2009. MC USA Archives, XII-9, Box 9 [CD-ROM].

40 MMA Board minutes and reports, June 29, 2009. MC USA Archives, XII-9, Box 9 [CD-ROM].

41 In addition, the MMA board had the power to approve the slate of potential directors put forward by the credit union's nominating committee.

42 E.g., on June 4, 2010, Everence agreed to provide $1.1 million to assure that CU could meet its capital requirements. Part of the problem was that the assets of the credit union were growing faster than the interest earnings on loans could generate the capital needed for new loans.

43 "The continuing need for capital is threatening our strategy for growing the credit union. We also have questions about the health and viability of the credit union system." MMA Board minutes and reports, Sept. 23, 2010. MC USA Archives, XII-9, Box 9 [CD-ROM].

44 MMA Board minutes and reports, Oct. 19–20, 2007. MC USA Archives, XII-9, Box 9.

45 MMA Board minutes and reports, Feb. 22–23, 2008. MC USA Archives, XII-9, Box 9. The report includes a helpful organizational diagram of the current and proposed structure.

46 "President's Report," ibid.

47 Interview with Larry Miller, Dec. 18, 2018.

48 MMA Board minutes and reports, Feb. 22–23, 2008. MC USA Archives, XII-9, Box 9.

49 Larry Miller, "President's Report—New Executive Leadership Team," June 2, 2008, MMA Board minutes and reports, June 20–21, 2008. MC USA Archives, XII-9, Box 9.

50 As another consequence of the restructuring, the vice president's offices were relocated from the departments they supervised to new locations close to Miller—a shift that some staff felt put them at greater distance from their supervisors, and from management in general.

51 MMA Board minutes and reports, Feb. 22–23, 2008. MC USA Archives, XII-9, Box 9.

52 MMA Board minutes and reports, Sept. 23, 2010. MC USA Archives, XII-9, Box 9 [CD-ROM].

53 Interview with Jane Bower, March 6, 2018.

54 MMA Board minutes and reports, MMA Board minutes and reports, June 20–21, 2008. MC USA Archives, XII-9, Box 9.

55 The distinctive design elements contributing to LEED certification included clerestory windows for consistent natural lighting; sunshades on the back of building; extensive use of bamboo for flooring, veneer, and cabinetry; window louvers; point-of-use hot water heaters; and modular furniture made out of recycled materials.

56 At the Dec. 18, 2008 board meeting, the group agreed to broaden the definition of MMA membership to include anyone who can "in good faith, adopt the following statement as a statement of belief and signs a document evidencing his/her adoption of this statement: 'I embrace the Anabaptist understanding of Christian stewardship and mutual aid and acknowledge God's ownership of all I am and have (Psalm 24). I commit to: practice stewardship of God's love towards all individuals; practice stewardship of all God's gifts: possessions, time, talents, health, and creation; practice stewardship of

God's generosity by sharing with others.'" MMA Board minutes and reports, Dec. 18, 2008. MC USA Archives, XII-9, Box. 9 [CD-ROM].

57 Although FutureBrand researchers assured the MMA team that none of their final recommendations had any inappropriate meanings in other languages, an MMA staff member did note later that the word "kefa" means "bug" in Pennsylvania Dutch.

58 Interview with Jim Alvarez, Aug. 21, 2018.

59 "Mennonite Mutual Aid—Mennonite Financial Federal Credit Union" folder, vertical file collection, Mennonite Historical Library, Goshen College, Goshen, Ind.

60 Paul Schrag, "MMA Renamed Everence," *Mennonite Weekly Review*, April 5, 2010.

61 Ibid.

62 Ibid.

63 Interview with Steve Bowers, March 8, 2018. See also the results of a survey as reported by Bowers, "Customers Satisfied Following Name Change," *The Mennonite* (Oct. 2011), 7.

64 "Mennonite Mutual Aid—Mennonite Financial Federal Credit Union" folder, vertical file collection, Mennonite Historical Library, Goshen College, Goshen, Ind.

65 A formal statement of the relationship can be found in "Statement of Expectations Between MMA and MC USA Executive Board/Executive Leadership," November, 2007. MMA Board minutes and reports, Feb. 22–23, 2008. MC USA, XII-9, Box 9.

66 For a description of the "Mennonite Creation Care Network" and its relationship to MMA, cf. MMA Board minutes and reports, Feb. 6, 2007. MC USA, XII-9, Box 9.

67 Included in most of the board dockets, the summaries of these encounters provide a rich source of information for a future researcher.

68 MMA Board minutes and reports, June 2–3, 2006. MC USA Archives, XII-9, Box 9.

69 MMA Board minutes and reports, March 18, 2008. MC USA Archives, XII-9, Box 9.

70 The initial conversation unfolded at a meeting of agency leaders and representatives of the MC USA executive board. Cf. minutes of the Governance Council, Mennonite Church USA, Chicago, Illinois, March 16–17, 2008. MMA board minutes and report, June 20–21, 2008. MC USA Archives, XII-9, Box 9. The response of the agency leaders noted in the minutes is bracing in the sharpness of the criticism—a moment of rare candor in church board minutes.

71 "Conference Call with Mennonite Mutual Aid Board (to process Executive Board Action)," May 15, 2008. MMA Board minutes and reports, June 20–21, 2008. MC USA Archives, XII-9, Box 9. In the call, MMA board member Pat Swartzentruber cited extensive research that suggested loyalty and contributions would decline. Other critics of the plan expressed deep skepticism that a general board would be capable of managing the institutional complexities of the various agencies it was seeking to consolidate; and seasoned development officers from those same church-related institutions were convinced that overall support for the church would decline if the plan were to move forward.

72 In the aftermath of the controversy around the "single board" proposal, the MMA board did clarify its policy to read: "The MMA Board will not adopt or approve any resolution amending the bylaws of MMAA without first informing and consulting with the Executive Board." Cf. MMA Board minutes and reports, Feb. 27, 2009. MC USA Archives, XII-9, Box 9 [CD-ROM].

73 The project team reported on a meeting of church representatives in March of 2008 where conference leaders shared stories of uninsured pastors. In addition to congregation and conference pastors, the pools included Associated Mennonite Schools and Camps, Covenant Mutual Benefit (COMB), Mennonite Health Services, Mennonite Educators Benefit Plan, MMA, and Mutual Aid Sharing Plan (MASP). Cf. MMA Board minutes and reports, June 19–20, 2008. MC USA board minutes and reports, XII-9, Box 9.

74 Amy Frykholm, "Health-care Option: A Mennonite Plan for Mutual Aid," *Christian Century* (September 22, 2009), 28–31; cf. "The Corinthian Plan and the Affordable Care Act." MC USA website, http://mennoniteusa.org/what-we-do/the-corinthian-plan/cp-aca/ [accessed November 2019].

75 Larry Miller, "Our Church's Commitment on Health-care Access," *The Mennonite* (July 1, 2013), 30.
76 Cf. http://mennoniteusa.org/what-we-do/the-corinthian-plan/ (accessed November 2019).

Chapter 8
1 Jim Miller, "Everence Joining Philly Neighborhood," *Everyday Stewardship* (Summer/ Fall, 2019), 11.
2 Ira David Landis, *The Missionary Movement Among Lancaster Conference Mennonites* (Scottdale, PA: Mennonite Publishing House, 1938), 46, 47. Since then the congregation, later renamed Diamond Street Mennonite Church, has dissolved.
3 Cf. Jeff Gingerich and Miriam Stoltzfus, *All God's Children: Philadelphia Mennonites of Lancaster Conference, 1899–1999* (Leola, PA: Imperial Graphics, 2000) .
4 Several Mennonite congregations in the Franconia region even created endowments to help manage their finances.
5 MEDA is an international economic development organization that helps to link the financial resources and skills of primarily Anabaptist-Mennonite business people in projects that address global poverty.
6 Cf. "Everence Names New President," *Mennonite World Review*, June 23, 2014. www.mennoworld.org/2014/06/23/news/everence-names-new-president.
7 "Everence Strategic Plan, 2020." Everence website [2020]. The plan, formulated in October of 2016, is reviewed each year and was updated on August 28, 2018.
8 Pat Swartzentruber, though not an MMA board chair, also exercised significant leadership on several key committees.
9 Mennonite Mutual Aid Personnel Listing, Dec. 31, 1972. Folder labeled "Early MMA History," Everence Archives.
10 According to the mandate, in circumstances where a male and female applicant had similar qualifications, for example, preference should be given to the woman. The Personnel Department was to create a list of fifteen to twenty-five women outside of MMA who showed potential for leadership with the goal of recruiting them as positions came open. And educational opportunities would be given to current female employees who wanted to complete their degrees. Steve Garboden to Administrative Services Committee, "Women in MMA Leadership," July 31, 1987. MMA Board minutes and reports, May 3, 1990. MC USA Archives, XII-9, Box 4/18.
11 Steve Garboden to Administrative Services Committee, "Women in Leadership," Dec. 8, 1989 and March 15, 1990, MMA Board minutes and reports, May 3, 1990. MC USA Archives, XII-9, Box 4/18.
12 Culp kept her position but was no longer in a senior management role when Larry Miller reorganized management. Under Hochstetler, however, she returned to an upper management position.
13 MMA *Office Mem-Oh!* (April 11, 1968), 1.
14 Cf. "CHIP: Congregational Health Improvement Plan," *Sharing* 5 (July 1971), 4–5; and a poetic description of CHIP in response to the question "Was MMA an 'insurance company' for middle-income American Mennonites?" "CHIP: A Celebration," 10 (July 1976), 5.
15 Cf. "MC USA Purposeful Plan" [2014]. http://mennoniteusa.org/what-we-do/undoing-racism/.
16 "Anti-racism Ends Statement Review," MC USA Executive Board (January, 2007), included in MMA Board minutes and reports, Feb. 23–24, 2007. MC USA Archives, XII-9, Box 9.
17 Ibid. All but one, according to the report, were managers.
18 Interview with Martin Navarro, Aug. 31, 2018.
19 For the draft of the 2019–2020 plan titled "Achieving Workplace Diversity, Enhancing and Growing the Everence Workforce," see Everence Board minutes and reports,

July 1–2, 2019, 39–43. Everence Connections [online web access to board reports and minutes].

20 MMA Board minutes and reports, Oct. 25–26, 2019. Everence Connections [online web access to board reports and minutes].

21 Everence has also developed a mentoring program for women that links new employees with experienced and successful female consultants and representatives.

22 "Everence Employment Philosophy," [2017], Everence Archives.

23 Report by Eunice Culp, Vice President of Human Resources, MMA Board minutes and reports, Oct. 25–26, 2019. Everence Connections [online web access to board reports and minutes]. In 2018 Everence hired a record number of sixty-four new employees and eighteen interns.

24 Cf. President and CEO Report, Everence Board minutes and reports, July 1–2, 2019. Everence Connections [online web access to board reports and minutes]. The initiative was originally known as the Sales and Contact Center.

25 Everence Board minutes and reports, Feb. 21–23, 2019. Everence Connection [online web access to board reports and minutes]. See also the results of a similar survey in 2015 that reported 90 percent of Everence members were "highly satisfied." "Everence Member Survey Shows the Importance of Faith," Dec. 11, 2015.

26 Steve Bowers, "Jim Kratz Looks Back on 17 Years at MMA," *Sharing* 25 (Winter, 1991), 10.

27 https://www.cigna.com/newsroom/news-releases/2018/new-cigna-study-reveals-loneliness-at-epidemic-levels-in-america [accessed March, 2019].

28 In 1994 MMA sold the MIS agency book of business, bringing this entity to a close. Cf. MMA board minutes and reports, Dec. 3, 1994. MC USA Archives, XII-9, Box 5.

29 MMA board minutes and reports, March 31, 1998. MC USA Archives, XII-9, Box 7.

30 In 2012, Everence took over Church Extension Services, a $5 million loan program started in 1958 by the General Conference Mennonite Church to support congregations in urban settings that had difficulty qualifying through traditional lending institutions. The program aligned well with the existing Everence Community Investments. Since 2015, support for these programs is brokered through Calvert Foundation. https://www.praxismutualfunds.com/news-and-stories/community-development-investing/.

31 www.everence.com/everence-articles/everence-federal-credit-union/product/20200116-myneighbor-aids-work-of-nonprofits.

32 Since 2005 Everence has been a primary financial supporter of the Mennonite Creation Care Network. Praxis Mutual Fund managers have also limited investments in major gas and oil companies, despite the fact that these stocks tend to drive the markets; and Praxis's Impact Bond Fund has invested over $125 million in bonds to improve the climate and global community, including funding solar and wind power.

33 In the first half of 2019, Everence directly engaged nineteen different companies on various issues related to these themes, and signed on to dozens of additional collaborative shareholder letters and investor statements, on issues like climate change, chemical safety concerns, and board diversity. For a more detailed report on Everence proxy voting, see www.praxismutualfunds.com/how-we-invest/proxy-voting.

34 Disagreements over these concerns have led numerous congregations and several conferences—including the Lancaster Conference with nearly 14,000 members—to withdraw from MC USA. Similar tensions have worked their way through the Brethren in Christ, the Mennonite Brethren, the Conservative Mennonite Conference, and a host of other smaller groups that have long had connections to Everence.

35 "Everence expands its Pastoral Financial Wellness Program," *Everence News*, Jan. 9, 2019.

36 The fuller description reads: "Everence is a Christian-based, member-owned financial services organization that offers banking, insurance, investments, asset management, financial planning and other financial services with community benefits and stewardship education."

37 Cf. Heather L. Klassen, *Faith at Work: Christian Spirituality and Ethics in Mennonite Church-Related Organizations* (M.A. thesis, Anabaptist Mennonite Biblical Seminary, 2001) and Eric Schnitger, *Community, Complicity, and the Coin: A Story of Anabaptist Relationships to Liberal Capitalism* (PhD. diss., Fuller Theological Seminary, 2019), esp. 208–236.

38 Conrad Kanagy, Elizabeth Miller, and John D. Roth, *Global Anabaptist Profile: Belief and Practice in 24 Mennonite World Conference Churches* (Goshen, IN: Institute for the Study of Global Anabaptism, 2017), 29.

39 In some contexts they are called "limited liability companies" since the board members who run an incorporated company are generally not personally liable for actions of the company.

The Author

John D. Roth is a professor of history at Goshen College, where he also serves as director of the Mennonite Historical Library, Institute for the Study of Global Anabaptism, and editor of the *Mennonite Quarterly Review*. Roth has degrees from Goshen College and the University of Chicago. He has edited and authored numerous books, including *Teaching that Transforms, Stories, Beliefs*, and *Practices*.